From. A. I. Norcott

Lillian E. Quinn
Mildred Quinn Bradley

THE RIVER

THE RIVER

BY
EDNAH AIKEN

ILLUSTRATED BY
SIDNEY H. RIESENBERG

NEW YORK
GROSSET & DUNLAP
PUBLISHERS

Copyright 1914
The Bobbs-Merrill Company

TO
CHARLES SEDGWICK AIKEN

CONTENTS

CHAPTER		PAGE
I	Marshall Sends for Rickard	1
II	A Bit of Oratory	9
III	The Blessing of Aridity	20
IV	The Desert Hotel	38
V	A Game of Checkers	50
VI	Red Tape	67
VII	A Garden in a Desert	80
VIII	Under the Veneer	87
IX	On the Wistaria	95
X	Fear	103
XI	The Rivals	111
XII	A Desert Dinner	117
XIII	The Fighting Chance	127
XIV	Hardin's Luck	137
XV	The Wrong Man	141
XVI	The Best Laid Schemes	150
XVII	The Dragon Takes a Hand	159
XVIII	On the Levee	169
XIX	The White Refuge	178
XX	Opposition	189
XXI	A Morning Ride	199
XXII	The Passing of the Waters	204
XXIII	More Oratory	214
XXIV	A Soft Nook	234
XXV	The Stokers	247
XXVI	The White Oleander	256
XXVII	A White Woman and a Brown	264
XXVIII	Betrayal	271
XXIX	Rickard Makes a New Enemy and a New Friend	278
XXX	Smudge	290
XXXI	Time the Umpire	297

CONTENTS—*Continued*

CHAPTER		PAGE
XXXII	THE WALK HOME	307
XXXIII	A DISCOVERY	319
XXXIV	THE FACE IN THE WILLOWS	329
XXXV	A GLIMPSE OF FREEDOM	337
XXXVI	THE DRAGON SCORES	346
XXXVII	A SUNDAY SPECTACLE	355
XXXVIII	THE WHITE NIGHT	367
XXXIX	THE BATTLE IN THE NIGHT	378
XL	A DESERTION	396
XLI	INCOMPLETENESS	405
XLII	A CORNER OF HIS HEART	417

THE RIVER

THE RIVER

CHAPTER I

MARSHALL SENDS FOR RICKARD

THE large round clock was striking nine as "Casey" Rickard's dancing step carried him into the outer office of Tod Marshall. The ushering clerk, coatless and vestless in expectation of the third, hot spring day, made a critical appraisement of the engineer's get-up before he spoke. Then he stated that Mr. Marshall had not yet come.

For a London tie and a white silk shirt belted into white serge trousers were smart for Tucson. The clerks in the employ of the Overland Pacific and of the Sonora and Yaqui Railroads had stared at Rickard as he entered; they followed his progress through the room. He was a newcomer in Tucson. He had not yet acquired the apathetic habits of its citizens. He wore belts, instead of suspenders. His white trousers, duck or serge, carried a newly pressed crease each morning.

The office had not reached a verdict on the subject of K. C. Rickard. The shirt-sleeved, collarless clerks would have been quick to dub him a dandy were it not for a page of his history that was puzzling them. He had held a chair of engineering in some eastern city. He had resigned, the wind-tossed page said, to go on the road as a fireman. His rapid promotion had been spectacular; the last move, a few weeks ago, to fill an office position in Tucson. The summons had found him on the west coast of Mexico, where the Overland Pacific was pushing its tracks.

"You can wait here," suggested the clerk, looking covertly at the shoes of the man who a few years before had been shoveling coal on a Wyoming engine. "Mr. Marshall said to wait."

"Ribbons, instead of shoe-laces!" carped the human machine that must ever write letters which other men sign. "And a blue pin to match his tie! I call that going some!"

It would never have occurred to Rickard, had he thought about it at all that morning as he knotted his tie of dark, brilliant blue silk, that the selection of his lapis pin was a choice; it was an inevitable result, an instinctive discretion of his fingers. It warped, however, the suspended judgment of Marshall's men who had never seen him shoveling coal, disfigured by a denim jumper. They did not know that they themselves were slovens; ruined by the climate that dulls vanity and wilts collars.

"Give him a year to change some of his fine habits!" wagered Smythe, the stoop-shouldered clerk, as the door of the inner office closed.

"To change his habits less!" amended the office wit. And then they fell to speculating what Marshall was going to do with him. What pawn was he in the game that every one in Tucson followed with eager self-interested concern? Marshall's was the controlling hand in Arizona politics; the maker of governors, the arbiter of big corporations; president of a half-dozen railroads. Not a move of his on the board that escaped notice.

On the other side of the door, Rickard was echoing the office question. This play job, where did it lead to? He had liked his work, under Stratton. There had been some pretty problems to meet—what did Marshall mean to do with him?

The note had set the appointment for nine. Rickard glanced at his watch, and took out his *Engineering Review*. It would be ten before that door opened on Tod Marshall!

He knew that, on the road, Marshall's work began at dawn. "A man won't break from overwork, or rust from underwork, if he follows the example of the sun," Rickard had often heard him expound his favorite theory. "It is only the players, the sybarites, who can afford to pervert the arrangement nature intended for us." But in Tucson, controlled by the wifely solicitude of his Claudia, he was coerced into a regular perversion. His office never saw him until the morning was half gone.

A half-hour later, Rickard finished reading a report on the diversion of a great western river. The name of Thomas Hardin had sent him off on a tangent of memory. The Thomas Hardin whose efforts to bring water to the desert of the Colorado had been so spectacularly unsuccessful *was* the Tom Hardin he had known! The sister had told him so, the girl with the odd bronze eyes; opal matrix they were, with glints of gold, or was it green? She herself was as unlike the raw boor of his memory as a mountain lily is like the coarse rock of its background. Even a half-sister to Hardin, as Marshall, their host at dinner the week before, had explained it,—

no, even that did not explain it. That any of the Hardin blood should be shared by the veins of that girl, why it was incredible! The name "Hardin" suggested crudity, loud-mouthed bragging; conceit. He could understand the failure of the river project since the sister had assured him that it was the same Tom Hardin who had gone to college at Lawrence; had married Gerty Holmes. Queer business, life, that he should cross, even so remotely, their orbits again. That was a chapter he liked to skip.

He walked over to the windows, shielded by bright awnings, and looked down on the city where the next few years of his life might be caught. Comforting to reflect that an engineer is like a soldier, never can be certain about to-morrow. Time enough to know that to-morrow meant Tucson! What was that threadbare proverb in the Overland Pacific that Tod Marshall always keeps his men until they lose their teeth? That defined the men who made themselves necessary!

His eyes were resting on the banalities of the modern city that had robbed "old town" of its flavor. Were it not for the beauty of the distant hills, the jar and rumble of the trains whose roar called to near-by pleasure cities, twinkling lights and crowded theaters, stretches of parks and recreation grounds, he, who loved the thrill and confinement of an engine, who had found enticement in a desert, a chapter of adventure in the barrancas of Mexico, would stifle in Tucson! American progress was as yet too thin a veneer on Mexican indifference to make the place endurable; as a city. Were it a village of ten thousand people, then he'd not be scolding at his hotel, The Rosales. He could find the limitations picturesque, even. The census it was that accused those dusty unswept floors, the stained cuspidors, the careless linen, and The Rosales the best place in town! One has a right to expect comforts in a city.

"I'm good for a lifetime here, if I want it," his thoughts would work back to the starting place. "If I knuckle down to it, let him grow to depend on me, it's as good as settled that I am buried in Tucson!" Hadn't he heard Marshall himself say that he "didn't keep a kindergarten —that his office wasn't a training-school for men!" He wanted his men to stay! That, one of the reasons of the great man's power; detail rested on the shoulders of his employees. It kept his own brain clear, receptive to big achievements.

"Perhaps as the work unrolls, as I see more of what he wants of me, why he wants me, I may like it, I may get to shout for Tucson!" It was improbable enough to smile over! Child's work, compared to Mexico. He was never tired—that was his grievance; he had it, now; he was never tired.

The distinction of serving Marshall well certainly had its drawbacks. He wanted to sweep on. Whether he had a definite terminal, a concrete goal, had he ever stopped to think? Specialization had always a fascination for him. It was that which had thrown him out of his instructorship into the fire-box of a western engine. It had governed his course at college—to know one thing well, and then to prove that he knew it well! Contented in the Mexican barrancas, here he was chafing, restive, after a few weeks of Tucson. For what was he getting here? Adding what scrap of experience to the rounding of his profession?

Retrospectively, engineering could hardly be said to be

the work of his choice. Rather had it appeared to choose him. From boyhood engineers had always been, to him, the soldiers of modern civilization. To conquer and subdue mountains, to shackle wild rivers, to suspend trestles over dizzy heights, to throw the tracks of an advancing civilization along a newly blazed trail, there would always be a thrill in it for him. It had changed the best quarter-back of his high school into the primmest of students at college. Only for a short time had he let his vanity side-track him, when the honor of teaching what he had learned stopped his own progress. A rut—! He remembered the day when it had burst on him, the realization of the rut he was in. He could see his Lawrence schoolroom, could see yet the face under the red-haired mop belonging to Jerry Matson—queer he remembered the name after all those years! He could picture the look of consternation when he threw down his book, and announced his desertion.

"Casey was off his feed," he had heard one of the students say as he passed a buzzing group in the hall. "He looks peaked."

He had handed in his resignation the next day. A month later, and he was shoveling coal on the steep grades of Wyoming.

"Marshall keeps his men with him!" The engineer's glance traveled around the fleckless office. A stranger to Marshall would get a wrong idea of the man who worked in it! Those precise files, the desk, orderly and polished, the gleaming linoleum—and then the man who made the negro janitor's life a proud burden! His clothes always crumpled—spots, too, unless his Claudia had had a chance at them! Black string tie askew, all the outward visible signs of the southern gentleman of assured ancestry,

Not even a valet would ever keep Tod Marshall up to the standard of that office. What did he have servants for, he had demanded of Rickard, if it were not to jump after him, picking up the loose ends he dropped?

Curious thing, magnetism. That man's step on the stair, and every man-jack of them would jump to attention, from Ben, the colored janitor, who would not swap his post for a sinecure so long as Tod Marshall's one lung kept him in Arizona, to Smythe, the stoop-shouldered clerk, who had followed Marshall's cough from San Francisco. Poor Smythe! as inextricably entangled in the meshes of red tape as was the hapless Lady of Shalott in the web of her own snarled loom. It was said in Arizona —he himself had met the statement in Tucson—that any man who had ever worked for Tod Marshall would rather be warmed by the reflection of his greatness than be given posts of personal distinction.

Rickard found his office the only attractive place in the desert city. Shining and airy, even in the hottest days, its gaily screened windows were far enough above the street to give a charitable perspective. Restive as he was under the inaction of the last few weeks, he could acknowledge a quaintness of foreign suggestion in the mixture of Indian and Mexican influence, hampered, rather than helped, by American aggressiveness. Over the heads of a group of low buildings he could see the roof of the old mission church, now the lounging place for roisterers and sponges. There, the fiery mescal, the terrible tequila, were sending many a white lad to destruction.

Those office buildings across the street, gay with canvas, suggested American enterprise. In the distance were the substantial structures of the lusty western university. Down by the track the new home of the Overland Pacific was nearing completion. In the street below, young girls with their crisp duck skirts and colored waists gave the touch of blossoming. Mexican women wrapped in the inevitable black shawl were jostling one another's baskets. The scene was full of color and charm, but to the watcher who was eager to be on and doing, it cried teasingly of inertia.

Was it office routine Marshall intended him for? He admired without stint Tod Marshall, but he preferred to work by the side of the other kind, the strong men, without physical handicap, the men who take risks, the men who live the life of soldiers. That was the life he wanted. He would wait long enough to get Marshall's intention, and then, if it meant—this! he would break loose. He would go back to the front where he belonged; back to the firing-line.

As the hands of the round clock in the outer office were pointing to ten, the door opened and Marshall entered. His clothes, of indefinite blackish hue, would have disgraced an eastern man. His string tie had a starboard list, and his hat was ready for a rummage sale. But few would have looked at his clothes. The latent energy of the dynamic spirit that would frequently turn that quiet office into a maelstrom gleamed in those Indian-black eyes. Beneath the shabby cloth, one suspected the daily polished skin; under the old slouch hat was the mouth of purpose, the lips that no woman, even his Claudia, had kissed without the thrill of fear.

Marshall glanced back at the clock, and then toward his visitor.

"On time!" he observed.

Rickard, smiling, put his book in his pocket.

CHAPTER II

A BIT OF ORATORY

MARSHALL threw his hat on a chair, the morning paper on his desk. He aimed his burned-out cigar at the nearest cuspidor, but it fell foul, the ashes scattering over Sam's lately scoured linoleum. Instantly there was appearance of settled disorder. Marshall emptied his pockets of loose papers, spreading them out on his flat-top desk.

"Sit down!"

Rickard took the chair at the other side of the desk.

Marshall rang a bell. Instantly the shirt-sleeved clerk entered.

"I shall not see any one," the chief announced. "I don't want to be interrupted. Take these to Smythe."

His eyes followed the shutting of the door, then turned square upon Rickard. "I need you. It's a hell of a mess!"

The engineer wanted to know what kind of a "mess" it was.

"That river. It's running away from them. It's always going to run away from them. I'm going to send you down to stop it."

"The Colorado!" exclaimed Rickard. It was no hose to be turned, simply, off from a garden bed!

"Of course you've been following it? It's one of the biggest things that's happened in this part of the world.

Too big for the men who have been trying to swing it. You've followed it?"

"Yes." Queer coincidence, reading that report just now! "I've not been there. But the engineering papers used to get to me in Mexico. I've read all the reports."

His superior's question was uncharacteristically superfluous. Who had not read with thrilled nerves of that wild river which men had been trying to put under work-harness? Who, even among the stay-at-homes, had not followed the newspaper stories of the failure to make a meek servant and water-carrier of the Colorado, that wild steed of mountain and desert? What engineer, no matter how remote, would not "follow" that spectacular struggle between men and Titans?

"Going to send me to Salton?" he inquired. The railroad had been kept jumping to keep its feet dry. His job to be by that inland sea which last year had been desert!

"No. Brainerd is there. He can manage the tracks. I am going to send you down to the break."

Rickard did not answer. He felt the questioning eyes of his chief.

"Down to the break," repeated Tod Marshall, his bright black eyes taking in every detail of the engineer's get-up, resting, finally, on his sunburned face. "Have one?" He offered Rickard his choice of two small black cigars.

"Thanks, no," said Rickard.

"Not smoking yet?"

"Not yet." Rickard was amused at the solicitude. It was as though he had asked: "Your mother is dying?"

"When will the penance be over?" Marshall lighted his cigar, watching the blue blaze of the sulphur-tipped match, the slow igniting of the tobacco—obviously an exquisite sensuous rite.

"It isn't a penance! It's an experiment. I never had to do anything I really hated to do. I've never had to deny myself anything. Some fellows have to give up studying the profession they love, go to some hard digging or other, to support somebody. I've been lucky. I discovered I did not know the meaning of the word 'sacrifice.' I buckled down, and gave up the thing I liked best. That's all that amounts to."

His words had a solemn effect. Marshall had stopped smoking. Rickard discovered that his confidence had been tactless. Few men had had to sacrifice so much as the one now somberly facing him. His home, first, because a civil war had crushed it; his refuge, then, after years in attics, and struggle with post-bellum prejudices, just as success met him there; the fulness of life as men want it—those eyes knew what sacrifice meant!

"When are you going to quit?" Marshall's face was still sober.

"When am I going to quit quitting?" laughed his subordinate. "I haven't thought it out, sir. When it comes to me, the inclination, I suppose. I've lost the taste for tobacco." The break—where those Hardins were—how in thunder was he going to get out of that, and save his skin? Marshall liked his own way—

Marshall had resumed his cigar. "We'll consider it settled, then." His minute of introspection was over. He had picked up his thread.

"Who's in charge there?" Rickard was only gaining time. He thought he knew the name he would hear. Marshall's first word surprised him.

"No one. Up to a few months ago, it was Hardin,

Tom Hardin. He was general manager of the company. He was allowed to resign, to save his face, as the Chinese say. I may tell you that it was a case of firing. He'd made a terrible fluke down there."

"I know," murmured Rickard. It was growing more difficult, more distasteful. If Marshall wanted him to supplant Hardin! It had been incredible, that man's folly! Reckless gambling, nothing else. Make a cut in the banks of a wild river, without putting in head-gates to control it; a child would guess better! It was a problem now, all right; the writer of the report he'd just read wasn't the only one who was prophesying failure. Let the river cut back, and the government works at Laguna would be useless; a nice pickle Hardin had made.

Still to gain time, he suggested that Marshall tell him the situation. "I've followed only the engineering side of it. I don't know the relationship of the two companies."

"Where the railroad came in? The inside of that story? I'm responsible—I guaranteed to Faraday the closing of that break. There was a big district to save, a district that the railroad tapped—but I'll tell you that later." He was leisurely puffing blue, perfectly formed rings into the air, his eyes admiring them.

"Perhaps you've heard how Estrada, the general, took a party of men into the desert to sell a mine he owned. After the deal was made, he decided to let it slip. He'd found something bigger to do, more to his liking than the sale of a mine. Estrada was a big man, a great man. He had the idea Powell and others had, of turning the river, of saving the desert. He dreamed himself of doing it. If sickness hadn't come to him, the Colorado would be meekly carrying water now, instead of flooding a country. Pity Eduardo, the son, is not like him. He's like his mother, you never know what they are dreaming about. Not at all alike, my wife and Estrada's."

Then it came to Rickard that he had heard somewhere that Marshall and General Estrada had married sisters, famous beauties of Guadalajara. He began to piece together the personal background of the story.

"It was a long time before Estrada could get it started, and it's a long story. As soon as he began, he was knocked down. Other men took hold. You'll hear it all in the valley. Hardin took a day to tell it to me! He sees himself as a martyr. Promoters got in; the thing swelled into a swindle, a spectacular swindle. They showed oranges on Broadway before a drop of water was brought in. Hardin has lots of grievances! He'd made the original survey. So when he sued for his back wages, he took the papers of the bankrupt company in settlement. He's a grim sort of ineffectual bulldog. He's clung with his teeth to the Estrada idea. And he's not big enough for it. He uses the optimistic method—gives you only half of a case, half of the problem, gets started on a false premise. Well, he got up another company on that method, the Desert Reclamation Company, tried to whitewash the desert project; it was in bad odor then, and he managed to bring a few drops of water to the desert."

"It *was* Hardin who did that?"

"But he couldn't deliver enough. The cut silted up. He cut again, the same story. He was in a pretty bad hole. He'd brought colonists in already, he'd used their money, the money they'd paid for land with water, to make the cuts. No wonder he was desperate."

It recalled the man Rickard had disliked, the roughshod, loud-voiced student of his first class in engineering. That was the man who had made the flamboyant carpets of the Holmes' boarding-house impossible any longer to him. He had a sudden disconcerting vision of a large unfinished face peering through the honeysuckles at a man and a girl drawing apart in confusion from their first, and last, kiss. He wanted to tell Marshall he was wasting his time.

"Overwhelmed with lawsuits," Marshall was saying. "Hardin had to deliver water to those colonists. It was then that he ran over into Mexico, so as to get a better gradient for his canal, and made his cut there. You know the rest. It ran away from him. It made the Salton Sea."

"Did he ever give you any reason," frowned Rickard reminiscently, "any *reasonable* reason why he made that cut without any head-gate?"

"No money!" shrugged Marshall, getting out another cigar. "I told you he's a raw dancer, always starts off too quick, begins on the wrong foot. Oh, yes, he has reasons, lots of them, that fellow, but as you say, they're not reasonable. He never waits to get ready."

Why was it that the face of the half-sister came to Rickard then, with that look of sensitive high-breeding and guarded reserve? And she, a Hardin! Sister to that loud-spilling mouth! Queer cards nature deals! And pretty cards Marshall was trying to deal out to him. Go down there, and finish Hardin's job, show him up to be the fumbler he was, give him orders, give the husband of Gerty Holmes orders—!

"It was Hardin who came to me, but not until he'd

A BIT OF ORATORY

tried everything else. They'd worked for months trying to dam the river with a few lace handkerchiefs, and perhaps a chiffon veil!" Marshall was twinkling over his own humor. "Hardin did put up a good talk. It was true, as he said; we'd had to move our tracks three, no, four times, at Salton. It was true that it ought to be one of the richest districts tapped by the O. P. But he clenched me by a clever bait—to put out a spur in Mexico which would keep any other railroad off by a fifty-mile parallel, and there the sand-hills make a railroad impossible.

"The government must eventually come to the rescue. Their works at Laguna hang on the control of the river down at the Heading. Once, he told me—I don't know how much truth there was in it—the Service, Reclamation Service, did try to buy up their plant for a paltry sum. He wouldn't sell. The short is, I recommended long-sighted assistance to Faraday. I promised to turn that river, save the district. We expected before the year was out to have the government take the responsibility off our hands."

Rickard made an impatient shrug. A nice problem Marshall had taken unto himself. He wanted none of it. Hardin—the thing was impossible.

He met laggardly Marshall's story. He heard him say: "Agreed with Faraday. The Desert Reclamation Company was as helpless as a swaddled infant. We made the condition that we reorganize the company. I was put in Hardin's place as president of the corporation, and he was made general manager. Of course, we had to control the stock. We put up two hundred thousand dollars—Hardin had estimated it would cost us less than half that! It's cost us already a million. Things haven't been going right. Faraday's temper burst out, and Hardin, a while back was asked to resign."

"And it is Hardin's position that you want me to fill?" His voice sounded queer to himself, dry, mocking, as if any one should know what an absurd thing he was being asked to do. He felt Marshall's sharp Indian eyes on him, as if detecting a pettiness. Well, he didn't care how Marshall interpreted it. That place wasn't for him.

"I want you in control down there." Rickard knew he was being appraised, balanced all over again. It made no difference—

"I'm sorry," he was beginning, when Marshall cut in.

"Good lord, you are not going to turn it down?"

He met Marshall's incredulous stare. "It's a job I'd jump at under most circumstances. But I can't go, sir."

Tod Marshall leaned back the full swing of his swivel chair, blankly astounded. His eyes told Rickard that he had been found wanting, he had white blood in his veins.

"It is good of you to think of me—pshaw, it is absurd to say these things. You know that I know it is an honor to be picked out by you for such a piece of work. I'd like to,—but I can't."

The president of railroads, who knew men, had been watching the play of feature. "Take your time," he said. "Don't answer too hastily. Take your time."

He was playing the fool, or worse, before Marshall, whom he respected, whose partisanship meant so much. But he couldn't help it. He couldn't tell that story—he knew that Marshall would brush it aside as a child's episode. He couldn't make it clear to the man whose stare was balancing him why he could not oust Tom Hardin.

"Is it a personal reason?" Marshall's gaze had returned to his ring-making.

Rickard admitted it was personal.

"Then I don't accept it. I wouldn't be your friend if I didn't advise you to disregard the little thing, to take the big thing. Maybe, you are going to be married." He did not wait for Rickard's vigorous negative. "That can wait. The river won't. Maybe it's some quixotic idea, like your smoking; for God's sake, Rickard, don't be quixotic. It's fine to be quixotic, magnificent, when you're young. Oh, you are young to me. But when you're no longer young? When you see the opportunity you did not take wasted, or made splendid, even, by some other man? Look at me! I could have foresworn the South, taken a different name after the war, said I was from England, or from New England. I could have made a decent living. What did I do? It seemed glorious to the youngster who had been fighting for his idea of justice to fight against such a handicap—a beaten southerner. And I did fight. I fought poverty, cold—I had a mother back there—I was hungry, often. Sick, and couldn't go to a doctor who might have warned me, because I hadn't a cent in my pocket. And so, when I was where I wanted to be, where I'd struggled up to be, had my hand on the life I loved, in the city I loved, with the woman I loved, I was knocked down, banished to this desert if I wanted to live a few more years! Where if I eat gruel, sleep a child's night sleep, give up all the things a man of red blood likes to do, I may live! If you'd call it that! Just because I'd had no one to talk to me, as I'm talking to you, to tell me I was a young fool."

Rickard was looking intently at a slit in the colored awning. He did not answer.

Marshall looked at the stiff figure facing him. "Your reason may be sounder than mine, less highfalutin. But look at it. Balance the other side. Drop yourself out of it. There's a river running away down yonder, ruining the valley, ruining the homes of families men have carried in with them. I've asked you to save them. There's a debt of honor to be paid. My promise. I have asked you to pay it. There's history being written in that desert. I've asked you to write it. And you say 'No—'"

"No! I say yes!" clipped Rickard. The Marshall oratory had swept him to his feet.

The dramatic moment was chilled by their Anglo-Saxon self-consciousness. An awkward silence hung. Then:

"When can you go?" Marshall's voice dropped from the declamatory. He had already taken up a pencil and was vaguely scribbling over a writing pad.

"To-day, to-morrow, the first train out." Rickard wondered if the scrawls had anything to do with him.

"Good!" Marshall's tone was hearty, but it had the finality of "good-by." He was tracing nebulous figures, letters. The word, "Oaxaca," ran out of the blur. Instantly his mind was diverted.

He had made his appeal, won his point. An hour later, perhaps, he would be honest in denying the paternity of some of his flowery phrases were he to be confronted by the children of his brain. His word of honor—he

A BIT OF ORATORY 19

had used as his climax. He had never thought of his business talk with Faraday in that light before, and never would again. It was a tool, picked up for his need and thrown away.

Already, he was revolving a spur he was planning for Oaxaca, in Southern Mexico. An inspiration had come to him on his walk from The Rosales that morning. His pencil made some rapid calculations.

A few minutes later he glanced up at the clock, and saw Rickard standing, as at attention.

"Ah!" He allowed his absorption to betray him.

"I should be off," discovered Rickard.

"Oh, no," replied the president of several railroads, looking at the clock again.

"Any instructions?"

"Just stop that river!"

Rickard again had a humorous vision of himself, asked to take away a bursting hose from a garden bed. "How am I limited?" he persisted. He stooped for his straw hat.

Marshall, still intrigued by his figures, looked up patiently, inquiringly, nibbling the end of his pencil.

"The expense?" demanded the engineer. "How far can I go?"

"Damn the expense!" cried Tod Marshall. "Just go ahead."

He had begun a swift pencil map of the province of Oaxaca before Rickard was out of the room.

CHAPTER III

THE BLESSING OF ARIDITY

WHEN Rickard left the main line at Imperial Junction the next afternoon, his eyes followed the train he was deserting rather than the one that was to carry him to his new labors. He felt again the thrill of detachment that invariably preceded his entrance into a new country. With the pulling up of the porter's green-carpeted stool, the slamming of the train gates, the curtain fell on the Tucson set scene.

The long line of cars was pushing off with its linen-covered Pullmans and diners, steaming down-grade toward the Sink, the depression which had been primeval sea, and then desert, and was now sea again. Old Beach, rechristened Imperial Junction for railroad convenience, was itself lower than the ancient sea-line where once the gulf had reached. Rickard knew he could find shells at that desert station should he look for them. He picked up his bag that the porter had thrown on the ground and faced the rung-down curtain.

Its painted scene was a yellow station house broiling under a desert sun; a large water-tank beyond, and in the distance the inevitable cardboard mountains, like property scene-shifts, flat and thin in their unreal hues of burnished pink and purple. A dusty accommodation train was backing and switching, picking up the empty refrigerator cars to carry into the valley for the early melon growers.

Already, the valley had asserted its industrial importance; the late rampage of the Colorado had made it spectacular. Those who would pay little attention to the opening of a new agricultural district in the heart of a dreaded desert opened their ears to the vagary of the river which had sportively made of a part of that desert an inland sea. Scientists were rushing their speculations into print; would the sea dwindle, by evaporation, as it had done before? Or would the overflow maintain the paradoxical sea?

The flood signs were apparent. There, cracks had split the desert sand; here, water fissures had menaced the track; and to the south, a fringe of young willows hid the path of the Colorado's debouch. The burning desert sands cried out a sharp antithesis. The yellow railway house bore all the parched signs of a desert station. Even the women, with children in their arms, did not attempt to sit in the stifling waiting-room; they preferred to stand in the glare.

The men crowding the platform wore the motley of a new country. In Tucson, the uniform of the male citizens, with the exception of those reckless ones who found inevitably that lotus is a liquid, was the wilted pretense of a gentle civilization; despondent ducks and khakis and limp collars. Imperial Junction marked the downfall of the collar. The rest of the composite costume was irregular, badly laundered and torn, faded and sunburned; the clothes of the desert soldier. Rickard saw buttonless shirts, faded overalls, shabby hats—the sombrero of Mexico. The faces under the broad-brimmed hats made a leaping impression upon him of youth and eagerness. He noted a significant average of intelligence and alertness. This was not the indolent group of men which makes a pretense of occupation whenever a train comes in!

"Going in?" asked a voice at his ear. A pair of faded eyes set in a young-old face, whether early withered or well-preserved he had not time to determine, was staring at him.

He assured his interlocutor that he was going in. His mood isolated the phrase; its significance vastly different from "going on."

"Buying?"

"I think not."

"It is a good time to buy." Rickard suspected a real-estate agent. "For land is low, rock-bottom prices on account of the uneasiness about the river. People are afraid. They want to see the company redeem some of its promises before they come in; and the company isn't in much of a hurry."

Rickard raised his chin that his collar might bind his suffering neck in a different place, and then asked what company he referred to.

The young-old face with the faded eyes looked at him in surprise. "The D. R. Company, Desert Reclamation, which brought us all here."

"Scamps?" The newcomer's survey of the long line of naked mountains and lean lands that formed the neck of the valley gave a snub of casualness to the question.

"No. Fools!" The answer was as swift as a bullet. "Though some people think them worse than that. I don't go so far, I'm willing to say they've tried. I'll say that much. But they haven't the know-how."

"I'd rather be a scamp than a fool," ventured Rickard. "It's more progressive." He drew a look of amused recognition from the faded valley man.

"Newspaper man? No? They are always coming in now since the break. I'm usually able to spot them."

"You've spotted wrong once," smiled Rickard, picking up his bag. The engine was backing the made-up train toward the station.

The crowd pushed forward. "No offense, I hope," called the sun-dried face over the heads of the press. "I've done a little of it myself."

The window seats, Rickard could see, were filled before the cars halted, by the experienced ones who had not waited for the train to be made up. In the scramble, he spied a vacant window on the sunny side, and made for it. Seated, he looked for his talkative friend who was already opening office farther down the car. A stranger dropped into the seat beside him.

Every window in the car was open. Each red-velveted, dusty seat was filled. A strong desert wind was blowing sand into their faces, discoloring the seats and covering the floor.

The engineer turned to his companion who was coughing.

"Do you mind this window being open?"

"I'd mind if it were not. It's always bad at the Junction. When we get into the cultivated country, you will see what the valley will be like when it is all planted. The wind is not bad when it blows over grain or alfalfa. It is the desert dust that nags one." He coughed again. "Going in?"

Rickard said he was going in.

"Are you going to settle in the valley?" The inquisitor was a man of about fifty, Rickard decided, with a desert tan of apparent health. His face was clear-cut and intelligent.

"I don't know."

"Just looking the country over?"

"You might call it that."

"Go slow," admonished his companion. "Don't let yourself be carried away. It is a wonderful country. But go slow. It's the ones who expect to make millions the first year that become the worst knockers. Go slow, I always tell them. Go slow."

"It's not a good time to buy then?"

"Not so good as it was ten years ago! But land is cheaper than it was a year back. In some districts you can buy a good farm for a ticket back home, the farmers are so discouraged. Cold feet." The slang sounded oddly, somehow. The man's voice had the cultivated precision of the purist. "Cold feet. The river's chilled them. The valley's losing faith in the company."

"What company?" inquired Rickard again.

"There's but one company to the valley, the one that brought them here, the D. R. They don't call the railroad The Company. They have nothing to do with that problem. They won't recognize that problem! It's had hard luck from the first, the D. R. At the very start, the wrong man got hold of it. Sather, the first promoter, was a faker; a pretty thorough faker. The company reorganized, but it's been in bad odor with the public ever since."

Rickard's eyes left the deep cuts in the land made by the ravaging waters, and looked at his companion.

"I thought Estrada was the original promoter?" he inquired.

"Estrada's a recent comer—oh, you mean the general. He started the ball rolling; that was all. Bad health, following the Bliss complication, tied his hands. Did you ever hear the story of the way he colonized his grant?"

Rickard shook his head.

"It is a good story. I wrote it once for the *Sun*. I was out here then. That was before the doctors sent me, giving me a year if I lived anywhere else. Reclamation was being talked even then. Estrada picked up the enthusiasm, and got hold of a big slice of land. The terms of his purchase were a few cents an acre, fifteen, if I remember correctly, and a hundred colonists to be established the first year. Estrada sent in his hundred families, and did not think it necessary to mention to the government that he was paying the so-called colonists a dollar a day. They earned their dollar—it was big money in those days, two dollars Mexican—by digging a canal. When the inspector came along—there were the hundred families. After he was safely out of the country, Estrada paid and dismissed his colonists. He had the mile or so of canal and his tract besides. What's the difference between fifteen cents and a hundred dollars? Multiply that by a million and a half, and you can see what those colonists were to bring to Estrada. Though they say he died poor."

The man in the seat ahead was listening. His head was leonine, his body shriveled. Rickard could see on the neck the ancient burns that had spared the magnificent head. The rest of the man had been shriveled and twisted into terrible deformity. Rickard found himself puzzling over the accident with its accompanying miracle. There was not a scar on the powerful face.

"Estrada's business methods were then not different from Sather's and Hardin's!" It was a deep rich organ.

"Oh, you can't class Hardin with Sather," protested Rickard's companion. "Sather *used* Hardin. Hardin's honesty can not be questioned. It's not money he's after. His whole heart is in this reclamation scheme."

"Hardin's a false alarm," growled the owner of the massive head. "He makes promises. He never keeps them."

The older man's smile was tolerant. "Barton," he indicated, "is the president of the water companies. And if you want to hear about a rogue and a scoundrel, ask the water companies their opinion of Hardin."

"Well, what sort of a hole has he got us into?" demanded the other with heat.

"Hardin's in a hole himself."

Rickard found himself admiring the distinction in the face beside him. The sharp-pointed beard in which the gray was appearing gave a dog-like keenness to the well-modeled head, but the sharpness of the features, of the long slender nose, the long chin and thin eyebrow lines were offset, curiously, by the mildness, the resignation, in the steady gray eyes. If fires had ever burned in them, there were but cold ashes left.

"No one seems to remember that he crucified himself to save the valley. I've a great respect for Thomas Hardin."

"Yes?" returned Rickard, whose liking had been captured by the speaker.

The impression of distinction sharpened. The stranger wore a laundered, pongee silk shirt, open at the neck, but restricted by a brown silk tie; and it was trimly belted. There were but two neckties in the entire car, and they occupied, Rickard observed, the same seat. "The beginning of the canal system."

Rickard looked out upon a flat one-toned country, marked off in rectangles by plows and scrapers. Farther south, those rectangles were edged by young willows. He fancied he could see, even at that distance, the gleam of water.

It was the passing of the desert. A few miles back, he had seen the desert in its primitive nakedness which not even cactus relieved. He was passing over the land which men and horses were preparing for water. And he could see the land where water was.

"That was the way Riverside looked when I first saw it," commented the other man who wore a tie. "Come out on the rear platform. We can see better."

Rickard followed to the back of the dust-swept stifling car. The glare on the platform was intense. He stood watching the newly made checker-board of a country slip past him. Receding were the two lines of gleaming steel rails which connected and separated him from the world outside. He was "going in." Not in Mexico even had he had such a feeling of ultimate remoteness. The mountains, converging perspectively toward the throat of the valley, looked elusive and unreal in their gauze draperies of rose and violet. The tender hour of day was clothing them with mystery, softening their sharp outlines. They curtained the world beyond. Rickard felt the suspense of the next act.

It was a torpid imagination, he thought, which would not quicken over this conquest of the desert. East of the tract, men and teams were preparing the newly-furrowed ground for the seed. The curved land-knives were breaking up the rich earth mold into ridges of soft soil as uncohesive and feathery as pulverized chocolate. It was the dark color of the chocolate of commerce, this silt which had been pilfered from the states through which the vagrant river wandered. The smell of the upturned earth, sweetly damp, struck against his nostrils. Rickard indulged a minute of whimsical fancy; this was California territory over which his train was passing, but the soil, that dark earth those blades were crumbling, was it not the tribute of other states, of despoiling Wyoming, of ravishing Colorado and Arizona?

To the west, new squares were being leveled and outlined. Shrubby rectangles were being cleared of their creosote-bush and tough mesquit. Compared with other countries, the preparation for planting was the simplest. Horses were dragging over the ground a railroad rail bent into a V angle which pulled the bushes by the roots and dragged them out of the way. Beyond, farther west, could be seen the untouched desert. The surface for many miles was cracked by water-lines, broken and baked into irregular sand-cakes; the mark of sand which has been imprisoned by water and branded by swift heat.

Close by, men were putting in with care the seed that was to quicken the river silt. They were passing a square where the green tips of the grain were piercing the ground. Now, they were abreast of a field of matured alfalfa over which the wind raced gratefully. Desert and grain field; death and life! The panorama embraced the whole cycle.

"Excuse me. I did not hear you." His new acquaintance had been endeavoring to get his attention.

The valley man tried to pitch his voice above the

rattle of the train, but the effort ended in spasmodic coughing. The attacks left him weak and gasping.

"Better go back," suggested Rickard. He followed the stranger who waved him to the seat by the open window. He busied himself with the sliding landscape, withholding his sympathy. He could hear the man drawing in long deep breaths. "Poor devil! He's had his sentence!" he gathered.

After a few minutes, the other leaned over his shoulder, his hand waving toward the passing mountains. "Those are the Superstition Mountains you can see over yonder. An unusually apt name."

"Yes?"

"An accidental hit of some tired traveler," hazarded the colorless lips. "He had probably been listening to the legends of some unusually garrulous Indian; could not find the germ of universal religion in the simple creed, so he called it,—the nameless mountains—'Superstition.' I've always wished I knew his own name, that we might credit him, this late, with the inspiration. Have you ever thought," he deflected, "how many familiar names are unsponsored? Take the Colorado, for instance. Melchior Diaz called it the Rio del Tizon; Alarçon, for diplomatic reasons, gave it Rio de la Buena Guia; Onate changed it to the Rio Grande de Buena Esperanza, and it was Kino, the Jesuit padre, who christened it in memory of the blessed martyrs Rio de los Martires. Who called it first the Colorado? History shuts her lips. And who will ever call it anything else?"

Rickard was attracted by the man's educated inflection, as well as by his musing. "Why Superstition?" he queried.

"Why is it good, you mean? That pile of dark rock stands as a monument to an effete superstition. It is the gravestone for a gigantic mistake. Why, it was only the grossest ignorance that gave to the desert the label of 'bad lands.' The desert is a condition, not a fact. Here you see the passing of the condition, the burial of the superstition. Are you interested in irrigation?"

Rickard was not given to explain the degree of interest his profession involved, for the stranger drew a painful breath, and went on.

"Of course you are, if you are a western man. You are, I think?"

The engineer said that he was, by choice.

"Irrigation is the creed of the West. Gold brought people to this country; water, scientifically applied, will keep them here. Look at this valley. What was it a few years ago? Look at Riverside. And we are at the primer stage only. We are way behind the ancients in information on that subject. I learned at school, so did you, that some of the most glorious civilizations flourished *in spite of the desert* which surrounded them. That was only half a truth. They were great *because* of it! Why did the Incas choose the desert when their strength gave them the choice of the continent of South America? Why did the Aztecs settle in the desert when they might easily have preempted the watered regions? Then there are the Carthaginians, the Toltecs, the Moors. And one never forgets Egypt!"

"For protection," Rickard gave the slighted question an interested recognition. "Was that not what we were taught at school? The forest held foes, animal and human. Those nations grew to their strength and power in the desert, by virtue of its isolation."

THE BLESSING OF ARIDITY 31

"Superstition!" retorted the man with the pointed beard. "We are babes at the breast measured by the wisdom of the men who settled Damascus, or compared with the Toltecs, or those ancient tribes who settled in Northern India. They recognized the value of aridity. They knew its threefold worth."

"An inherent value?" demanded the college-bred man, turning from the window.

"An inherent value," declared the exponent of aridity.

"Will you tell me just what you mean?"

"Not in one session! Look yonder. That's Brawley. When I came through here, ten years ago, I could have had my pick of this land at twenty-five cents an acre. They were working at this scheme then—on paper. I was not alive to the possibilities then; I had not yet lived in Utah!"

The train was slowing up by a brand-new, yellow-painted station. There were several dusty automobiles waiting by the track, a few faded surreys, and the inevitable, country hotel bus. The platform was swarming with alert vigorous faces, distinctly of the American type.

The man in the seat beside him asked Rickard if he observed the general average of intelligence in the faces of the crowd below. Rickard acknowledged that he had been struck by that, not only here, but at Imperial Junction, where he had waited for the train.

"There is a club in the valley, lately started, a university club which admits as members those who have had at least two years of college training. The list numbers three hundred already. The first meeting was held last week in an empty new store in Imperial. If it had not been for the setting, we might have been at Ann Arbor or Palo Alto. The costumes were a little motley, but the talk sounded like home."

The dust, blowing in through the car doors, brought on another fit of strangling. Rickard turned again to the window, to the active scene which denied the presence of desert beyond.

"The doctors say it will have to be the desert always for me." The stranger tapped his chest significantly. "But it is exile no longer—not in an irrigated country. For the reason of irrigation! It is the progressive man, the man with ideas, or the man who is willing to take them, who comes into this desert country. If he has not had education, it is forced upon him. I saw it worked out in Utah. I was there several years. Irrigation means cooperation. That is, to me, the chief value of aridity."

The wind, though still blowing through the car and ruffling the train dust, was carrying less of grit and sand. To the nostrils of Rickard and his new acquaintance, it brought the pleasing suggestion of grassy meadows, of willow-lined streams and fragrant fields.

"It is the accepted idea that this valley is attracting a superior class of men because of its temperance stand. It is the other way round. The valley stood for temperance because of the sort of men who had settled here, the men of the irrigation type."

The engineer's ear criticized "irrigation type." He began to suspect that he had picked up a crank.

"The desert offers a man special advantages, social, industrial and agricultural. (I would invert that arrangement if I made over that sentence!) It is no accident that you find a certain sort of man here."

"I suppose you mean that the struggle necessary to

develop such a country, under such stern conditions, develops of necessity, strong men?" evolved Rickard. "Oh, yes, I believe that, too."

"Oh, more than that. It is not so much the struggle, as the necessity for cooperation. The mutual dependence is one of the blessings of aridity."

"One of the blessings of aridity!" echoed his listener. "You are a philosopher." He had not yet touched the other's thought at the spring.

"You might as well call me a socialist because I praise irrigation in that it stands for the small farm unit," retorted the valley man. "That is one of its fiats; the small unit. It is the small farm that pays. That fact brings many advantages. What is the charm of Riverside? It comes to me always like the unreal dream of the socialist come true. It is a city of farms, of small farms, where a man may make his living off his ten acres of oranges, or lemons; and with all the comforts and conveniences of a city within reach, his neighbors not ten miles off! A farmer in Riverside, or in any irrigated community, does not have to postpone living for himself or his family, until he can sell the farm! He can go to church, can walk there; the trolley car which passes his door takes him to a public library, or the opera-house. His children ride to school. His wife does not need to be a drudge. The bread wagon and the steam laundry wagon stop at her door."

Rickard observed that perhaps he did not know anything about irrigation after all! He had not thought of it before in its sociological relation, but merely as it touched his profession.

"Not going into soil values, for that is a long story," began the older man, "irrigation is the answer which science gives to the agriculturist who is impatient of haphazard methods. Irrigation is not a compromise, as so many believe who know nothing about it. It is a distinct advantage over old-fashioned methods."

"I am one of those who always thought it a compromise," admitted the engineer.

"Better call rain a compromise," retorted the irrigationist. "The man who irrigates gives water to the tree which needs it; rain nourishes one tree, and drowns out another. Irrigation is an insurance policy against drought, a guarantee against floods. The farmer who has once operated an irrigated farm would be as impatient were he again subjected to the caprice of rain as a housewife would be were she compelled to wait for rain to fill her wash-tub. There is no irregularity or caprice about irrigation."

"Wonder how the old fellow picked it all up?" mused Rickard with disrespect. Aloud he said—"You were speaking of the value of the soil?"

"Look at the earth those plows are turning over. See how rich and friable it is, how it crumbles? You can dig for hundreds of feet and still find that sort of soil, eight hundred feet down! It is disintegrated rock and leaf mold brought in here in the making of a delta. Heavy rainfalls are rare here, though we have had them, in spite of popular opinion. Were we to have frequent rains, the chemical properties, which rain-farmers must buy to enrich their worn-out soils, would be leached out, drained from the soil. I can't make this comprehensive, but I've a monograph on desert soil. If you are interested, I'll send it to you."

"I should like it—immensely," assented the engineer, still amused.

"It explains the choice of the Aztecs, of the Incas, of Carthaginians, the Moors," observed the stranger. "They chose the desert, not in spite of the soil, but because of it. I doubt if they were awake to the social advantages of the system, but it was their cooperative brotherhood that helped them to their glory. We are centuries behind them. Look what the acceptance of the superstition has already cost California! The Mexican Boundary Survey Commission did its work pretty thoroughly until familiarity with the bad lands they were plodding through confirmed the old superstition. The international line was to cut across at the mouth of Hardy's Colorado. When the surveyors struck the Gila, they assumed it was the river they wanted it to be; anyway, it did not matter; it was 'bad land,' where even the Indians were thinning, where only scorpions and rattlers could flourish. The line was drawn there, and California lost all that area of desert land. However, a lady got her silk gown!"

The last words were as spice to a tasteless pudding. "A silk gown!" It sounded piquant.

"That's a page of unwritten history," said the stranger, rising. "I'm getting out here; Imperial. If you come up to Imperial, look me up. Brandon's my name. I've no card these days!"

"There are several things I want to hear from you," answered Rickard, rising also, and following the pointed beard to the platform. "I'll be sure to look you up. Mine's Rickard."

"There's my residence," waved Brandon. "That tent over yonder?" All of Imperial was easily seen from the car platform. "No, that is a canvas house. There is a great difference,—in distinction!"

Rickard liked the nicety of speech which to the critical ear is as pleasing as wit. He watched Brandon step off the car, saw him greeted and surrounded by a knot of station watchers.

"Hello, Brandon," Rickard could hear them hail him. "Back home, Brandon?" "Treated you well at Palm Springs?"

"Poor devil," he thought again. "Trying Palm Springs for his cough. Wonder who the old duck is. Country newspaper, I fancy. He did say he had reported for the *Sun*."

The young-old man who had spoken to him at the Junction, pushed past with some bundles. He stopped when he saw Rickard.

"I get out here. If you come to Imperial, hunt me up. I run the *Star*, the only newspaper in the valley. Glad to meet you."

"Disposing of my theory about Brandon," smiled the engineer, going back into the dusty car. He was interested enough to lean over and ask Barton who was the man called Brandon. They could see him from the windows, still surrounded, still smiling that sweet ascetic smile.

"Captain Brandon they call him. He's one of the old settlers. Was with Powell, on the second expedition down the river. Then was one of the big men on the *Sun*." He tapped his chest significantly. "Bad; came West, folks thought to die. There's lots of grit in the old fellow. He's written a history of the Colorado River that reads like a novel, they say. I've never read it. I never read books. I'm lucky if I can get time for a newspaper, and I don't often get a newspaper."

THE BLESSING OF ARIDITY

Rickard observed that "Captain Brandon" seemed to be well informed on the subject of irrigation.

"That's his hobby, that and desert soil. He's writing a book on irrigation, not half done yet, but it's already sold. He's published a pamphlet on desert soil. Oh, he knows his subject."

"College man?"

"Harvard, I think, and then either an English or German university. I've heard, but I've forgotten by now. He's lived in the West, everywhere they've tried irrigation; in Utah, Colorado, California, and he's been to Egypt and Syria and all the classic places. Studying, but he came back again, nearly dead. He goes up to Palm Springs every little while to get toned up, taken care of. Poor devil!"

The breeze, which was now entering the car windows, had blown over clover-leafed fields. Its message was sweet and fresh. Rickard could see the canals leading off like silver threads to the homes and farms of the future; "the socialists' dream come true!" Willows of two or three years' growth outlined the banks. Here and there a tent, or a ramada, set up a brave defiance against the hard conditions of the land it was invading. Rickard leaned out of the window, and looked back, up the valley which was dominated by the range now wrapping around itself gauzy iridescent draperies.

"The monument to an effete superstition!" he repeated. "That wasn't a bad idea. I hope he won't forget to send me his monograph."

CHAPTER IV

THE DESERT HOTEL

HE left the dusty car with relief when the twin towns were called. The sun, plunging toward the horizon, was sending out long straight shafts of yellow light, staining the railroad buildings a deeper hue and playing queer tricks with faces and features. The yellow calcium isolated two stalwart Indians whose painted faces and streaming black hair, chains of tawdry beads and floating ribbons made the vacuity of their brown masks a grotesque contrast. Their survey of the train and the jostling passengers, was as dispassionate and incurious as though this brisk invasion carried no meaning nor menace to them.

Rickard had expected to see a Mexican town, or at least a Mexican influence, as the towns hugged the border, but it was as vividly American as was Imperial or Brawley. There was the yellow-painted station of the Overland Pacific lines, the water-tank, the eager American crowd. Railroad sheds announced the terminal of the road. Backed toward the station was the inevitable hotel bus of the country town, a painted board hanging over its side advertising the Desert Hotel. Before he reached the step, the vehicle was crowded.

"Wait, gen'lemen, I'm coming back for a second load," called the darky who was holding the reins.

"If you wait for the second trip, you won't get a room," suggested a friendly voice from the seat above.

Rickard threw his bag to the grinning negro, and swung on to the crowded steps.

Leaving the railroad sheds, he observed a building which he assumed was the hotel. It looked promising, attractive with its wide encircling veranda and the patch of green which distance gave the dignity of a lawn. But the darky whipped up his stolid horses. Rickard's eyes followed the patch of green.

The friendly voice from above told him that that was the office of the Desert Reclamation Company. His next survey was more personal. He saw himself entering the play as the representative of a company that was distrusted, if not indeed actively hated by the valley folk. It amused him that his entrance was so quiet as to be surreptitious. It would have been quieter had Marshall had his way. But he himself had stipulated that Hardin should be told of his coming. He had seen the telegram before it left the Tucson office. He might be assuming an unfamiliar rôle in this complicated drama of river and desert, but it was not to be as an eavesdropper.

"Going in to settle?" The friendly voice belonged, he could see through the press of arms and limbs, to a pair of alert eyes and a faded buttonless shirt that had once been blue.

"I did that before I left!" He was tired of the question.

There was a laugh from the seats above.

"Going to try Calexico?"

"I think Calexico is going to try me! If this dust is a sample!"

"Wonder if they are so eager to welcome settlers because they are all real-estate agents, or if the valley movement is a failure?" reflected the newcomer.

The heavy bus was plowing slowly through the dust of the street. Rickard was given ample time to note the limitations of the new town. They passed two brick stores of general merchandise; lemons and woolen goods, stockings and crackers disporting fraternally in their windows. A board sign swinging from the overhanging porch of the most pretentious building announced the post-office. From a small adobe hung a brass plate advising the stranger of the Bank of Calexico. The 'dobe pressed close to another two-storied structure of the desert type. The upper floor, supported by posts, extended over the sidewalk. Netted wire screened away the desert mosquito, and gave the overhanging gallery the grotesque appearance of a huge fencing mask. From the street could be seen rows of beds; as in hospital wards. Calexico, it was seen, slept out-of-doors.

"Desert Hotel," bawled the darky, reining in his placid team.

"Yes, sah, I'll look out for your bag. Got your room? The hotel's mighty sure to be full. Not many women yit down this a-way. . . . All the men mostly lives right heah at the hotel."

Rickard made a dive from a swirl of dust into the hotel. The long line he anticipated at the desk was not there. He stopped to take in a valley innovation. One end of the long counter had been converted into a soda-water bar. The high swivel stools in front of the white marbled stand, with its towering silver fixtures, were crowded with dust-parched occupants of the bus. A white-coated youth was pouring colored sirups into tall glasses; there was a clinking of ice; a sizzling of siphons.

"That's a new one on me," grinned Rickard, turning toward the desk where a complacent proprietor stood waiting to announce that there was but one room left.

"With bath?"

"Bath right across the hall. Only room left in the house." The proprietor awarded him the valley stare. "Going to be here long?" He passed the last key on the rack to the darky staggering under a motley of bags and suit-cases. Rickard recognized his, and followed.

"I may get you another room to-morrow," called the proprietor after him as he climbed the dusty stairs.

Rickard decided that the one room was not only hot and stifling, but dirty. The darky thrust his bag through the door and left the guest staring at the bed. He pulled back the covers; dust and sand of apparently a week's accumulation lined the sheets. The red, gaily-flowered, Brussels carpet was gritty with sand. Rickard rubbed a reflective finger over the surface of the golden-oak bureau.

A middle-aged chambermaid with streaming rusty hair, entering without ceremony, caught his grimace.

"It's not as bad as it looks. I cleaned it up this morning. It's the wind. Ain't it awful? I've known people to come into this place when the wind has been blowing as it has to-day, and seen them leave as soon as they seen their bed. They had to come back, as there's no other place to go, and they'd be no better if there was. But Mr. Patton, that's the boss, has me go around regular now, and explain. It saves his time. I'll fix it up for you, so you can be easy as to its being new dirt. It'll be just as bad as this when you come to go to bed."

Rickard washed his hands, and fled, leaving the berserker to the clouds of fury she had evoked. The soda-counter was deserted. The youth, divested of his white coat, was relieving Mr. Patton at the register. Rickard followed the sound of voices.

The signals of a new town were waving in the dining-room. The majority of the citizens displayed their shirt-sleeves and unblushing suspenders. One large table was surrounded by men in khaki; the desert-soldiers, engineers. The full blown waitresses, elaborately pompadoured, were pushing through the swing-doors, carrying heavy trays. Their transparent shirt-waists of coarse embroidery or lace were pinned to rusty, badly hung skirts of black alpaca. An apron, the size of a postage stamp, was the only badge of servitude. Coquetry appeared to be their occupation, rather than meal-serving, the diners accepting both varieties of attention with appreciation. The supremacy of those superior maidens was menaced only by two other women who sat at a table near the door. Rickard did not see them at first. The room was as masculine as a restaurant in a new mining town.

A superior Amazon inquired if the gentleman would like vermicelli soup? As he did not even glance at her magnificent pompadour, he was punished by being served last through the entire bill of fare.

He had two men at his table. They were engrossed with their course of boiled beef and spaghetti. Iced tea, instead of wine, was the only variation from the conventional, country hotel dinner.

Rickard left his indoor view to look through the French windows opening on a side street. He noticed a slender but regular procession. All the men passing fell in the same direction.

THE DESERT HOTEL

"Cocktail route," explained one of his neighbors, his mouth full of boiled beef.

"Oyster cocktail?" smiled the newcomer.

"The real thing! Calexico's dry, like the whole valley, that is, the county. See that ditch? That is Mexico, on the other side. Those sheds you can see are in Mexicali, Calexico's twin sister. That painted adobe is the custom house. Mexicali's not dry, even in summer! You can bet your life on that. You can get all the bad whisky and stale beer you've the money to buy. We work in Calexico, and drink in Mexicali. The temperance pledge is kept better in this town than any other town in the valley. But you can see this procession every night."

The Amazon with a handkerchief apron brought Rickard his soup. He was raising his first spoonful to his mouth when he saw the face, carefully averted, of the girl he had met at the Marshalls' table, Innes Hardin. His eyes jumped to her companions, the man a stranger, and then, Gerty Holmes. At least, Mrs. Hardin! Somehow, it surprised him to find her pretty.

She had achieved a variety of distinction, preserving, moreover, the clear-cut babyish chin which had made its early appeal to him. There was the same fluffy hair, its ringlets a bit artificial to his more sophisticated eyes, the same well-turned nose. He had been wondering about this meeting; he found that he had been expecting some sort of shock—who said that the love of to-day is the jest of to-morrow? The discovery that Gerty was not a jest brought the surprised gratification which we award a letter or composition written in our youth. Were we as clever as that, so complete at eighteen or twenty-one? Could we, now, with all our experience, do any better, or indeed as well? That particular sentence with wings! Could we make it fly to-day as it soared yesterday? Rickard was finding that Gerty's more mature charms did not accelerate his heart-beats, but they were certainly flattering to his early judgment. And he had expected her to be a shock!

He was staring into his plate of chilled soup. Calf-love! For he had loved her, or at least he had loved her chin, her pretty childish way of lifting it. She was prettier than he had pictured her. Queer that a man like Hardin could draw such women for sister and wife —the blood tie was the most amazing. For when women come to marry, they make often a queer choice. It occurred to him that that might have been Hardin—he had not wanted to stare at them.

That was not Hardin's face. It held strength and power. The outline was sharp and distinct, showing the strong lines, the determined mouth of the pioneer. There was something else, something which stood for distinction—no, it couldn't be Hardin.

And then, because an outthrust lip changed the entire look of the man, Rickard asked his table companions, who was the man with the two ladies, near the door.

"That, suh," his neighbor from Alabama became immediately oratorical, "that is a big man, suh. If the Imperial Valley ever becomes a reality, a fixtuah, it will be because of that one man, suh. Reclamation is like a seed thrown on a rock. Will it stick? Will it take root? Will it *grow?* That is what we all want to know."

Rickard thought that he had wanted to know something quite different, and reminded the gentleman from Alabama that he had not told him the name.

THE DESERT HOTEL

"The father of this valley, of the reclamation of this desert, Thomas Hardin, suh."

Rickard tried to reset, without attracting their attention, the group of his impressions of the man whose personality had been so obnoxious to him in the old Lawrence days. The Hardin he had known had also large features, but of the flaccid irritating order. He summoned a picture of Hardin as he had shuffled into his own class room, or up to the long table where Gerty had always queened it among her mother's boarders. He could see the rough unpolished boots that had always offended him as a betrayal of the man's inner coarseness; the badly fitting coat, the long awkward arms, and the satisfied, loud-speaking mouth. These features were more definite. Could time bring these changes? Had *he* changed, like that? Had they seen him? Would Gerty, would Hardin remember him? Wasn't it his place to make himself known; wave the flag of old friendship over an awkward situation?

He found himself standing in front of their table, encountering first, the eyes of Hardin's sister. There was no surprise, no welcome there for him. He felt at once the hostility of the camp. His face was uncomfortably warm. Then the childish profile turned on him. A look of bewilderment, flushing into greeting—the years had been kind to Gerty Holmes!

"Do you remember me, Rickard?"

If Hardin recognized a difficult situation, he did not betray it. It was a man Rickard did not know who shook him warmly by the hand, and said that indeed he had not forgotten him.

"I've been expecting you. My wife, Mr. Rickard, and my sister."

"Why, what are you thinking of, Tom? To introduce Mr. Rickard! I introduced you to each other, years ago!" Gerty's cheeks were red. Her bright eyes were darting from one to the other. "You knew he was coming, and did not tell me?"

"You were at the Improvement Club when the telegram came," put in Innes Hardin, without looking at Rickard. No trace of the Tucson cordiality in that proud little face! No acknowledgment that they had met at the Marshalls'!

"Oh, you telegraphed to us?" The blond arch smile had not aged. "That was friendly and nice."

Rickard had not been self-conscious for many a year. He did not know what to say. He turned from her upturned face to the others. Innes Hardin was staring out of the window, over the heads of several crowded tables; Hardin was gazing at his plate. Rickard decided that he would get out of this before Gerty discovered that it was neither "friendly nor nice."

"If I had known that you were here, I would have insisted on your dining with us, in our tent. For it's terrible, here, isn't it?" She flashed at him the look he remembered so vividly, the childish coquettish appeal. "We dine at home, till it becomes tiresome, and then we come foraging for variety. But you must come to us, say Thursday. Is that right for you? We should love it."

Still those two averted faces. Rickard said Thursday, as he was bidden, and got back to his table, wondering why in thunder he had let Marshall persuade him to take this job.

Hardin waited a scant minute to protest: "What possessed you to ask him to dinner?"

"Why shouldn't I? He is an old friend." Gerty caught a glance of appeal, from sister to brother. "Jealous?" she pouted charmingly at her lord.

"Jealous, no!" bluffed Hardin.

He thought then that she knew, that Innes had told her. The Lawrence episode held no sting to him. Once, it had enchanted him that he had carried off the boarding-house belle, whom even that bookman had found desirable—bookman! A superior dude! He had always had those grand airs. As if it were not more to a man's credit to struggle for his education, even if he were older than his class, or his teacher, than to accept it off silver plates, handed by lackeys? Rickard had always acted as if it had been something to be ashamed of. It made him sick.

"They've done it this time. It's a fool choice."

Again, that look of pleading from Innes. Gerty had a shiver of intuition.

"Fool choice?" Her voice was ominously calm.

Hardin shook off Innes' eyes. Better be done with it! "He's the new general manager."

"He's the general manager!"

"I'm to take orders from him."

Gerty's silence was of the stunned variety. The Hardins watched her crumbling bread on the table-cloth, thinking, fearfully, that she was going to cry.

"Didn't I tell you?" Her voice, repressed, carried the threat of tears. "Didn't I tell you how it would be? Didn't I say that you'd be sorry if you called the railroad in?"

"Must we go over this again?" asked her husband.

"Why didn't you tell me? Why did you let me make a goose of myself?" She was remembering that there had been no protest, no surprise from Innes. She knew! A family secret! She shrugged. "I'm glad, on the whole, that you planned it as a surprise. For I carried it off as if we'd not been insulted, disgraced."

"Gerty!" expostulated Hardin.

"Gerty!" implored Innes.

"And we are in for a nice friendly dinner!"

"Are you quite finished?" Hardin got up.

As the three passed out of the dining-room, Rickard caught their several expressions: Hardin's stiff, indifferent; Gerty's brilliant but hard, as she flashed a finished, brave little smile in his direction. The sister's bow was distinctly haughty.

In the hall, Gerty's laugh rippled out. It was the laugh Rickard remembered, the light frivolous cadence which recalled the flamboyant pattern of the Holmes' parlor carpet, the long, crowded dining-table where Gerty had reigned. It told him that she was indifferent to his coming, as she meant it should. And it turned him back to a dark corner in the honeysuckle draped porch where he had spent so many evenings with her, where once he had held her hand, where he told her that he loved her. For he had loved her, or at least he thought he had! And had run away from her expectant eyes. A cad, was he, because he had brought that waiting look into her eyes, and had run from it?

Should a man ask a woman to give her life into his keeping until he is quite sure that he wants it? He was revamping his worn defense. Should he live up to a minute of surrender, of tenderness, if the next instant brings sanity, and disillusionment? He could bury now forever self-reproach. He could laugh at his own vanity. Gerty Hardin, it was easy to see, had forgotten what he had whispered to Gerty Holmes. They met as sober old friends. That ghost was laid.

CHAPTER V

A GAME OF CHECKERS

THE uneasy mood of the desert, the wind-blown sand, drove people indoors the next morning. Rickard was served a substantial, indifferently cooked breakfast in the dining-room of the Desert Hotel, whose limitations were as conspicuous to the newcomer as they were non-existent to the other men. They were finding it a soft contrast to sand-blown tents, to life in the open.

Later, he wandered through the group of staring idlers in the office, past the popular soda-stand and the few chair-tilters on the sidewalk, going on, as if without purpose, to the railroad sheds, and then on, down to the offices of the Desert Reclamation Company. He discovered it to be the one engaging spot in the hastily thrown-together town. There were oleanders, rose and white, blooming in the patch of purple blossoming alfalfa that stood for a lawn. Morning-glories clambered over the supports of the veranda, and on over the roof. Rickard's deductions led him to the Hardins.

What school of experience had so changed the awkward country fellow? He had resented his rivalry, not that he was a rival, but that he was a boor. His kisses still warm on her lips, and she had turned to welcome, to coquet with Tom Hardin! The woman who was to be his wife must be steadier than that! It had cooled his fever. Not for him the aspen who could shake and bend her pretty boughs to each rough breeze that blew!

Men tossed into a desert, fighting to keep a foothold, do not garland their offices with morning-glories! Was it the gracious quiet influence of a wife, a Gerty Hardin? The festive building he was approaching was as unexpected—as Captain Brandon! Rickard walked on, smiling.

He was fairly blown into the outer room, the door banging behind him. Every one looked up at the noisy interruption. There were several men in the long room. Among them two alert, clean-faced youths, college-graduates, or students out on furlough, the kind of stuff in his class at Lawrence. Three of the seasoned, road-coached type were leaning their chairs against the cool thick walls. One was puffing at a cigar. The other, a big shy giant, was drawing clouds of comfort from a pipe. There was a telegraph operator at work in one end of the room, her instrument rapidly clicking. In an opposite corner was a telephone exchange. A girl with a metal band around her forehead was punching connections between the valley towns. Rickard lost the feeling of having gone into a remote and isolated region. The twin towns were on the map.

One of the older men returned his nod. The young men returned their hastily withdrawn attention to their game of checkers. The other smoker was watching with cross-eyed absorption the rings his cigar was sending into the air. Rickard might not have been there.

One of the checker players looked up.

"Anything I can do for you? Do you want to see any one in particular?"

"No," it was admitted. "No one in particular. I was just looking round."

"It's the show place of Calexico. I'll take you around. It is the only place in town that is comfortable when it's hot, or when the wind blows, and that's the program all summer. Take my place, Pete."

Pete, the young giant, with the face of his infancy enlarged rather than matured, slipped into the vacant chair. He had been the first to discover the stranger, but he had evaded the responsibility. The game immediately absorbed him.

"It's nice here," repeated the young fellow, leading the way. They were followed by a few idle glances.

Rickard looked with approval at the tall slim figure which was assuming the courtesy of the towns. The fine handsome face was almost too girlish, the muscles of the mouth too sensitive yet for manly beauty, but he liked the type. Lithe as a young desert-reared Indian, his manner and carriage told of a careful home and rigid school discipline.

It was the type Rickard liked, he was thinking, because it was the type he understood. He preferred the rapier to the bludgeon, the toughened college man to the world-veneered man of the field. He revered the progress of a Jefferson or a Hamilton; he would always distrust the evolution of a contemporary Lincoln. It is easier, he maintained, to skip classes, or grades in world discipline, than in a rigorous college. This was the kind which in his own classes had attracted him. He had missed them in his years on the road—in Mexico, Wyoming, North Dakota, where rough material had been his to shape.

He was ushered into a large cool room. The furnishings he inventoried: a few stiff chairs, a long table and a typewriter desk, closed for the Sabbath.

"The stenographer's room," announced the lad superfluously.

"Whose stenographer?"

"General property, now. Every one has a right to use her time. She used to be Hardin's, the general manager's. She is his still, in a way. But Ogilvie keeps her busy most of the time."

Rickard had not heard of Ogilvie. He made a mental register.

"When did Hardin go out?" He knew the date himself. He expected the answer would trail wisps of other information. He had a very active curiosity about Hardin. The man's failures had been spectacular.

The young fellow was thinking aloud. "The dam went November twenty-ninth. Hardin was given a decent interval to resign. Of course, he was fired. It was an outrage—" He remembered that he was speaking to a stranger, and broke off suddenly. Rickard did not question him. He made another note. Why was it an outrage, or why did it appear so? In perspective, from the Mexican barranca, where he had been at the time, the failure of that dam had been another bar sinister against Hardin.

"I see that you are from the University of California?" he said, following his courier to the door that opened on a long covered inner porch. Another lawn of alfalfa rested the eyes weary of dust and sand. A few willows and castor-beans of mushroom habit shut out the desert, denied the lean naked presence just beyond the leafy screen. Rickard nodded at the pin of gold and blue enamel.

"Out for a year," glowed the lad. "Dad wanted me to get some real stuff in my head. He said the Colorado would give me more lessons—more real knowledge in a year than I'd get in six at college. I kicked up an awful row—"

The older man smiled. "Of course. You didn't want to leave your class."

"You're a college man, then." Rickard uncovered his "frat" pin under his vest lapel. "Father wasn't. He couldn't understand. It was tough."

"You don't want to go back now?"

The boy made a wry face. "He expects me to go back in August. Says I must. Think I'd leave the desert if the Colorado goes on another rampage? Miss the chance of a lifetime? I'll make him see it. If I don't, I'll buck, that's all."

"You did not tell me your name," was suggested.

"MacLean, George MacLean," said the young man rather consciously. It was a good deal to live up to. He always felt the appraisement which followed that admission. George MacLean, elder, was known among the railroad circles to be a man of iron, one of the strongest of the heads of the Overland Pacific system. He was not the sort of man a son could speak lightly of disobeying.

"Of course, every one calls me Junior."

"I guess you'll go back if he wants you to," smiled Rickard.

"Oh, but what a rotten trick it would be!" exclaimed the son of the man of iron. "To throw me out of college—I was daffy to finish with my class, and to get me here, to get me interested—and then after I've lost my place to pull me back. Why, there are things happening every day that are a liberal education. They are only just beginning to understand what they are bucking up against. The Colorado's an unknown quantity, even old engineers are right up against it. There are new problems coming up every day. The Indians call her a yellow dragon, but she's a tricky woman, she's an eel; she's giving us sums to break our teeth on."

The man smiled at the eager mongrel imagery.

"I'll not go," said MacLean.

"Fathers seem wise the year after where they seem blind the year before!"

"I'll not go!" the boy blustered. Rickard suspected that he was bolstering up his courage.

"Who has the next room?"

"Used to be the general manager's. Ogilvie uses it now."

"And who did you say was Ogilvie?" They turned back into the room.

"You can go in. He's not here. He is the new auditor, an expert accountant from Los Angeles. Put in by the O. P. when it assumed control last year. He used to come down once a month. After Hardin went out, he came down to stay."

"Whose say-so?"

"I don't know. The accounts were rotten, that's no office secret. The world knows that. Hardin is blamed for it. It isn't fair. Look at Sather's stone palace in Los Angeles. Look at Hardin's tent, his shabby clothes."

"I'd like to meet Ogilvie," observed the general manager.

"Oh, he's not much to meet. A pale white-livered vegetarian, a theosophist. You've seen 'em. Los Angeles is full of 'em. He was here when Hardin was fired. You could see him see his opportunity. His chest swelled up. He looked as if he had tasted meat for the first time. He thought that he could woozle into the empty place! He went back to Los Angeles, convinced them that the auditor should be here, protect the company's interests. It sounded mysterious, sleuth-like, as if he had discovered something, so they let him bring the books down here. He is supposed to be ferreting. But he's 'woozling.' He used to be in the outer office. Said the noise made his head ache, so he moved in here. All the committee meetings are held here, and occasionally the directors' meetings. Water companies', too. Ogilvie's taking notes—wants to be the next general manager, it sticks out all over him."

"What's the derivation of woozle?" this with deep gravity.

"Wait till you see Ogilvie!" laughed his entertainer. Then as an afterthought: "This is all public gossip. He's fair game."

The door opened behind them, and Rickard saw the man whose description had been so deftly knocked off. He recognized the type seen so frequently in Southern California towns, the pale damaged exile whose chance of reprieve is conditioned by stern rules of diet and sobriety. It was the temperament which must perforce translate a personal necessity into a religious dogma.

"This gentleman's just,—is just looking around," stammered MacLean, blundering, confused.

The vegetarian nodded, taking off his felt sombrero and putting it on a chair with care.

The stranger observed that he had pleasant quarters.

Ogilvie said that they answered very well.

"Are there other offices than those I have seen?" Rickard demanded of MacLean.

He shook his head. "Dormitories. We sleep here, a lot of us when we are not on duty. At least, we don't sleep inside, unless it blows us in. We sleep out there." He nodded in the direction of the lawn. "We dress and 'gas' in there." His hand waved toward the rooms beyond.

By this time it was apparent that no one, save Hardin, knew of his coming. He was ahead of Marshall's letters. He did not like the flavor of his entrance.

"What provision is being made for a new general manager?"

The question, aimed carelessly, hit the auditor.

"They are not talking of filling the position just yet," he responded. "There is no need, at present. The work is going along nicely, better I might say, adjusted as it now is, than it did before."

"I heard that they had sent a man from the Tucson office to represent Mr. Marshall."

"Did you hear his name?" stammered Ogilvie.

"Rickard."

The auditor recovered himself. "I would have heard of it, were it true. I am in close touch with the Los Angeles office."

"It is true."

"How do you know?" Ogilvie's dismay was too sudden; the flabby facial muscles betrayed him.

"I'm Rickard." The new general manager took the swivel chair behind the flat-top desk. "Sit down. I'd like to have a talk with you."

"If you will excuse me," Ogilvie's bluff was as anemic as his crushed appearance. "I—I am busy this morning. Might I—trouble you—for a few minutes? My papers are in this desk."

Rickard now knew his man to the shallow depths of his white-corpuscled soul. "If I won't be in your way, I'll hang around here. I've the day to kill."

His sarcasm was lost in transit. Ogilvie said that Mr. Rickard would not be in his way. He would move his papers into the next room to-morrow.

The engineer moved to the French windows that opened on the alfalfa lawn. A vigorous growth of willows marked the course of New River which had cut so perilously near the towns. A letter, "b," picked out in quick river vegetation told the story of the flood. The old channel, there it was; the curved arm of the "b," one could tell that by the tall willows, had been too tortuous, too slow for those sweeping waters. The flow had divided, cutting the stem of the letter, carrying the flood waters swifter down-grade. The flow had divided,—hm! divided perhaps the danger, too! An idea in that! He would see that better from the water-tower he'd spied at entering. Another flood, and a gamble whether Mexicali or Calexico would get the worst of it. Unless one was ready. A levee—west of the American town!

"Excuse me, sir—do you need me?" He turned back into the room. He could see that MacLean was aching to get out of the room. Ogilvie had visibly withered. A blight seemed to fall on him as his white blue-veined fingers made a bluff among his papers.

"Thank you." Rickard nodded at MacLean, who burst into the outer office.

"It's the new general manager from Tucson—Rickard's his name." His whisper ran around the walls of the room where other arrivals were tilting their chairs. "The new general manager! Ogilvie woozled for nothing. You should have seen his face!"

"Did any one know that he was coming?" Silent, the tanned giant, spoke.

"That's Marshall all over," said Wooster, bright-eyed and wiry, removing his pipe. "He likes to move in a mysterious way his wonders to perform. (Used to sing that when I was a kid!) No announcement. Simply: 'Enter Rickard.'"

"More like this," said Silent. "Exit Hardin. Enter Ogilvie. Enter Rickard."

"And exit Ogilvie," cried MacLean.

"It's a—damned shame," burst out Wooster. No one asked him what he meant. Every man in the room was thinking of Hardin whose shadow this reclamation work was.

"What's Rickard doing?" asked the infantile Hercules at the checker-board. The force called him Pete, which was a short cut to Frederick Augustus Bodefeldt.

"Taking Ogilvie's measure," this from MacLean.

"Then he's doing something else by this time. That wouldn't take him five minutes unless he's a gull," snapped Wooster, who hated Ogilvie as a rat does a snake.

The door opened and Rickard came in. Almost simultaneously the outer door opened to admit Hardin. Who would introduce the new general manager to the dismissed one? The thought flashed from MacLean to Silent, to the telegraph operator. Bodefeldt doubled over the checker-board, pretending not to see them. Confusion, embarrassment was on every face. Nobody spoke. Hardin was coming closer.

"Hello, Hardin."

"Hello, Rickard."

It appeared friendly enough to the surprised office. Both men were glad that it was over.

"Nice offices," remarked Hardin, his legs outspread, his hands in his pockets.

"Ogilvie is satisfied with them." The men rather overdid the laugh.

"Finding the dust pretty tough?" inquired Hardin.

"I spent a month in San Francisco last summer!" was the rejoinder. "This is a haven, though, from the street. Thought I'd loaf for to-day." Was Hardin game to do the right thing, introduce him as the new chief to his subordinates? Nothing, it developed, was further from his intention. Hardin, his legs outstretched, kept before his face the bland impenetrable smile of the oriental. It was clearly not Rickard's move. The checker players fidgeted. Rickard's silence was interrogative. Hardin still smiled.

The outer door opened.

The newcomer, evidently a favorite, walked into a noisy welcome, the "boys'" embarrassment overdoing it. He was of middle height, slender; a Mexican with Castilian ancestry written in his high-bred features, his grace and his straight dark hair.

"Good morning, Estrada," said Hardin with the same meaningless smile.

"Good morning, gentlemen." The Mexican's greeting paused at Rickard.

"Mr. Estrada, Mr. Rickard."

Every one in the office saw Hardin snub his other opportunity. He had betrayed to every one his deep hurt, his raw wound. When he had stepped down, under cover of a resignation, he had saved his face by telling every one that a rupture with Maitland, one of the directors of the reorganized company, had made it impossible for them to serve together, and that Maitland's wealth and importance to the company demanded his own sacrifice. Two months before Rickard's appearance, Maitland had been discovered dead in his bath in a Los Angeles hotel. Though no one had been witless enough to speak of their hope to Hardin, he knew that all his force was daily expecting his reinstatement. Rickard's entrance was another stab to their chief.

"The son of the general?" The new manager held out his hand. "General Estrada, friend of Mexican liberty, founder of steamship companies and father of the Imperial Valley?"

"That makes me a brother of the valley," Estrada's smile was sensitive and sweet.

"He did good work in his day," added Rickard rather stupidly.

Estrada looked at Hardin, hesitated, then passed on to the checker players, and stood behind MacLean.

"I saw your father in Los Angeles."

MacLean's eager face flushed. "Did you speak to him? Did you tell him how hard it would be for me to go back?"

"I did what I could. But it was a busy time. There were several meetings of the board. At the last two, he was present."

"You mean?"

"He was chosen to fill the vacancy made by Maitland's death."

MacLean's eyes wavered toward Hardin, whose nonchalance had not faltered. Had he not heard, or did he know, already?

"I'd like to have a meeting, a conference, to-morrow morning." Rickard was speaking. "Mr. Hardin, will you set the hour at your convenience?"

Because it was so kindly done, Hardin showed his first resentment. "It will not be possible for me to be there. I'm going to Los Angeles in the morning." He turned and left the office, Estrada following him.

"Oh, Mr. Hardin, you mustn't take it that way," he expostulated, concern in each sensitive feature.

"I'll take orders from him, but he gave me none," growled Hardin. "It's not what you think. I'm not sore. But I don't like him. He's a fancy dude. He's not the man for this job."

"Then you knew him before?" It was a surprise to Estrada.

"At college. He was my—er, instructor. Marshall found him in the class room. A theory-slinger."

Estrada's thoughtful glance rested on the angry face. Was this genuine, or did not Hardin know of the years Rickard had served on the road; of the job in the heat-baked barrancas of Mexico where Marshall had "found" him? But he would not try again to persuade Hardin to give up his trip to Los Angeles. It might be better, after all, for the new manager to take charge with his predecessor out of the way.

"MacLean's coming down to-night," he threw out, still watching Hardin's face. "With Babcock."

"I won't be missed." Hardin's mouth was bitter. "Estrada, if I had the sense of a goat, I'd sell out, sell my stock to MacLean, and quit. What's in all this, for me? Does any one doubt my reason for staying? It would be like leaving a sinking ship, like deserting the passengers and crew one had brought on board. God! I'd like to go! But how can I? I've got hold of the tail of the bear, and I can't let go!"

"No one doubts you—" began Estrada. Hardin turned away, with an ugly oath. The Mexican stood watching his stumbling anger. "Poor Hardin!"

In the office, Rickard was speaking to MacLean, whom he had drawn to one side, out of ear-shot of the checker players.

"I want you to do something for me, not at all agreeable!" His tone implied that the boy was not given the chance to beg off. "What time does the train pull out in the morning?"

"Six-fifteen."

"I'll have a letter for you, at the hotel at six. Be on time. I want to catch Hardin before he leaves for Los Angeles. If he's really going. I'll give him to-day to think it over. But he can't disregard an order as he did my invitation. I didn't want to rub it in before the men."

MacLean stared; then said that he thought he was not likely to!

Rickard left the office in time to see Hardin shutting the outer gate behind him. His exit released a chorus of indignant voices.

"An outrage!"

"A damned shame!" This from Wooster.

"Hardin's luck!"

On the other side of the door, Rickard deliberated. The hotel and its curious loungers, or his new office, where Ogilvie was making a great show of occupation? He had not seen Estrada. He was making a sudden dive for his hotel, when the gentle voice of the Mexican hailed him.

"Will you come to my car? It's on the siding right here. We can have a little lunch, and then look over some maps together. I have some pictures of the river and the gate. They may be new to you."

Rickard spent the afternoon in the car. The twin towns did not seem so hostile. He thought he might like the Mexican.

Estrada was earning his father's mantle. He was the superintendent of the road which the Overland Pacific was building between the twin towns and the Crossing; a director of the Desert Reclamation Company; and the head of a small subsidiary company which had been created to protect rights and keep harmonious relation with the sister country. Rickard found him full of meat, and heard, for the first time consecutively, the story of the rakish river. Particularly interesting to him was the relation of Hardin to the company.

"He has the bad luck, that man!" exclaimed Estrada's soft tuneful voice. "Everything is in his hands, capital is promised, and he goes to New York to have the papers drawn up. The day he gets there, the *Maine* is destroyed. Of course, capital is shy. He's had the devil's own luck with men: Gifford, honest, but mulish; Sather, mulish and not honest—oh, there's a string of them. Once, he went to Hermosillo to get an option on my father's lands. They were already covered by an option held by some men in Scotland. Another man would have waited for the three months to pass. Not Hardin. He went to Scotland, thought he'd interest those men with his maps and papers. He owned all the data, then. He'd made the survey."

Estrada repeated the story Brandon and Marshall had told, with little discrepancy. A friendly refrain followed the narrative. "He has the bad luck, that man!"

"And the Scotched option?" reminded Rickard, smiling at his own poor joke.

"It was just that. A case of Hardin luck again. He stopped off in London to interest some capital there; following up a lead developed on the steamer. He was never a man to neglect a chance. Nothing came of it, though, and when he reached Glasgow, he found his man had died two days before. Or been killed, I've forgotten which. Three times Hardin's crossed the ocean trying to corner the opportunity he thought he had found. It isn't laziness, is his trouble. It's just infernal luck."

"Or over-astuteness, or procrastination," criticized his listener to himself. He knew now what it was that had so changed Hardin. A man can not travel, even though he be hounding down a quick scent, without meeting strong influences. He had been thrown with hard men, strong men. It was an inevitable chiseling; not a miracle.

"I want to hear more of this some day. But this map. I don't understand what you told me of this by-pass, Mr. Estrada."

Their heads were still bending over Estrada's rough work-bench when the Japanese cook announced that dinner was waiting in the adjoining car. MacLean and Bodefeldt and several young engineers joined them.

It had been, outwardly, a wasted day. Rickard had lounged, socially and physically. But before he turned in that night, he had learned the names and dispositions of his force; and some of their prejudices. Nothing, he summed up, could be guessed from the gentleness of the Mexican's manner; Wooster's antagonism was open and snappish. Silent was to be watched; and Hardin had already shown his hand.

The river, as he thought of it, appeared the least formidable of his opponents. He was imaging it as a high-spirited horse, maddened by the fumbling of its would-be captors. His task it was to lasso the proud stallion, lead it in bridled to the sterile land. No wonder Hardin was sore; his noose had slipped off one time too many! Hardin's *luck!*

CHAPTER VI

RED TAPE

AT ten o'clock the next morning, Hardin, entering the office, again the general manager's, found there before him, George MacLean, the new director, and Percy Babcock, the treasurer, who had been put in by the Overland Pacific when the old company was reorganized. They had just come in from Los Angeles, the trip made in MacLean's private car.

"Where's Estrada?" inquired Hardin of Ogilvie, who was making a great show of industry at the desk in the center of the room.

Before Ogilvie could open his deliberate lips, Hardin's question was answered by Babcock, a thin nervous man, strung on live wires. "Not here yet."

Hardin stood in his characteristic attitude, legs outstretched, his hands in his pockets. "Rickard?"

"Coming back, Ogilvie says. He went out a few minutes ago."

"Just like Marshall, that." Hardin moved over to the leather lounge where MacLean was sitting. Neither man answered him. It was Hardin's method of acknowledging the situation.

Rickard entered a few minutes later, Estrada behind him. Ogilvie followed Rickard to his desk.

"Well?" inquired the new manager.

Ogilvie explained lengthily that he had the minutes of the last meeting.

"Leave them here." Rickard waved him toward Estrada, who held out his hand for the papers.

Ogilvie's grasp did not relax. He stammered: "There is no secretary. I've been taking the minutes—"

"Thank you. Mr. Estrada will read them. We do not need you, Mr. Ogilvie."

Ogilvie stood, turning his expressionless eyes from one director to the other as if expecting that order to be countermanded. Babcock and MacLean appeared to be looking at something outside through the vine-framed windows. An ugly smile disfigured Hardin's mouth.

Rickard spoke again. "Mr. Estrada! We won't detain you any longer, Mr. Ogilvie."

Reluctantly, the accountant relinquished the papers. His retreating coat tails looked ludicrously whipped, but no one laughed. Hardin's scowl deepened.

"Showing his power," he thought. "He's going to call for a new pack."

Estrada pushed the minutes through with but a few unimportant interruptions. He was sitting at the same desk with Rickard. Hardin, sensitive and sullen, thought he saw the meeting managed between them. "It's all slated," ran his angry blood. "The meeting's a farce. It was all fixed in Los Angeles, or in Marshall's office." He whipped himself into rebellion. He was no baby. He knew about these matters better than these strangers, this fancy dude! He'd show them!

It took their silent cooperation to hold him down. It became more apparent to him that they were all pitted against him. He was being pressed against the wall.

Several times he attempted to bring the tangled affairs

of the water companies before the directors. Rickard would not discuss the water companies.

"Because he's not posted! He's beginning to see what he's up against," ran Hardin's stormy thoughts. He felt Rickard's hand in this, although it was Estrada, apparently, who shelved the mystifications of the uneasy companies, their rights, their dissatisfactions and their lawsuits. Babcock seconded the Mexican's motion to discuss those issues at the next meeting. "It is a put-up job," sulked Tom Hardin.

He was on his feet the next minute with a motion to complete the Hardin head-gate. Violently he declaimed to Babcock and MacLean his wrongs, the injustice that had been done him. Marshall had let that fellow Maitland convince him that the gate was not practicable; had it not been for him, the gate would be in place now; all this time and money saved. And the Maitland dam, built instead! Where was it? Where was the money, the time, put in that little toy? Sickening! His face purpled over the memory. Why was he allowed to begin again with the gate? "Answer me that. Why was I allowed to begin again? It's all child's play, that's what it is. And when I am in it again, up to my neck, he pulls me off."

This was the real Hardin, the uncouth, overaged Lawrence student! The new manner was just a veneer. Rickard had been expecting it to wear thin.

"Why did we begin it, I ask you?" repeated Hardin, his face flushed and eager. "To make laughing-stocks of ourselves down here? That's a costly game for the O. P. to play. What does Marshall know about conditions, sitting in his office, and looking at maps, and reading letters and reports from his spies? I'll give you the answer: he wants the glory himself. Why did he tell me that he thought my gate would go, and then start another ten times as costly? He wants all the credit. He'd like to see my gate a failure. Why does he push the concrete gate ahead, and hold up mine every few days?"

"I think," interjected Rickard, "that we all agree with Mr. Marshall, Mr. Hardin, that a wooden head-gate on silt foundation could never be more than a makeshift. I understood that the first day he visited the river with you he had the idea to put the ultimate gate, the gate which would control the water supply of the valley, up at the Crossing on rock foundation. Mr. Marshall does not expect to finish that in time to be of first use. He hopes the wooden gate will solve the immediate problem. It was a case of any port in a storm. He has asked me to report my opinion."

"Why doesn't he give me a chance to go ahead then?" growled the deposed manager. "Instead of letting the intake widen until it will be an impossibility to confine the river there at all?"

"So you do think that it will be an impossibility to complete the gate as planned?"

Hardin had run too fast. "I didn't mean that," he stammered. "I mean it will be difficult if we are delayed much longer."

"You are in charge of the construction of that gate?"

Hardin said he was. If it had not been for the floods—

"Have you the force to re-begin work at once?" demanded Rickard.

"I had it," evaded Hardin. "I had everything ready to go on—men, material—when we stopped the last time."

"And you haven't it now?"

Hardin hated to the soul of him to have to acknowledge that he had not; he shrank from uncovering a single obstacle that stood between his gate and completion. He tried to hedge. MacLean, a big man whose iron wheels moved slowly, was weighing the caliber of the two opposing men. Babcock, wiry, alert, embarrassed Hardin with his challenging stare.

"Answer my question, please."

"I should have to assemble them again," admitted Hardin sulkily.

Rickard consulted his note-book. "I think we've covered everything. Now, I want to propose the laying of a spur-track from Hamlin's Junction to the Heading." His manner cleared the stage of supernumeraries; this was the climax. Hardin looked ready to spring.

"And in connection with that, the development of a quarry in the granite hills back of Hamlin's," continued Rickard, not looking at Hardin.

Instantly Hardin was on his feet. His fist thundered on the table. "I shall oppose that," he flared. "It is absolutely unnecessary. We can't afford it. Do you know what that will cost, gentlemen?"

"One hundred thousand dollars!" Rickard interrupted him. "I want an appropriation this morning for that amount. It is, in my opinion, absolutely necessary if we are to save the valley. We can not afford *not* to do it, Mr. Hardin!"

Hardin glared at the other men for support; he found MacLean's face a blank wall; Estrada looked uncomfortable. Babcock had pricked up his ears at the sound of the desired appropriation; his head on one side, he looked like an inquisitive terrier.

Hardin spread out his hands in helpless desperation. "You'll ruin us," he said. "It's your money, the O. P.'s, but you're lending it, not giving it to us. You are going to swamp the Desert Reclamation Company. We can't throw funds away like that." One hundred thousand dollars! Why, he could have stopped the river any time if he had had that sum; once a paltry thousand would have saved them— "I didn't ask the O. P. to come in and ruin us, but to stop the river; not to throw money away in hog-wild fashion." He was stammering inarticulately. "There's no need of a spur-track if you rush my gate through."

"If," Rickard nodded. "Granted. If we can rush it through. But suppose it fails? Marshall said the railroad would stand for no contingencies. The interests at stake are too vital—"

"Interests!" cried Tom Hardin. "What do you know of the interest at stake? You or your railroad? Coming in at the eleventh hour, what can you know? Did you promise safety to thousands of families if they made their homes in this valley? Are you responsible? Did you get up this company, induce your friends to put their money in it, promise to see them through? What do you know of the interests at stake? You want to put one hundred thousand dollars into a frill. God, do you know what that means to *my* company? It means ruin—" Estrada pulled him down in his seat.

Rickard explained to the directors the necessity in his opinion of the spur-track and the quarry. Rock in great quantities would be needed; cars must be rushed in to the break. He urged the importance of clenching the issue. "If it's not won this time, it's a lost cause," he maintained. "If it cuts a deeper gorge, the Imperial Valley is a chimera; so is Laguna Dam."

The other men were drawn into the argument. Babcock leaned toward Hardin's conservatism. MacLean was judicial. Estrada upheld Rickard. The spur-track, in his opinion, was essential to success. Hardin could see the meeting managed between the newcomer and the Mexican, and his anger impotently raged. His temper made him incoherent. He could see Rickard, cool and impersonal, adding to his points, and MacLean slowly won to the stronger side. Hardin, on his feet again, was sputtering helplessly at Babcock, when Rickard called for a vote. The appropriation was carried. Hardin's face was swollen with rage.

Rickard then called for a report on the clam-shell dredge being rushed at Yuma. Where was the machinery? Was it not to have been finished in February?

Hardin said that the machinery was ready, waiting in San Francisco. The hull of the dredge could not be finished for a couple of months at least.

"Why not get the machinery here? What's the use of taking chances?" demanded Rickard.

Hardin felt the personal implication. He was on his feet in a second. "There are no chances." He looked at MacLean. "The machinery's done. It's no use getting it here until we're ready."

"There are always chances," interrupted his opponent coolly. "We are going to take none. I want Mr. Hardin, gentlemen, appointed a committee of one to see that the machinery is delivered at once, and the dredge rushed. What's the date?"

"April eleventh," clicked the nickel-in-the-slot-machine-

Babcock again. Had any one asked the time, his answer as swift without consultation would have been as exact. He lived with his watch under his eye. Every few minutes he assured himself as to his gain on eternity.

"Get it in before the heavy summer traffic begins," instructed Rickard.

The working force was informally discussed. Hardin said they could depend on hobo labor. His enthusiasm took fire; he saw the work begun on his gate. "That class of men flock like bees to such work as this. There's no trouble getting them; they just drop in. Curious, isn't it, how such fellows keep track of the world's work? You build a levee, you begin a bridge, and there's your hobo on the spot. It's good labor, too, though it's fickle." It was the other Hardin, the chiseled man of affairs and experience. Rickard agreed that they would find such help, but it would not do to rely on it. The big sewer system of New Orleans was about completed; he had planned to write there, stating the need. And there was a man in Zacatecas, named Porter—

"Frank Porter?" sneered Hardin, "that—murderer?"

"His brother," Rickard answered pleasantly. "Jim furnishes the men for the big mines in Sonora and Sinaloa. He'll send us all the labor we want, the best for our purpose. When it gets red-hot, there's no one like a peon or an Indian."

"You'll be infringing on the international contract law," suggested MacLean.

"No. The camp is on the Mexican side," laughed Casey. "I'd thought of that. We'll have them shipped to the nearest Mexican point, and then brought to the border. Mr. Estrada will help us."

The meeting had already adjourned. They were standing around the flat-top desk. Estrada invited them all to lunch with him, in the car on the siding. MacLean said that he had to get back to Los Angeles. Mr. Babcock was going to take him out to Grant's Heading in the machine. He had never been there. They had breakfasted late. He looked very much the colonel to Rickard, his full broad chest and stiff carriage made more military by his trim uniform of khaki-colored cloth.

"May I speak to you about your boy, Mr. MacLean?"

Hardin caught a slight that was not intended. He pushed past the group at the door without civility or ceremony.

The steady grave eyes of the big frame looked at Rickard inquiringly.

"He wants to stay out another year. I hope you will let him. It's not disinterested. I shall have to take a stenographer to the Heading this summer. There is a girl here; I couldn't take her, and then, too, I'm old-fashioned; I don't like women in offices. My position promises to be a peculiar one. I'd like to have your son to rely on for emergencies a stenographer could not cover."

MacLean's grave features relaxed as he looked down on the engineer, who was no small man himself, and suggested that his son was not very well up in stenography.

"That's the least of it."

"I hope that he will make a good stenographer! Good morning, gentlemen."

At table, neither Estrada nor his guest uncovered their active thought which revolved around Hardin and his hurt. Instead, Rickard had questions to ask his host on river history. As they talked, it came to him that something was amiss—Estrada was accurate; he had all his facts. Was it enthusiasm, sympathy, he lacked? Presently he challenged him with it.

Estrada's eyes dreamed out of the window, followed the gorge of the New River, as though out there, somewhere, the answer hovered.

"Do you mean, do you *doubt* it?" exclaimed Rickard, watching the melancholy in the beautiful eyes.

Estrada shook his head, but without decision. "Nothing you'd not laugh at. I can laugh at it myself, sometimes."

Rickard waited, not sure that anything more was coming. The Mexican's dark eyes were troubled; a puzzle brooded in them. "It's a purely negative sense that I've had, since I was a child. Something falls between me and a plan. If I said it was a veil, it would be—something!" His voice fell to a ghost of tunefulness. "And it's—nothing. A blank—I know then it's not going to happen. It is terribly final! It's happened, often. Now, I wait for that—veil. When it falls, I know what it means."

"And you have had that—sense about this river business?"

Estrada turned his pensive gaze on the American. "Yes, often. I thought, after father's death, that that was what it meant. But it came again. It kept coming. I had it while you were all talking, just now. I don't speak of this. It sounds chicken-hearted. And I'm in this with all my soul—my father—I couldn't do it any other way, but—"

"You think we are going to fail?"

"I can't see it finished," was Estrada's mournful answer. He turned again to stare out of the window.

An odd sense of unreality rested for an instant on Rickard. Swiftly he rejected it. Outside, the sunshine, the work to be done, the river running wild—

"You've been too much in the valley, Mr. Estrada!"

Estrada looked at him, and then his glance went back to the car window. His silence said plainly: "Oh, I knew you would not believe me!"

"I mean, this country gets on men's nerves. It's so— omnipotent! The victories are all to the river's side, as yet. We're pygmies, fighting Titans. We fear what we have never conquered."

"Oh, that!" He could see that Estrada would not argue with him. "Oh, we all get that. The personal feeling, as if it were really a dragon, and we trying to shackle it with our wisps of straw!"

"A few lace handkerchiefs and a chiffon veil!" sang Rickard's memory.

"We get the sense of being resented, of angry power. We feel like interlopers in this desert. She tells us all, in her own terrible, silent way, 'You don't belong here!'"

"That has been quoted to me, silently, too!" laughed Rickard. And they were on solid ground again.

"Who are the river-men in the valley?" demanded the newcomer. "I want to meet them, to talk to them."

"Cor'nel, he's an Indian. He's worth talking to. He knows its history, its legends. Perhaps some of it *is* history."

"Where's he to be found?"

"You'll run across him! Whenever anything's up, he is on hand. He senses it. And then there's Matt Hamlin."

"I'll see him, of course. Has he been up the river?"

"No, but I'll tell you two who have. Maldonado, a

half-breed, who lives some twenty miles down the river from Hamlin's. He knows the Gila as though he were pure Indian. The Gila's tricky! Maldonado's grandfather was a trapper, his great-grandfather, they say, a priest. The women were all Indian. He's smart. Smart and bad."

Estrada's Japanese servant came back into the car to offer tea, freshly iced.

"That's what I want, smart river-men, not tea!" laughed Rickard. "I want river history."

"There's another man you ought to meet." Before he spoke the name, Rickard had a flash of telepathy; he knew Estrada would say, "Brandon."

"He was with the second Powell expedition. He's written *the* book on the river. He knows it, if any man does."

"That's so. I'd forgotten about him. I think I'll run up and have a talk with him."

"This instant?" smiled the Mexican, for his guest had risen. "There's no train out until to-night."

"I'll ask Mr. MacLean to take a passenger. That will save me several hours; and an uncomfortable trip."

"You wanted these maps." Estrada was gathering them together.

Queer, how that name had flashed from Estrada's mind to his. He hadn't thought about Brandon—there *was* something in it, in the vitality, the force of thought. If that were true, then why not the other, that odd sense that Estrada spoke of? Seeing clear!

"Your maps, Mr. Rickard!"

"Thank you. And you can just strangle that foreboding of yours, Mr. Estrada. For I tell you, we're going to govern that river!"

Estrada's pensive smile followed the dancing step of the engineer until it carried him out of sight. Perhaps? Because he was the son of his father, he must work as hard as if conviction went with him, as if success waited at the other end of the long road. But it was not going to be. He would never see that river shackled—

CHAPTER VII

A GARDEN IN A DESERT

HIS dwelling leaped into sight as Hardin turned the corner of the street. There was but one street running through the twin towns, flanked by the ditches of running water. The rest were ditches of running water edged by foot-paths. Scowling, he passed under the overhanging bird-cages of the Desert Hotel without a greeting for the loungers, whose chairs were drawn up against the shade of the brick walls. His abstraction aborted the hallo of jovial Ben Petrie, who was leaving his bank for his vineyard, the more congenial half of his two-sided life. Petrie stood for a minute on the narrow board-walk watching the hunched shoulders, the angry blind progress. He shrugged. Hardin was sore. It *was* pretty tough. Such infernal luck! He got thoughtfully into his English trap.

Fred Eggers left his motley counter, and joined the group of lounging Indians outside his store. He had a morning paper in his hand. His pale blue eyes looked surprised as Hardin's momentum swept him past. "Mr. Hardin," he called ineffectually.

The momentum slackened as Hardin neared the place he called his home. An inner tenderness diluted the sneer that disfigured his face. He could see Innes as she moved around in the little fenced-in strip that surrounded her desert tent. She insisted on calling it a garden, in spite of his raillery.

"Gerty's in bed, I suppose," thought Tom. He had a sudden vivid picture of her accusing martyrdom. His mouth hardened again. Innes, stooping over a rose, passed out of his vision.

It came to Hardin suddenly that a man has made a circle of failure when he dreads going to his office and shrinks from the reproaches at home.

"A 'has-been' at forty!" he mused. Where were all his ships drifting?

Innes, straightening, waved a gay hand.

"She's raising a goodly crop of barrels." His thought mocked and caressed her. Her garden devotion was a tender joke with him. He loved the Hardin trait in her, the persistence which will not be daunted. An occupation with a Hardin was a dedication. He would not acknowledge the Innes blood in her. Like that fancy mother of hers? Innes was a Hardin through and through!

"It's in the blood," ran his thought. "She can't help it. All the Hardins work that way. The Hardins always make fools of themselves!"

Innes, lifting her eyes from a crippled rose, saw that the black devils were consuming him again.

"Will you look at this wreck!" she cried.

The wind-storm the previous week had made a sickening devastation of her labors. The morning-glories alone were scatheless. A pink oleander drooped many broken branches from which miracles of perfect flowers were unfolding. The prettiest blossom to Hardin was the gardener herself. She was vivid from eager toil. Hardin looked at her approbatively. He liked her khaki suit, simple as a uniform, with its flowing black tie and leather belt. She looked more like herself to-day. She had bleached out, in Tucson. She had been letting herself get too tanned, running around without hats. Sunburn paled the value of those splendid yellow eyes of hers. He could always tease her by likening them to topazes.

"Cat's eyes, why don't you say it?"

She pushed a teasing lock of hair out of her eyes with one of her mud-splashed garden gloves. It left a ludicrous smudge across her cheek.

"Each time I leave this garden," she complained, "I declare I won't again. Not even for the Marshalls." She bent over again to adjust a bottomless keg around a wind-whipped, moribund plant.

"Quite a keg plant!" he quizzed. "Raising anything else?"

"And the glory of the morning he does not see!" she exclaimed with theatric intent.

His eyes ran over the pink and purple lines of cord-trained vines which made floral screens for her tent. Free of the strings overhead, they rioted over the ramada, the second roof, of living boughs. He acknowledged their beauty. They gave grace to bare necessity; they denied the panting, thirsty desert just beyond.

He remembered his own ramada. Gerty had hated it, had complained of it so bitterly when she came home from New York that he had had it pulled down and replaced by a V roof of pine boards, glaring and ugly. Gerty was satisfied, for it was clean; she no longer felt that she lived in a squaw-house. Let the Indians have ramadas; there was no earthly reason she should. He had urged that the desert dwellers had valuable hints to give them. But what was a ramada to him, or anything else?

He nodded at Innes.

"They are doing so much better than the ones you planted at the office. I wonder if Sam doesn't water them enough?" His mood was faultfinding. "Didn't he water your roses while you were gone?"

"Oh, he *waters* enough," smiled his sister. "But Sam's not for progress. He won't see the difference between watering and irrigating."

"It looks like a train wreck, or a whipped prize-fighter, next day," observed Hardin.

"It's really my fault. I staked it." She was still mourning over her calamity. "I forgot to barrel it. Stakes won't do here. The keg's the thing."

"That's what they think in Mexicali." Hardin turned to leave.

"The joke's as stale as their beer," retorted Innes. She did not want him to go so soon. She pointed out a new vine to him. She had brought it from Tucson; "Kudzu," they called it; a Japanese vine. And there was another broken rose, quite beyond the help of stripped handkerchiefs and mesquit splints.

He followed her around the tent, her prattle falling from his grim mood. He was not thinking of her flowers except as a mocking parallel. The desert storm had made a havoc of his garden—a sorry botch of his life. He and Innes had been trying to make a garden out of a desert; the desert had flouted them. It was not his fault. Something had happened; something quite beyond his power. Luck was turning against him.

Innes, why, she was playing as with a toy. It was the natural instinct of a woman to make things pretty around her. But he had sacrificed his youth, his chances. His domestic life, too—he should never have carried a dainty little woman like Gerty into the desert. He had never reproached her for leaving him, even last time when he thought it was for good. The word burned his wound. Whose good? His or Gerty's? Somehow, though they wrangled, he always knew it would turn out all right; life would run smoothly when they left the desert. But things were getting worse; his mouth puckered over some recollections. Yet he loved Gerty; he couldn't picture life without her. He decided that it was because there had never been any one else. Most fellows had had sweethearts before they married; he had not, nor a mistress when she left him, though God knows, it would have been easy enough. His mouth fell into sardonic lines. Those half-breed women! No one, even when a divorce had hung over him. Oh, he knew what their friends made of each of Gerty's lengthened flights; he knew! But that had been spared him, that vulgar grisly spectacle of modern life when two people who have been lovers drag the carcass of their love over the grimy floor of a curious gaping court. He shuddered. Gerty loved him. Else, why had she come back to him? Why had she not kept her threat when he refused to abandon his desert project and turn his abilities into a more profitable dedication? He could see her face as she stared flushing up into his that nipping cold day when he had run into her on Broadway. He remembered her coquetry when she suggested that there was plenty of room in her apartment! His wife! She spoke of seeing his pictures in the papers. "He had grown to be a great man!"

That piquant meeting, the week following had been the brightest of his life. He was sure then that Gerty loved him. The wrangles were only their different ways of looking at things. Of course, they loved each other. But Gerty couldn't stand pioneer life. She had loved him, or she would not so easily have been persuaded to try it over again. She yearned to make him comfortable, she said. So she had gone back, and pulled down his ramada, and put his clothes in the lowest bureau drawer!

"It wasn't either of our faults," he ruminated. "It was the fault of the institution. Marriage itself is a failure. Look at the papers, the divorce courts. A man's interests are no longer his wife's. Curious that it should be so. But it's a fact. It is the modern discontent. Women want different careers from their husbands."

Yet, how could he help throwing his life into his work? He had committed himself; it was an obligation. Besides, he was a Hardin; they take things that way. And, too, a man can not live in the desert the best years, the vivid years of his life without absorbing its grim indomitable spirit; without learning to love, to require the great silent mornings, the vast star-brilliance of the nights; without falling under the spell of the land, the spell of elusiveness and mystery, of false distances, illusions; of content.

If it were not for that indefinable something, his allegiance to the cause which mocked at reasons and definitions; oh, he knew!—he had tilted with Gerty and been worsted!—he would have resigned from the company, his company which had dishonored him. Why should he stay to get more stabs, more wounds? MacLean, what in God's name had MacLean ever done for the valley?

And Rickard? It was he, Tom Hardin, who had pulled the valley, and therefore the company, from ruin, and it was that very act which had ruined him. Yet for his life, were he to go over it again, he knew he could not do differently. A curious twist of the ropes which had pulled the company back from the edge of the precipice and mangled him. Where was the loyalty of his associates? Loyalty, there was no such thing! They were cowards, all of them. Afraid of the power of the O. P. Truckling to it! Kotowing to Marshall, shivering every time he opened those profane lips of his. Bah! It made his stomach turn. Oh, he saw through their reason for kicking him out. He hadn't been born yesterday. This was a big thing, too big not to rouse cupidity, cupidity of men and corporations. He had been fooled by Marshall's indifference; play, every bit of it; theatric. Faraday's reluctance? Sickening. It was a plot. Some one had put him up to it, given him the first suggestion, made him think it was his own. Hot chestnuts, all right! He was burned all right, all right! And the last scorch, this pet of Marshall's! Hardin gave a scantling in his path a vicious kick.

The girl's prattle had died. She walked with him silently.

At the door of her tent, she stopped, looking at him wistfully. She wished he could hide his hurt. If he had only some of the Innes' pride!

"How are things?" She used their fond little formula.

"Oh, rotten!" growled Hardin, flinging away. The gate slammed behind him.

CHAPTER VIII

UNDER THE VENEER

AN hour later Innes, blinking from the sun, stepped into the tent, which had been partitioned with rough redwood boards into a bed-chamber on the right, a combination dining-room and "parlor" on the left. Her glance immediately segregated the three stalks of pink geraniums in the center of the Mexican drawn-work cloth that covered the table. Gerty, herself, in a fresh pink gingham frock, was dancing around the table to the tune of forks and spoons. It was just like Gerty to dress up to her setting, even though it were only a pitiful water-starved bouquet. She had often tried to analyze her sister-in-law's hold on her brother; certainly they were not happy. Was it because she made him comfortable? Was it the little air of formality, or mystery, which she drew around her? Her rooms when Innes was allowed to enter them were always flawless; Gerty took deep pride in her housekeeping. Why was it, Innes wondered, that she could never shake off her suspicion of an underlying untidiness? There was always a closed door on Gerty's processes.

"May I help?" The sun was still yellowing the room to her.

"Hello!" Hardin looked up from the couch where he was lying. Innes suspected it of being a frequent retreat.

She had found it tumbled once when she ran over early. It was then that Gerty made it understood that she liked more formality. Innes was rarely in that tent except for meals now, or during her alternating week of house-chores.

"I was afraid I was late," said the girl.

"Lunch will be ready in a few minutes," announced Gerty Hardin. "Won't you sit down? There's the new *Journal*. Sam came to clean this morning, and I couldn't get to the lunch until an hour ago."

Innes, settling herself by the reading table, caught herself observing that it would not have taken her an hour to get a cold lunch. Still, it would never look so inviting! If Gerty's domestic machinery was complicated and private, the results always were admirable. The early tomatoes were peeled as well as sliced, and were lying on a bed of cracked ice. The ripe black olives were resting in a lake of California olive oil. A bowl of crisp lettuce had been iced and carefully dried. The bread was cut in precise triangles; the butter had been shaved into foreign-looking roses. A pitcher of the valley's favorite beverage, iced tea, stood by Hardin's plate. There was a platter of cold meats.

It came home to Innes for the hundredth time, the surprise of such a meal in that desert. A few years ago, and what had a meal been? She threw the credit of the little lunch to sulky Tom Hardin lying on the portière-covered couch, his ugly lower lip outthrust against an unsmiling vision. It was Tom, Tom and his brave men, the sturdy engineers, the dauntless surveyors, the Indians who had dug the canals, those were the ones who had spread that pretty table, not the buxom little woman darting about in pink gingham.

"Is it because I don't like her?" she mused, her eyes on the pictures in the style-book which had just come in that morning. Certainly Gerty did have the patience of a saint with Tom's humors. If she would only lose that set look of martyrdom! It was not for an outsider to judge between a husband and wife, even if the man were her own brother. She could not put her finger on the germ of their painful scenes; she shrank from the recollection of Tom's temper; his coarse streak, the Gingg fiber, her own mother had called it. Tom was rough, but she loved him. Why was it she was sure that Gerty did not love her husband? Yet there was the distrust, as fixed and as unjust perhaps as the suspicion of Gerty's little mysteries.

She said aloud: "This is your last day. My week begins to-morrow."

Mrs. Hardin adjusted a precise napkin before she spoke.

"I think I will keep the reins for a month this time." Her words were reflective, as though the thought were new. "I get my hand in just as I stop. I will be running out for my visit in a few weeks. It will be only fair for me to do it as long as I can."

Again the girl had a sense of subtlety. Whenever Gerty put on that air of childish confidential deliberation, she hunted for the plot. This was not far to seek. Her sister-in-law was passing out the hot season to her.

"It's all ready." Gerty's glance was winging, bird-like, over the table. Nothing had been forgotten. She gave a little sigh of esthetic satisfaction. Hardin misinterpreted it.

"I ought to be able to keep a servant for her." It was like him to have forgotten the Lawrence days; he was never free of the sense of obligation to the dainty little woman who was born, he felt, for the purple. There was nothing too good for Gerty. He felt her unspoken disappointments; her deprivations. "Of course, she can have no respect for me. I'm a failure."

"Doesn't this give you an appetite?" demanded Innes heartily. "And I'm to be a lady for three more weeks." The remark was thoughtless. A bright flush spread over Gerty's face. She caught an allusion to her origin.

Innes saw the blush and remembered the boarding-house. She could think of nothing to say. The three relatives sat down to that most uncomfortable travesty, a social meal where sociability is lacking. Innes said it had been a pleasant morning. Gerty thought it had been hot. And then there was silence again.

Innes began to tell them of her Tucson visit, when Gerty laid down her fork. "I've meant to ask you a hundred times. Did you attend to my commission in Los Angeles?"

"I forgot to tell you. I raked the town, really I did, Gerty." For there was a cloud on Gerty's pretty brow. "I could have got you the other kind, but you said you did not want it."

"I should think not." The childish chin was lifted. "Those complicated things are always getting out of order. Besides, if I had an adjustable form, everybody'd be borrowing it."

"What are you talking about?" demanded Tom, waking up. "Who'd borrow your what, Gert?"

"Please don't call me Gert, Tom," besought his wife plaintively. "A figure. I wanted Innes to try to get one for me in Los Angeles."

"I did try," began Innes.

"Yours is good enough for any one. Why should you get another?" He was openly admiring the ample bust swelling under the pink gingham.

"Don't, Tom."

Innes tried to explain the sincerity of her search. She had visited every store "which might be suspected of having a figure." She could not bring a smile to her sister's face. "There was none your size. They offered to order one from Chicago. They have to be made to order, if they are special sizes. You are not stock size, did you know that?"

"I should think not," cried Gerty, bridling. "My waist is absurdly small for the size of my hips and shoulders."

Innes wondered if it would be safe to agree with her.

"When will it be here?"

"You'll be disappointed." Innes found herself stammering. "But not for six weeks. I did not know whether to order it or not."

"And I in Los Angeles with my summer sewing all done! What good will it do me then?" The pretty eyes looked ready for childish tears.

"I know. That is, I *didn't* know what to do," apologized Innes Hardin. "I decided to order it as I'd found the place, and was right there, but I made sure that I could countermand the order by telegram. So I can this very afternoon. I knew you would be disappointed. I was sorry."

"I'll need it next winter," admitted Gerty, helping herself to some of the chilled tomatoes. "I'm sure I'm much obliged to you. I hope it did not put you to much trouble."

The words raised the wall of formality again. Innes bent over her plate.

"What made you change your plans?" suddenly demanded his wife of Hardin. "When Sam came in with your bag, he surprised me so."

"My boss kept me." Hardin's face looked coarse, roughened by his ugly passion. "Rickard, your old friend. He served a subpœna on me at the station."

"Oh," cried Gerty. "Surely, he did not do that, Tom!"

"Sure he did." Hardin's face was black with his evil mood. "I'm only an underling, a disgraced underling. He's my boss. He's going to make me remember it."

"You mustn't say such things," pouted his wife. "If it does not hurt you, if you do not care, think how I must feel—"

"Oh, rot!" exclaimed Hardin. The veneer was rubbed down to the rough wood. Innes saw the coarseness her mother had complained of, the Gingg fiber.

"I suppose you think I like to take orders, to jump at the snap of the whip?" He was deliberately beating up his anger into a froth. "Oh, sure, I do. That's a Hardin, through and through."

Again the angry blood flooded his wife's cheeks. He, too, was throwing the boarding-house at her.

"You did it yourself." Gerty with difficulty was withholding the angry tears. "I told you how it would be. You would do it."

"Oh, hell!" cried Tom, pushing back his plate.

His sister looked drearily out the wire-screened door. Her view was a dusty street. Hardin got up, scraping his chair over the board floor.

"And to keep it from me," persisted the wife. "To let me ask him to dinner—"

"Does that dismal farce have to go on?" demanded

Hardin, turning back to the table. "You'll have to have it without me, then. I'll not stay and make a fool of myself. Ask him to dinner. Me! I'll see myself."

Innes wished she were in the neighboring tent. Tom was lashing himself into a coarse fury.

To her dismay, Gerty burst into tears. It was killing her, the disgrace, she cried. She couldn't endure it. She couldn't stand it there; she had not the courage to go to Los Angeles, where her friends would pity her. It was crushing her. *She* was not a Hardin; *she* was sensitive; she could not justify everything a Hardin did as right, no matter what the consequences. The pretty eyes obscured, she rushed, a streaming Niobe, from the room.

The brother and sister avoided each other's eyes. Innes rose and cleared the table of the dishes. She made a loud noise with the running water in the shed, racketing the pans to drown the insistence of Gerty's sobbing.

She kept listening for Tom's step. She wanted to go with him when he left; he must not reach the office in the blackness of that mood. She wished he would not betray his feelings; yet she knew it was not he who was to blame.

When she heard the screen door slam, she flashed out the back way.

"Going?" she called after him. "Wait for me." She dashed into her tent for her hat. She had to run to catch up with him.

"I thought I'd go and see Mrs. Parrish," she caught up, panting. "I've not seen her since I came back, and I felt anxious. Have you heard how she was?"

"A man's a fool who'll bring in a nervous silly woman like that," growled Hardin, stalking along. "Any man is a fool," he added to himself, "who expects to keep the love or the respect of a woman in a place like this. Women want luxury, modern women. They can't stand hardships." He was a fool, like Parrish.

"Any of the rigs going over in that direction to-day?" inquired his sister. She told herself that if Gerty had made that conversational opening, she would have convicted her of tactlessness. The Parrish theme was certainly an inspired one!

"I should send MacLean over to the Wistaria. Those Indians shirk if we don't jump in on them every day." Then his face blackened again. "I was going to send the new machine. But I suppose the boss will be using it."

All topics were equally dangerous with Tom in this mood!

The telegraph operator told Hardin that Rickard had gone to Imperial with MacLean.

"Truckling," sneered Hardin, thrusting out his lip.

Innes felt a thud of anger.

"Wish he could stand a hurt like an Innes," she thought.

"A toady," concluded Tom. "How do you like your new boss, boys?" The men crowded around him. Innes, through an open window, saw MacLean, Jr., in the company's new machine, leaving the sheds. She ran out of the office.

"I won't listen to you," she defied her disloyal thoughts. "He's my brother. I'll not listen to you."

A wide-open smile was on MacLean's face as he swung the long gray machine around to the morning-glories.

"Coming to Wistaria? Oh, that's bully."

CHAPTER IX

ON THE WISTARIA

"YOU are sure you are feeling better?" insisted Innes.

Mrs. Parrish's answer was careful. She *thought* she was feeling better! She had not had one of those bad nervous headaches for a week. "It was a week come Sunday, no, it was more than that, it was of a Saturday when the last bad spell came on. It was one of those hot days, the second of the three, you remember; oh, but you were in Tucson. Did you get to Los Angeles?" Her sigh was almost ecstatic. "Los Angeles is nice. I haven't been there for two years come September."

"You surely will go out this summer?" The hectic color, the snapping restlessness of her hostess' black eyes disquieted the girl.

"I've not decided," evaded Mrs. Parrish. "Oh, I'm all right! That last medicine I got from Los Angeles helped me a lot. As I was saying, it was that hot Saturday, and I had my baking to do. I can't cook on Sunday; Jim hates to see me working; I have to get at it when he's out of the way. I think the oil must have been bad; I don't know what Coulter was thinking of—I always insist on paying for the best; the cheap sort will smell. Maybe, it wasn't the oil, but by noon I could hardly see. I sent back that can, and had them send out new wicks—it's a blue-flame stove I use—but of course that didn't cure the headache. And the cooking not done."

Innes suggested that there were two cooks in that family! Everybody knew that Jim Parrish had developed, through the exigency of desert conditions and his wife's headaches, into the most helpful of cooks.

Mrs. Parrish smiled with sad pride. "He's had to do it too much. He's too good to me, Jim is." She was wishing she had not been grinding coffee in the lean-to when Miss Hardin came. The automobile was on her before she had time to get away, and Miss Hardin speaking to her through the screening. With the old purple flannelette waist on! She had put it on that morning for "the last time." She hoped Miss Hardin would not notice the missing buttons. She stretched a torn and faded apron of gingham that had once been brown across her knees. She did not dare take it off. She had put on, too, her old blue alpaca skirt, promising herself that she would use it for rags, tear it up before she could ever yield to the temptation of wearing it again. She looked like a slouch, she knew; and her hands fidgeted over the deficiencies of her dress. The desert was excuse enough! The washing had to be sent out of the valley, or it had to be done by one's self, the water boiled niggardly on a blue-flame stove. She had good things to wear, but she could see down the road a long way, and visitors were scarce; she could sight them a mile off, and get into clean clothes and be sitting waiting in the tent parlor when the folk drove up. But the new automobile of the company, seen for the first time, changed that. A puff, a rumble, and there it was upon her, with Miss Hardin smiling at her through the screen window!

"Washing or no washing, I'll have to keep ready to see folks," she resolved. She tried to make the hand look casual that was holding the rebellious waist together over her meager bust.

"It's been cool since I got home," cheered Innes.

Mrs. Parrish hoped that Miss Hardin could not see behind the rough screen into the space that was called a bedroom. The bed was tossed and tumbled; the night clothes lying around. And she had not washed last week. "I'd be ashamed to have her see those clothes," she thought. "Take this chair, Miss Hardin," she begged. "It's more comfortable." Innes asked to be allowed to stay where she was, but she had to surrender to the other's nervous persistence.

Mrs. Parrish kept her hand over her gaping placket as she made the change. "Yes, it's been cool," she answered, "but, oh, the wind! Ain't it terrible? They say as these tents won't blow down, they are so well put together. Do you believe it, Miss Hardin? That the 'spider' coming down so low shelters it so that it couldn't blow over?"

"Of course they won't blow over!" chirped Innes Hardin.

Mrs. Parrish sighed. "That's what Jim says. I wish I could believe it. I'm not doubting you, or him, neither, Miss Hardin; I know you mean what you say. But when the wind blows, and the tent creaks, and strains, oh, I know then as it's coming down; I can't sleep those windy nights. I just lie and plan which way I'll jump when it goes."

Innes tried to laugh at her, but the woman's fear was too real.

"I've made myself learn to love the wind," she urged. "Don't you think you could, too? Try to think of it as gay; as the air of the world on some mad, reckless romp. It gets into your blood, then, and you want to run, to dance. 'Oh, the whole world is glad of the wind!'"

"The wind in Nebraska's like that, but this! Why, it sounds like angry devils to me, all shrieking to me to get out; that I don't belong here. I cover up my ears with the bedclothes, but it's no use. I can hear them just the same: 'I'll blow you away. I'll blow you away.' And then the dust it brings; the dirt! There's no use trying to be clean." The mouth muscles twitched unpleasantly.

"How is the neuralgia?" inquired Innes, helpless against this determined pessimism.

"Better. That new medicine is helping that. I seemed to wear out the good effects of those powders."

"Have you begun to sleep out-of-doors yet?"

Mrs. Parrish shivered. "I wouldn't sleep a wink. I'd be waiting for Indians all night."

"The Indians are harmless," cried Innes. "They wouldn't hurt any one."

"They're Indians!" persisted Mrs. Parrish. "I'll never get over being afraid of their dark faces. They're heathens."

Innes turned her eyes hopelessly away from the woman's twitching face. She looked out the wire-meshed door beyond the line of stakes which stood for the proposed canal. She wondered when MacLean, Jr., would be coming back for her.

"Is that a company rig?" she asked.

"I declare if it isn't the Busby wagon!" exclaimed Mrs.

Parrish, jumping up and going to the door. Her dress threatened to leave her. "She's driving the roans. There's somebody with her. It must be Mr. Busby!"

The wretched room was then fully revealed to the guest. There was a rent in the loud-patterned couch cover of green and red; the table cover, a fringed imitation damask, was askew. Disorder leaped from beneath the couch, from the boxes by the door, from the room beyond. A graphophone perched uncertainly on the edge of the table. A pile of *Youth's Companions* toppled uncertainly away over a pine box. There were a few pictures from *Life* tacked upon the board walls; a few were pasted to the canvas top-walls. Innes segregated the two influences. The graphophone, the file of *Youth's Companions*, the pictures from *Life*, these were the contributions of Jim Parrish toward the elevating of their sordid life. The dirt, the disorder made up no less a heroic subscription from the wife, who was too frail for the sacrifice, too fond and too proud for a surrender.

"How can you see so far?" Innes asked. "I thought I could see farther than most people, but this glare blinds me."

"If you lived over here in Number Six, miles off from everybody, with nobody to see, unless it's the engineers or those black Indians, you'd learn to know folks miles off. It's—yes, it is Mr. Busby. He's been promising to bring her over here to sit with me the first time he came to inspect the Wistaria. It's to come right past here when it's finished. I'll be seeing folks then. But I shouldn't complain of not having visitors. Two in one day!"

To Innes Hardin the excitement seemed all out of proportion to the cause. Dark somber blotches were coming out on the woman's skin. "Sit down. It's too warm for you by the door."

"They might go past," began Mrs. Parrish, when a smell of burning food smote both their nostrils. "The rice and codfish's burning," she exclaimed, and fled to the kitchen in the lean-to.

She was not back in time to greet her guest, whose vigorous entrance struck at once the note of middle-aged, experienced authority. Innes had met her but once before, but she recognized the species, the woman who has the best recipe for bread, the most valuable hints for housekeepers; handy in the sick room, indispensable at accouchements; a kindly irresistible vulture.

Their talk was of the coming heat, the new canal; the difference it would make to "Number Six"; the melon crop.

Mrs. Parrish came fluttering back, her brown apron changed for a clean white one. A few pins sealed the gap in the unutterable purple waist. She could not get another without passing through the sitting-room, and she had a feeling of shame to emphasize her embarrassment before Miss Hardin. Her cheeks were redder, her eyes more glittering.

She established Mrs. Busby on the wire-collapsible couch, with the green and red flowered cover. The guest preferred a straight chair, but Mrs. Parrish would not hear of it. She herself had a rocker. Perched on one edge of it, she rocked back and forth violently, until her chair kept grating against Innes'. The girl pitied the woman's excitement, wondering at it.

Mrs. Parrish was worked up to almost hysterical sociability. It was as if a deep desert well had been tapped. Her rocker swaying interminably, she told them of her life at home, of the farm they were just clearing of the mortgage; of her love for Nebraska. She would never forget that day when a friend, they wouldn't know him, but it was Sam Kirkland, anyway! when he came through on his way back East to get his family. He told the wonderful story of the Imperial Valley—of the country below sea-level, where even cactus would not grow. To their skeptical ears he had unfolded a tale of rich soils, of desert redemption—of irrigation "which made Jim Parrish just sit up, I can tell you." The early crops, the water scientifically applied, the hothouse heat, the millions in sight. Was he, Sam Kirkland goin' back? Well, sure. He was no man's fool. He knew opportunity when he saw it.

And then the pamphlets! When they began to come she fell to watching her Jim uneasily. All their friends were in Nebraska; and her doctor. "Let well enough alone," says I. "How can I live without Doctor Pratt, who knows all my symptoms? But Jim just would come!" She related the weary minute details of their home-breaking; of their move from Nebraska. Her impressions of California, deeply registered, were passed on to her guests. Her horror of the valley. Her fear of the Indians—her fear of the wind, of centipedes, and she knew that the water was typhoidal—

"Typhoidal? Bosh!" interjected Maria Busby. She had something to say about the water, but she could not get it in. The rocker grew more agitated. "The very rocker which had been brought in on a wagon from Old Beach! That was before the railroad came in; every one had to wagon it from Old Beach. But that was before their time!

"I don't sleep. That's the trouble with me," she

jumped back to her ailments, her nervous eyes passing from Mrs. Busby's face to Innes Hardin's. "Jim calls me the desert watch-dog. I feel as I must keep an ear and eye trained on the desert to see what it's going to do next; or the river; or the Indians."

Mrs. Busby thought she saw a chance to talk of the water, and why it was not typhoidal. But she was not swift enough. Innes was cheered to hear the chug of the company automobile. Before another stream of talk started on its irresistible flow, she made her escape. Through the screen door, as she was borne away, she could see Mrs. Parrish, still wildly rocking.

CHAPTER XI

FEAR

MRS. Parrish's chair continued to plunge. It rocked and pitched like a ship in a storm. Her tongue gathered excitement from the motion. Mrs. Busby looked with anxiety at the graphophone perching uncertainly on the pine box. The curved rocker was threatening it. Mrs. Parrish drew back, and the danger was once again averted. She was plowing her way now toward the wire couch covered with the red and green tapestry ordered from a circular from Howe and Wort's, Chicago. Mrs. Busby, usually placid, caught a little of the excitement. If she had nerves she told herself, she would be turned crazy. As it was, nerveless, and poised by the support of a newly acquired philosophy, she watched, hypnotized, the menace of that desperate rocker. Two lurid spots glowed in the cheeks of her hostess. The excitement of hostess-ship was consuming her. Entertaining, in simple folk vocabulary, means talking. So Mrs. Parrish talked.

When her ailments were exhausted, she began on her neighbors'. Mrs. Busby caught her breath as the rocker jabbed the pine box carrying the talking-machine. "I wonder why she wants a talking-machine?" she asked herself with the grim humor which had won sturdy Sam Busby twenty years before when he had acquired the habit of buying bread at the Home Bakery in a suburb of Boston where Maria Mathes served.

Mrs. Parrish was embarked now on the sea of a neighbor's woe, the rocker working toward the couch. A newcomer into the valley, Mrs. Dowker, was the subject of another Æneid. It transpired that Mr. Dowker had been reading desert literature, too. He had heard of wonderful cures effected by desert air. He dreamed to make a fortune and recreate a sickly wife. Mrs. Dowker from a hospital bed begged to be left behind for a year. Mrs. Parrish dwelt on the Dowker pilgrimage with ghoulish realism. Mrs. Dowker was failing under the labors of desert life; the little boy was always ailing. It was hard to get bottled water "in there." Mrs. Dowker had to boil every drop they drank.

Mrs. Busby saw her chance and grabbed it. "I don't believe in boiled water," she announced. Mrs. Parrish was ready to pick up her thread, but Mrs. Busby was not to be ousted.

"I don't believe in all this fuss about bottled water, nor in boiled water, either. The water of a place is the water one should drink. You breathe the air, why shouldn't you drink the water?" Her logic was terrifically convincing to herself. "To be consistent, why shouldn't you bring in bottled air? The water of a place is the water that agrees with one in that place. Why, that's as plain as poverty! Look at the Indians. They've been drinking this water for a hundred years, and over. Did you ever hear of an Indian dying because he drank too much water?" It was a touch of the Maria Mathes sardonic humor.

Mrs. Busby quoted Mrs. Hadley. "Didn't every one scare her into thinking that the canal water was not fit to drink, and didn't she boil every drop that went down a Hadley throat?"

"But that was different," tried to interpose Mrs. Parrish, but Mrs. Busby held the rostrum.

"And that first year, wasn't the three of them, herself and her two grown sons, down with typhoid? Where'd they get it? Out of the air? You can't talk to me of boiled water."

"Do you think it was the boiled water that killed Joe Hadley?" demanded Mrs. Parrish, fear reducing her black eyes to points of startled light.

"There's the facts," said her guest with an oracular wave of the hand. "Take 'em, or leave 'em." And then she practised passing on her second lesson. "It was the *fear* of the water as killed them. That's my belief."

"Fear?"

"Fear," declaimed Mrs. Busby, rising out of reach of the suspended rocker, and taking the Morris chair deserted by Innes Hardin. "Fear is *poison.*" She watched the effect of her words, for a careful second. She had no intention of being entertained any more!

She answered the round question in Mrs. Parrish's eyes.

"I'm only just beginning it—I see it as plain as prophecy, but it's hard to explain. The fear of a thing gives you a thing itself. There is no such thing as pain." A loud protest from Mrs. Parrish warned her into guarding her outposts. "There is no such thing as pain. It is only *fear* of the pain which gives it to you. It is so clear to me; I wish I could explain it. But I've some pamphlets; I'll send them over by Sam, the next time he comes over to the Wistaria. This new canal ought to be helping you over here," she hazarded.

"I heard as you were taking that up, the new thoughts," Mrs. Parrish returned to the main issue. "Is that a part of it?"

"Fear? you mean. Have you never thought yourself into a toothache?"

Parrish toothache had been too recent to be imaginary. "It's decay, usually, with me," she faltered. "Decay, and then the nerves get exposed. Mine die easily. I just lie awake sometimes, all night, dreading as one of my nerves will die, and with no good dentist this side of Los Angeles."

"Didn't I tell you so?" Mrs. Busby thrilled over this unexpected ally. "Well, if you agree that you can think yourself into a pain, can't you think yourself out of it? It must work both ways. That's logic."

"Not a toothache." The black beady eyes, shut obstinately over their conviction. "That's real. Perhaps you never had one?"

"Not since I've begun to study. And besides, they're false. They're not mine, the teeth, I mean. Didn't you never guess it? Pretty good work, I tell Sam. They fool every one. He put in two large gold fillings in the front teeth, so as they'd look just like the ones I lost. There's Sam coming now. I promised I'd not keep him waitin'. I'll send you those leaflets. And I'll come out and explain them some day. But I'm busy now, getting ready for the hot weather. Goin' out this year?"

Mrs. Parrish thought not.

Sam Busby shouted through the door that he was in a hurry; that he had to leave her at home, and get out to Grant's Heading. There was trouble there. A messenger had just caught him.

Mrs. Busby's farewell to Mrs. Parrish had to be casual.

FEAR

She clambered up into the seat beside her short stubby master. Sam had a short blackened pipe between his teeth, obviously his own. No store or dentist would acknowledge them. His sombrero, battered and sunburned, was pulled low over his jolly blue eyes.

She opened a large black cotton umbrella.

"She'll never grasp it," she was thinking aloud.

"Grasp what?" the humorous eyes turned toward her.

"The new thoughts. If I could only get her to throw away that shelf of medicines."

"Now, for the lord's sake, don't go proselyting, Maria."

"How can I, when I haven't learned to hold a thought yet, myself?"

"Hold a—what? Whatever you are talking about?"

"You hold a good thought—it's like the Catholics crossing themselves with holy water, only it isn't. It keeps off bad thoughts—trouble. It sounds easy, but it's terribly hard."

"Jew Peter!"

She mistook his exclamation. "Well, you just try it yourself. Sometime, when you're just a-dyin' for a smoke, just you hold the thought that you are smokin', and see if it's easy."

He looked at her a few minutes reflectively before speaking. Was Maria losing all her humor? He had been noticing a tendency to dictate, a growing dogmatism. Jew Peter! Like her mother! How he had dreaded the corpulent and dogmatic Mrs. Mathes, whom he had learned to respect at a distance, a very complete distance! He had loved Maria not only for herself, but for the dissimilarity to her mother. Come to think of it, matronhood, middle-aged matronhood, brought dictatorial authority with the dreaded double chin. On every hand, one sees young girls and gaiety. Does the gaiety go with the girlhood? He stole a distrustful look at Mrs. Busby. He had not heard her laugh or crack a joke for a long while. He felt cheated, as though he had bought a piece of goods that did not wear well.

"Maria Busby," he said solemnly, "when it's time for me to take to holdin' thoughts, it'll be time for me to quit holdin' anything. Now, what I've always liked about you was that you were not eternally meddlin' and fussin' like other men's wives. You've minded your own business. That's what I liked. Keep to it. I don't care what new fad you pick up. Pick 'em all up. Only don't force 'em down other folks' throats. That's what I could never understand in women. They can never do anything alone. If they find a new medicine, they've got to make some one else try it. They love company so much that they want to carry some one along to the other side if the drug happens to be fatal. That's all I can make out of it."

"Sam," Mrs. Busby's voice was tremulously earnest, "this is so wonderful. You aren't willing to let me help you with it?"

"Am I needin' help?" His sturdy rotund body deflected her missionary zeal for an instant.

"You might be sick." She yearned to protect his unguarded body with the shining wonderful armor she had discovered. She could not be happy in this new religion with her Sam stalking alone outside in the black terrors of the night. She began to realize why religion demands its martyrs. She sighed deeply.

"What's the matter? Feelin' poorly?"

"Oh, no. I'm all right. It's you."

"Oh, I'm poorly, am I? Well, if this is feelin' poorly, I'd be afraid to feel well. Something would bust." He shook such a vigorous repudiation that the mares took it as a command, and several miles had flown past before he had them calmed.

"Frightened?" He threw the word over his shoulder to a disheveled Maria Busby, clinging to her bonnet. The mares were still quivering.

Through white lips, Mrs. Busby murmured that she was all right, now!

"What's that you were tryin' to tell me a way back?" he asked when the mares had settled down into a sober gait.

"There's no such thing as pain," began Mrs. Busby. She must always begin there. It was the initial letter of her creed.

"I thought you said something about not having fear?"

"Oh, I knew I couldn't explain it to you, you're such a mocker, Sam Busby. But I've got books for you to read. They'll show you."

"It's not another sort of Electropoise?" grinned her spouse. "Do you remember, Maria, how you used to have me sittin' there, one end of that infernal machine in a pail of water, the other tied around my leg, keep me sittin' like a fool waitin' for currents. Nary a current, or a raison Paddy would say. Holy smoke!"

She held up a solemn finger. "See that?"

"Anything the matter? Another felon?"

"I can think a pain in that finger."

"Why should you?"

His levity threw her argument off the track. She had planned a physical, scientific proof. How by taking thought, she could gather the blood at a stated point;

how congestion would inevitably follow. The sequence evaded her.

"I thought there was no such thing as pain?"

"Don't try to trap me. Just listen. If I can think a pain there, why can't I think it away?" The sequence came to her. "See, I think the blood to the tip of my finger. It congests. There is inflammation; a swellin'."

"Does it hurt much?" She saw a twinkle in his eyes.

"Of course not."

The two drove on in silence, busy with the thoughts which must divide them. Sam decided that Maria had parted with her charm, her sense of fun. And then he gave himself up to his routine. Baldwin's alfalfa was fine this spring. If the railroad could handle it, what a crop of melons the valley would harvest that year! There was a stoppage in the canal. The water looked stagnant. He forgot Maria.

She was facing a noble lonely martyrdom. This truth which was being revealed to her, which was dawning above her sky as a wonderful shimmer of light, she must follow where it led. Sam's obstinacy would keep him out. No, they would not bicker; she was above that. She never quarreled with any one. It must be a closed subject between them; their first barrier. She felt very righteous and holy. He stopped at their house, a square pine cottage, built by jovial Sam Busby, and bossed by Maria.

As he was driving through the pine-board gate, he pulled the gray mares on their startled haunches. Real concern was in his honest face.

"Sure nothing's the matter with that finger, Maria?"

"Shucks!" tossed Maria Busby.

CHAPTER XI

THE RIVALS

FROM the window of the adobe office building of the company, Hardin saw Rickard jump from the rear platform of the train as it slowed into the station. He noticed that the new manager carried no bag.

"Wonder what he's decided to do about the head-gate. He didn't waste much time out there." Hardin was fidgeting in his seat, his eyes on the approaching figure. His desk was cluttered with untouched papers; there was a report to be made; Hardin had several times made a great show of getting out his books, sharpening his pencils, but he was as restless as a girl when a lover's declaration lingers. Marshall had held up the gate—what did Marshall know about it, he'd like to know, sitting at his office desk in Tucson? They were losing valuable time. He wondered what Rickard would report to his chief; he vowed to himself that he would not show his eagerness by inquiring. "Ask him, please him by truckling? I'd see the gate rot first."

Rickard passed through the room, nodding to his office force. The door of the inner office shut behind him. Hardin stared at the blank surface. He moved restlessly in his swivel chair. Did the fellow think a big thing like that could hang on while he unpacked his trunks and settled his bureau drawers? He picked up a pencil, jabbing at the paper of his report. He covered the sheet with figures—three hundred—six hundred. Six hundred feet. Whose fault that the intake had widened, doubling its width, trebling its problem? Whose but Marshall's, who had sent down one of his office clerks to see what Hardin was doing? Wouldn't any man in his senses know that the way Maitland would distinguish himself would be by discrediting Hardin, by throwing bouquets to Marshall; praising *his* plan? They all go at it the same sickening way! Office clerks, bah! Sure, Maitland had advised against the completion of the gate. Said it would cost more in time and money than Hardin's estimates. "Thanks to Maitland it did," growled Hardin, scrawling figures over the page. "By the time Maitland finished monkeying with that toy dam of his the river had widened the break from three hundred to six hundred feet. For that, they throw mud at me. Oh, it makes me sick." Hardin flung his broken pencil out of the window.

Rickard reentered the room. The question leaped from Hardin.

"The head-gate—are you going on with it?"

Rickard looked curiously at the flushed antagonistic face of the man he had supplanted. The thought crossed his mind that perhaps Hardin had taken to drinking. It made his answer curt.

"I don't know."

"You don't know!"

"I have no report to make, Mr. Hardin, until I see the gate."

"And you went to the Crossing without going down to the head-gate?" Hardin did not try to conceal his disgust.

"I did not go to the Crossing."

"Didn't go—!" Hardin's mouth was agape. Then he rudely swiveled his chair. The door slammed behind Rickard.

Hadn't been to the Crossing? Then where in Hades did he go? "Truckling to MacLean! Those office clerks! I know them. Jumping for favors from the man higher up." He ticked off on his fingers the days the new manager had already squandered. Saturday, he threw in perversely the day of Rickard's arrival, Saturday, Sunday, he loafed all day Sunday, Monday—and this was Wednesday. What could a man find in the valley to do if he didn't rush straight to the gate? The gate upon which the whole valley hung? Gerty's dinner occurred to him. "He never intended to come," he reflected with satisfaction. "He'll have to be starting for the Heading to-morrow. Already, it's a farce, five days!"

He halted MacLean who was passing him, a stenographic pad under his arm, a battered copy of *Thorns and Orange Blossoms* in his hand. He was cramming night and day, requisitioning the good-natured to read aloud at a snail's pace. He had found the novel under Bodefeldt's bureau and had held up Pete to give him a page of dictation from the classic.

"Are you going to the Crossing to-morrow?" Hardin knew he should be too proud to betray his eagerness, but the words ran away with him.

"Not to-morrow. Mr. Rickard just told me he might not be able to get off until next week."

Hardin's anger sputtered. "Next week. Why does he rush so? Why doesn't he go next year? The Colorado's so gentle, it'd wait for him, I'm sure. Next week! It's a put-up job, that's what it is. Oh, I can see through a fence with a knot-hole as big as your head. He doesn't want to finish the head-gate. He wants to put off going until it's too late to go on with it; I know him. He'd risk the whole thing, and all the money the O. P. has chucked into it, just to start with a clean slate; to get the glory of stopping the river himself. It turns my stomach; it's a plot." The lower lip shot out.

MacLean's attention was deferential. He had always liked Hardin; all the fellows did. But he was jumping off wrong this time. He'd brought it all on himself.

"One would think he'd been brought up in a convent, he finds the valley so distracting. Time to go to dinners. Sickening!"

MacLean did not understand the allusion.

"He said," MacLean hesitated, wondering if the statement had been a confidence. But Bodefeldt had been there. "He said something about a levee for the towns. He's got to investigate that before he goes to the front."

"A levee? Well, wouldn't that jar you?" Hardin addressed the stenographer in the transparent shirt-waist. "Does he think we're going to have another flood this season? Thinks it's going to reach the hotel and wet his clothes? Take the starch out of his shirts?" He flung out of his chair, throwing the papers back into a drawer.

He stamped out of the office, mad clear through. To this crisis they had sent down a dandy, a bookman who wanted to build a levee. Oh, hell! He laughed out his bitterness aloud, and did not care that Coulter, who kept the store, and two gaily dressed squaws turned to look after him. For it was a crisis, and the O. P. was making it so. They should have learned their lesson by this time. Trust *Maitland?* And now, Rickard!

"They'll come crawling after me to help them after this fellow's buried himself under river mud, come calling to me as they did after Maitland failed. 'Please, Mr. Hardin, won't you come back and finish your gate!' I'll see them dead first. No, I'll be fool enough to do it. I can't help myself. I'm a Hardin. I have to finish what I've begun."

It was not because this was a pet enterprise, the great work of his life, that he must eagerly eat humble pie, take the buffets, the falls, and come whining back when they whistled to him. He told himself that it was because of his debt to the valley, to the ranchers. He saw himself sacrificing everything to a great obligation. "Who was the Bible fellow who led his people across the desert? I must polish up my Bible," he resolved. He remembered that he had not opened one since his mother's death, and that was so long past that the thought brought no physical thrill.

The colonists were about desperate. Who could blame them? The last year's floods had worked havoc with their crops; this year had been a horror. The district they called Number Six was a screaming irony of ruin. The last debauch of the river had made great gashes through the ranches, had scoured deep gorges which had undermined the canals on which the water supply for Number Six depended. The suits were piling up against the D. R., damage suits, and they hold up his gate, while he gets the curses of the valley. And Mr. Rickard thinks he'll build a levee!

Hardin was in the mood to fancy slights. He was convinced that Petrie went back into the bank to avoid him. Two ranchers, Hollister and Wilson, from the Palo Verde, busy with their teams, did not return his halloo. The ranchers hated him. "That's what you get for crucifying yourself."

He flung himself on the couch in the tent. Gerty was laying a careful cloth for supper. A brave determined smile was arranged on her lips. The noon storm had passed. She hummed a gay little tune. If there was anything Hardin hated, it was humming.

"You'll have your dude to dinner all right," her husband announced. "He's in town."

"Yes, I know," rejoined his spouse. "I had a letter from him yesterday. From Imperial."

Tom sat up glaring. "He wrote to you from *Imperial?*"

His wife misplaced the accent. She misunderstood Tom's scowl. It was the old story over again. Whenever those two men came together, the old feeling of jealousy must be revived again! It was unpleasant, of course, very unpleasant to have men care like that, but it made life exciting. Life had been getting a little stale lately; like a book of obvious even plot. Rickard's entrance into the story gave a new interest, a new twist. She hummed an air from a new opera that had set the world waltzing.

Hardin's thoughts did not touch her at the hem. He was at the head-gate, his gate. What the deuce had Rickard gone to Imperial for? If he wasn't the darndest ass! Imperial! And the gate hung up!

"For God's sake stop that buzzing!"

The happy little noise was quenched. Innes, entering at that moment, heard the rough order. She looked imploringly at her sister-in-law.

"Supper's on the table," cried Gerty, the fixed determined smile still on her lips.

CHAPTER XII

A DESERT DINNER

INNES HARDIN was completing her simple toilet. Not even to please Gerty would she "dress up" for this dinner! It would have been easy for her sister-in-law to postpone it. How could she expect Tom to go through with it! She couldn't understand Gerty!

An hour ago, hearing distinctly the whir and splash of egg-beating, she had run over to the neighboring tent. The clinking of cake-tins had suddenly silenced. "Excuse me, won't you?" Gerty's voice had come from the lean-to, the little kitchen shed. "I'm lying down."

"Lieing, yes!" grimaced the Hardin mouth to its reflection in the mirror. How many times that week had she been repulsed by a locked door, a sudden curtain of silence, or a "Run away for a while. I'm trying to catch a nap." Easy now to see why Gerty had wanted to "hold the reins" that week!

She didn't need to pierce those canvas walls to know that there had been feverish activity for this dinner. A new gown would appear to-night, made secretly. An exquisite meal, and no one must comment on its elaboration. Twice Tom and she had been asked to take their lunch at the hotel. "Because of a headache!" A headache!

Tom's wife could not even shop openly! Bundles had

always the air of mystery, never opened before Tom or herself. She must have yards of stuff laid away, kept for sudden emergencies.

"She can't help it. It's her disposition. She can't help being secretive. Look at your face, Innes Hardin!" What was it to her, the pettiness of a woman whom an accident of life had swept upon the beach beside her? Gerty was not her kind, not the sort she would pick out for a friend. She was an oriental, one of the harem women, whose business it is in life to please one man, keep his home soft, his comforts ready, keep him convinced, moreover, that it is the desire of his life to support her. Herself dissatisfied, often rebellious, staying by him for self-interest, not for love—ah, that was her impeachment. "Not loving!"

Soberly, she covered her plain brassière with a white waist of cotton ducking. A red leather belt and crimson tie she added self-consciously. "Where is my bloodstone pin?"

Hadn't she spent an hour at least matching that particular leather belt? But he was a man, in battle. The head-gate held up; it was too bad. Silent, Bodefeldt, Wooster, Grant, all of them fighting mad because of the deadlock at the Heading. All up in arms, at last, against Marshall, because of this cruel cut to their hero, Hardin. Her eyes glowed like yellow lamps, as she recalled their fervid partisanship.

"Only one man who can save the valley, and that's Tom Hardin." Wooster had said that; but they all believed it. The loyalty of the force made her ashamed of her soft woman fears. For there were times when she questioned her brother's executive ability. He had a large loose way of handling things. He was too optimistic. But those men, those engineers must know. It was probably the man's way of sweeping ahead, ignoring detail. The verdict of those field-tried men told her that the other, the careful planning way, was the office method. Rickard, as a dinner neighbor, she had found interesting; but for great undertakings, a man who would let a Gerty Holmes jilt him, ruin his life for him! The whole story sprang at last clear, from the dropped innuendos.

She adjusted a barrette in her smoothly brushed hair. Slowly, she walked over to the neighboring tent.

Gerty frowned at the white duck. "You might at least have worn your blue!"

"You're elegant enough for the two of us. Isn't that something new?"

Gerty said carelessly that she had had it for a long time. For she had had the material a long time! It wasn't necessary to explain to her husband's sister that it had been made up that week. She hoped that she didn't look "fussed-up." Would Mr. Rickard think she was attaching any importance to the simple little visit? For it was nothing to him, of course. A man of his standing, whom the great Tod Marshall ranked so high, probably dined out several times each week, with white-capped maids and candelabra! If Tom had only made the most of his opportunities. What a gamble, life to a woman!

She made a trip into her bedroom and took a reassuring survey in her mirror. The lingerie frock *would* look simple to a man who would never suspect it of handmade duplicity. Her glass declared the hand-whipped medallions casual and elegant. And a long time ago, a lifetime ago, Rickard had told her that she always should wear blue, because of her eyes.

Innes from the next room could hear Gerty teasing Tom to wear his Tuxedo.

"Isn't one dude enough for you?" growled her surly lord. Innes recognized the mood, and shrank from the ordeal ahead. It was the mood of the Hardin in the rough, the son of his frontier mother, the fruit of old Jasper Gingg, whose smithy had been the rendezvous for the wildest roughs, the fiercest cattlemen in Missouri.

"I'd let him see you know what's what, even if we do live like gipsies."

The answer to that was another growl. Innes could hear him dragging out the process, grumbling over each detail. That confounded laundry had torn his shirt. He hadn't a decent collar to his name. Where was his black string tie? If Gert *would* keep his things in the lowest drawer! Hang that button! Gerty emerged from the encounter, her face very red. Innes could see her biting her lips to keep the tears back as she put the last touches to the table.

"She's tired out," thought the sister of Tom Hardin. "She's probably fussed herself to death over this dinner."

A few minutes later Rickard arrived in a sack suit of tweeds. Gerty's greeting was a little abstracted. How could she make Innes understand to tell Tom to change his coat? The duty of a host, she suddenly remembered, was to dress down rather than up, to the chances of his guest. She regretted bitterly her insistence. Was ever any one so obtuse as Innes? Mr. Rickard would see that they thought it a big event. She was watching the curtain where Tom would emerge. And his coat was a style of several seasons ago and absurdly tight! She made an unintelligible excuse, and darted behind the portière.

Tom's face was apoplectic. He was wrestling with a mussed tie; the collar showed a desperate struggle.

Gerty made wild signals for him to change his clothes. She waved a hand indicating Rickard; she pointed to Tom's sack suit lying on the floor where he had walked out of it.

"What is it all about?"

"Ssh," whispered his wife. Again the wild gestures.

"Well, aren't you satisfied? Don't I look like a guy?"

He could be heard distinctly in the next room. Gerty gave it up in despair. She dabbed some more powder on her nose, and went out looking like a martyr; a very pretty martyr!

Rickard praised the miracles of the tent. Gerty's soft flush reminded Innes of their old relation. "Exit Innes," she was thinking, when Tom, red and perspiring, brought another element of discomfort into the room.

Gerty ushered them immediately to the table. She covered the first minutes which might be awkward with her small chatter. Somewhere she had read that it was not well to make apologies for lack of maid or fare. Besides, Mr. Rickard remembered Lawrence! That dreadful dining-room, the ever-set table! How she had hated it, though she had not known how fearful it was until she had escaped.

"We are simple folk here, Mr. Rickard," she announced, as they took their places around the pretty table. That was her only allusion to deficiencies, but it covered her noiseless movements around the board between courses, filled up the gaps when she made necessary dives into kitchen or primitive ice-chest, and set the key for the homeliness of the meal itself. The dinner was a triumph of apparent simplicity. Only Innes could guess the time consumed in the perfection of detail, details dear to the hostess' heart. The almonds she had blanched, of course, herself; had dipped and salted them. The cheese-straws were her own. She did not make the mistake of stringing out endless courses. An improvised buffet near at hand made the serving a triumph.

Rickard praised each dish; openly he was admiring her achievement. Innes, remembering the story Gerty had told her in dots and dashes, the story of the old rivalry, glanced covertly at Tom sulking at the head of his own table.

"Poor sulky Achilles," she thought. "Dear, honest old bear!"

"Innes!" cried Mrs. Hardin.

She turned to find that the guest was staring at her. She had not heard his effort to include her in the conversation.

"Mr. Rickard asked you if you like it here?"

"Thank you, why, of course!" Her answer sounded pert to herself.

Her sister-in-law hastened to add that Miss Hardin was very lonely, was really all alone in the world; that they insisted on her making her home with them.

Innes had with difficulty restrained a denial. After all, what other home had she? Still the truth had been deflected. She recalled the sacrifice it had been to cut her college course in order to make a home in the desert for the brother who had always so gently fathered her, who had helped her invest her small capital that it might spell a small income. She recalled his resistance when she had called in a mortgage; who could watch that mad scapegoat of a river playing pranks with desert homes, and not yearn to help? Not a Hardin. She still gloried in remembering that she had at least driven one pile into that rebellious stream, even if when she left the valley it would be as a breadwinner. She was prepared. She was a good draftsman; she would go as an apprentice in an architect's office. She had already settled on the architect!

"Are you going to Los Angeles again soon?" She heard the new manager address his host.

"I'm taking orders!"

There was another awkward moment when Hardin pushed back his plate declaring he had reached his limit; it was too big a spread for him! It was the stupid rudeness of the small bad boy; even Innes flushed for her sister-in-law.

With resolution, Gerty assumed control of the conversation. Her rôle sounded casual; no one could have suspected it of frequent rehearsal. They must not talk of the river; that was taboo. Railroad matters were also excluded. Equally difficult would be reminiscences of Lawrence days. So she began brightly with a current book. Had Mr. Rickard read *The Home of Joy* that every one was discussing? Rickard confessed he was a barbarian; he had not read a book that was not on engineering for many a month. He had read a review or two, and several minutes were contributed to a discussion of the problem it covered. The theater proved a safe topic, and by that natural route, they reached New York. Innes, who had never been farther East than Chicago, was grateful to play audience. Hardin, who knew his New York perhaps better than either, refused to be drawn into the gentle stream. Gerty skimmed easily the cream of modern issues; she read her newspaper religiously each morning; they talked of popular movements. There had been a demonstration in the streets of London, rock-throwing mobs of suffragettes the week before.

"Surely, they proved their equality," observed Casey Rickard. Innes was angry with herself for smiling.

"What about their right?" She wanted to urge the right of the wage-earners, the taxpayers. Taxation without representation, but she heard her chance pass by. Gerty had danced on to another topic.

Things must be kept sprightly. Had Mr. Rickard met many of the valley people? And it was then that she threw her bomb toward the listening silent Hardins. She would like Mr. Rickard to meet some of their friends.

He said that he would be delighted, but that he was planning to leave shortly for the Heading.

"Of course." She did not give her husband time to speak. She meant afterward! She was planning to give something, a bit novel, in his honor. She refused to see the glare from the angry man in his outgrown dinner coat. She did not glance toward the sister. What did Mr. Rickard think about a progressive ride?

"It sounds very entertaining, but what do you do?"

There was a loud guffaw from Tom. With deepened color, Gerty told her idea. A drive, changing partners, so he could meet all the guests. There was such a handsome girl in the valley, a Miss Morton. Visiting her brother, young Morton, of Philadelphia, the Mortons. His father a millionaire, himself a Harvard graduate, and he was running a melon ranch in the desert! There were the Youngbergs; Mr. Youngberg, the manager of the great A B C ranch, which belongs to Senator

Graves, you know? Mrs. Youngberg, the senator's own niece. And the Blinns, Mr. and Mrs. Blinn, not *quite* the same class of people, but so jolly and entertaining. Mr. Blinn makes you scream! And young Sutcliffe, the English zanjero, a remittance man, of course. Englished, the word wasn't so pretty; it meant ditch-tender.

"And the Wilson girls. I was forgetting about them. They are with their brother, who owns one of the big ranches here. He is picking grapes, think of it, off vines not four years old."

"Yes, it is a wonderful land," agreed her guest.

"I think it will surprise you to find so many nice people in here; it certainly did me. One doesn't expect to find congenial people in a new country like this. They say it is the quick rewards which attract ambitious men. Why, how much was it Jones cleared off his place last year, Tom? He was sending tomatoes east in February, grown in the open. This is really a huge forcing bed, isn't it? I've heard it said, too, that there is an intellectual stimulus which attracts one class, and develops the other. Do you agree with that, Mr. Rickard?"

Just like the sparrow, darting from bough to bough! He answered, gravely, that they certainly used a dictionary of their own! He had been to a meeting of the water companies, up at Imperial the other day. He turned to his host. "The fluency of some of those men surprised me!"

"We're not all dubs!" gruffed Hardin.

Gerty swept up her ruffles; her laugh sounded hard instead of gay. It was a kindness for a newcomer to bring in a breath of fresh air from the outside. They did get stale, they couldn't help it.

Rickard remembered that he had to get back to his

hotel. He had letters to write. It had been a splendid dinner! And what a wonderful home she had made out of a sand-baked lot, out of a tent! He spoke of the roses and the morning-glories. His eyes fell on the open piano, the reading table with the current magazines. Now, he couldn't understand why they ever went to that hotel!

Gerty's eyes were shining as deep pools of water on which the sun plays. She looked almost infantile as she stood by the two tall men, her head perched bird-like. "Good-by! and I hope you'll come again!"

Of course he'd come again!

"And you will let me know when you return, so that I may set the date for my party?"

Innes did not get his answer. She had been observing that he was not taller than her brother. He looked taller. He was lean, and Tom was growing stocky. She wished he would not slouch so, his hands in his pockets! In Tucson, before she knew that she must dislike Rickard, she had had an impression of virile distinction, of grace, a suggestion of mastered muscles. He had *known* that it was her brother he was supplanting—did he get any satisfaction from the fact that it was the husband of the woman who had jilted him? Anyway, she did not like him. She could never forgive a hurt that was done to her own. She was a Hardin.

"Innes! Mr. Rickard said good night!"

She gave him the tips of her cool browned fingers. Her eyes did not meet his; she would not meet that laughing scrutiny.

"Good night, Mr. Rickard."

CHAPTER XIII

THE FIGHTING CHANCE

"CASEY'S back; spying!" announced Wooster at mess one evening. By that time, the feeling against "Marshall's man" was actively hostile. There had been a smudge of slumbering fires before Rickard had left the towns. Fanned by much talk during his absence, it had burst into active blaze. They were ready to show their resentment against the man who had supplanted Hardin, their Napoleon, if it cost them their places. By this time the cause of the desert was as compelling to these hardy soldiers as were the lily banners of France to the followers of the Little Corporal.

Rickard was not expected. He had been gone less than a week. The effect of his return was that of a person who returns suddenly into a room, hushing an active babel of tongues. He knew what he would find, ample reasons why! He was not given the satisfaction of locating any particular act of disobedience. The men presented a blank wall of politeness, reasonable and ineffectual. Silent explained, briefly, that he had not been able to collect enough men. Most of the force was busy in the Number Six District, trying to push the shattered Wistaria through by a new route before that year's crops were entirely ruined. A gang was at Grant's Heading; the floor needed bracing. Another squad, Irish's, was in the Volcano Lake Region, where they were excavating for the new head-gate.

"No hurry for that." Rickard was glad to pick a flaw in such a perfect pattern. "You might have withdrawn those men, and put them to work on the levee."

"I was given no authority to do that."

The chief pretended to accept the reason; else it were a case of changing horses in mid-stream. What he had seen at the Heading, his peep at the exposed valley, his gleaning of the river's history had convinced him that in haste and concentration lay the valley's only chance. He must refuse to see the insubordination of the engineers, the seasoned desert soldiers. He needed them, must win their confidence if he could. If not, they must save the valley, anyway! The imperturbable front of Silent, his bland big stare, exasperated him; easier to control the snapping terrier of a Wooster. He had told Silent distinctly to gather his men and rush the levee. A good soldier had made a better guess than his, and had stopped the casual work at Black Butte, or had found Indians! Thoughtfully, Rickard followed that last suggestion across the ditch into Mexicali.

He gathered all the recruits he needed that morning. The Indians, lazy Cocopahs, crept out of their huts to earn a few of the silver dollars held out to them by the new white boss. A few Mexican laborers were bribed to toss up earth to the west of the town. Estrada, at his request, put a squad of his road force at the service of the manager. He could not spare many men.

The railroad had already started the line projected by Hardin to Marshall the year before, a spur across the desert, dipping into Mexico between the lean restless sand-hills, from Calexico to Yuma. The Mexican government had agreed to pay five thousand dollars a mile were the road completed at a certain period. Estrada was keeping his men on the jump to fill the contract, to make his nation pay the price. The completion of the road meant help to the valley; supplies, men, could be rushed through to the break.

In spite of his haunting sense of ultimate failure, the growing belief in the omnipotence of the Great Yellow Dragon as the Cocopahs visualized it, Estrada's work was as intense as though he were hastening a sure victory. The dauntless spirit of the elder Estrada pushed the track over the hot sands where he must dance at times to keep his feet from burning. Many of the rails they laid at night.

"Hog-wild!" exclaimed Hardin when he saw the levee for the first time. "Gone hog-wild." To him, the growing ridge of fine earth, like a soft heap of pulverized chocolate, was an absurd proof of misdirected energy. He walked down with Silent after dark to the gorge the river had cut on its last wild debauch, and stood on the newly upturned mound of earth. There was no water running now in the flood channel; it was a deep dry scar.

"It would be a good idea if it were necessary. It can do no harm."

"Do no harm, and the gate hung up! He makes me sick. We've had all the floods coming to us this twenty years. He's locking the barn after the horse is gone."

The calm beauty of that desert night was wasted on the man whose life, he told himself, had been dishonored. He did not smell the pungent breath, the damp moist sweetness of the newly turned earth; did not see the star-pricked canopy spreading out toward illimitable horizons. The moon trailed its cold pale light across the sky, but

Hardin could not see. His view was a world of his making, a country peopled by his energy, the people who had turned him down. The eyes that were looking at the levee were no longer seeing another man's folly; they were visualizing his head-gate, the gate that meant safety to the valley, the gate he was not allowed to complete. He was living over again, step by step, the chain of events that led to this exasperating deadlock; himself, incapacitated, helpless, seeing the thing which should be done, powerless to do it. The men who might win, petty enough to let the wish to put him in the wrong override the big opportunity to save the valley! He wondered again why he had not the sense to get out.

"And kick the whole bucket over," he grumbled. "I would, too, if I had the sense I was born with. Get out, and begin over again somewhere. Not stay for more kicks. They'd find they'd be wanting me back again. I will get out. I'll not stay a month longer."

"Rickard's gone hog-wild," he told his family the next morning. "Building a levee between the towns! The man's off his head."

"There really isn't any danger?" Gerty's anxiety made the deep blue eyes look black.

Innes looked up for Tom's answer. His face was ugly with passion.

"Danger! It's a bluff, a big show of activity here, because he's buffaloed; he doesn't know how to tackle the job out there."

It had begun to look that way to more than one. It was talked over at Coulter's store; in the outer office of the D. R. Company where the engineers foregathered; among the chair-tilters who idled in front of the Desert Hotel.

"The man does not know how to tackle his job!" A levee, and the gate held up! What protection to the towns would be that toy levee if the river should return on one of its spectacular sprees? A levee, and the intake itself not guarded? He was whispered of as an incompetent; one of Marshall's clerks. He was given a short time to blow himself out. A bookman, a theorist.

"As well put sentinels a few miles from prison, and leave the jail doors open!" This was Wooster's gibe. All saw the Colorado as a marauder at large. "And a little heap of sand stacked up to scare it off! It's a scream!"

Mrs. Hardin found it difficult to meet with diplomacy the confidences which inevitably came her way. As Hardin's wife, she was expected to enjoy the universal censure the new man was acquiring. Gerty's light touches, too slight for championship, passed as a sweet charity. Her own position those days was trying. She did not yet know her diplomatic lesson.

Apparently unaware of the talk, Rickard spent the greater part of his time superintending the levee. He could trust no one else to do it, no one unless it were Estrada, who was rushing his steel rails through to the front, and was needed there.

Things were moving under his constant goading. The extra pay was showing results. He should be at the Heading now, he kept telling himself, but he was convinced that the instant he turned his back, the work on the levee would stop; and all the reasons excellent! Some emergency would be cooked up to warrant the withdrawal of the hands. Chafe as he might at the situation, it was to be guerrilla warfare. Not a fight in the open, he knew how to meet that, but this baffling resistance, the polite silence of the office when he entered,—"Well, they'll be doing my way pretty soon, or my name isn't Rickard. That's flat."

He was fretting to be at work, to start the wheels of the O. P., its vast machinery toward his problem. He knew that that organization, like well-drilled militia, was ready for his call. The call lagged, not that he did not need men, but there was no place ready for them. The camp, that was another rub. There was no camp! It was not equipped for a sudden inflation of men. The inefficiency of the projectors of this desert scheme had never seemed so criminal as when he had surveyed the equipment at the intake. "Get ready first; your tools, your stoves, your beds." That was the training of the good executive, of men like Marshall and MacLean. Nothing to be left to chance; to foresee emergencies, not to be taken by them unaware. The reason of Hardin's downfall was his slipshod habits. How could he be a good officer who had never drilled as a soldier? There was the gap at the intake, Hardin's grotesque folly, widened from one hundred feet to ten times the original cut; widening every day, with neither equipment nor camp adequate to push through a work of half the original magnitude. Cutting away, moreover, was the island, Disaster Island; it had received apt christening by the engineers, its baptismal water the Colorado. The last floods had played with it as though it were a bar of sugar. There was no rock at hand; no rock on the way, no rock ordered. Could any one piece together such recklessness?

Rickard knew where he would get his rock. Already he had requisitioned the entire output of the Tacna and Patagonia quarries. He had ordered steam shovels to be installed at the quarry back of old Hamlin's. That rock pit would be his first crutch, and the gravel bed, —that was a find! As he paced the levee west of the towns, he was planning his campaign. Porter was scouring Zacatecas for men; he himself had offered, as bait, free transportation; the O. P. he knew would back him. He was going to throw out a spur-track from the Heading, touching at the quarry and gravel pit, on to the main road at Yuma. Double track most of the way; sidings every three miles. Rock must be rushed; the trains must be pushed through. He itched to begin. It never occurred to him that, like Hardin, he might fail.

"Though it's no pink tea," he told himself, "it's no picnic." At Tucson, he knew that the situation was a grave one, but his talk with Brandon, who knew his river signs as does a good Indian, made the year a significant, eventful one. Matt Hamlin, too, whose shrewd eyes had grown river-wise, he, too, had had tales to tell of the tricky river. Maldonado, the half-breed, had confirmed their portents while they sat together under his oleander, famous throughout that section of the country. And powerfully had Cor'nel, the Indian who had piloted Estrada's party across the desert, whom Rickard had met at the Crossing, deeply had he impressed him. The river grew into a malevolent, mocking personality; he could see it a dragon of yellow waters, dragging its slow sluggish length across the baked desert sands; deceiving men by its inertness; luring the explorer by a mild mood, to rise suddenly with its wild fellow, the Gila, sending boat and boatmen to their swift doom.

Rickard was thinking of the half-breed, Maldonado, as he inspected the new stretch of levee between the towns. He had heard from others besides Estrada of the river knowledge of this descendant of trapper and squaw, and had thought it worth while to ride the twenty miles from down the river to talk with him. The man's suavity, his narrow slits of eyes, the lips thin and facile, deep lines of cruelty falling from them, had repelled his visitor. The mystery of the place followed him. Why the 'dobe wall which completely surrounded the small low dwellings? Why the cautious admittance, the atmosphere of suspicion? Rickard had seen the wife, a frightened shadow of a woman; had seen her flinch when the brute called her. He had questioned Cor'nel about the half-breed. He was remembering the wrinkles of contempt on the old Indian's face as he delivered himself of an oracular grunt.

"White man? No. Indian? No! Coyote!"

Though he suspected Maldonado would lie on principle, though it might be that two-thirds of his glib tissue were false, yet a thread of truth coincident with the others, Brandon and Hamlin and Cor'nel, might be pulled out of his romantic fabric.

"When the waters of the Gila run red, look for trouble!" He doubted that they ever ran red. He would ask Cor'nel. He had also spoken of a cycle, known to Indians, of a hundredth year, when the Dragon grows restless; this he had declared was a hundredth year.

On the road from Maldonado's, Rickard had met several Indians swaying from their saddles; a half-breed lurching unsteadily toward Yuma. He had made note of that. Who was selling liquor to those Indians, those half-breeds? Maldonado could have told him, Maldonado who wore the dirty unrecognizable uniform of a rurale. Rickard was going to use Indian labor; must depend, he knew, for steady work, the brush clearing and the mattress weaving, on the natives. If any one was selling mescal and tequila within a day's ride of the Heading, it was his place to find out.

Following his talk with Maldonado, and the accidental happy chance meeting with Coronel at the Crossing, Rickard had written his first report to Tod Marshall. Before he had come to the Heading, he had expected to advise against the completion of the wooden head-gate at the Crossing. Hamlin had given him a new view-point. There was a fighting chance. And he wanted to be fair. Next to being successful, he wanted to be fair.

He smiled as he remembered MacLean's cramped fingers after the dictation was done. "Holy Minnie," he had exclaimed, rubbing his joints. "If you call that going slow!"

"It's time to be hearing from Marshall," Rickard was thinking, as he walked back to the hotel. "I wonder what he will say." He felt it had been fair to put it up to Marshall; personally, he would like to begin with a clean slate; begin right. Clumsy work had been done, it was true, yet there were urgent reasons now for haste; and the gate was nearly half done! He had gone carefully over the situation. The heavy snowfall, unprecedented for years, a hundred, according to the Indians,—on the Wind River Mountains—the lakes swollen with ice, the Gila restless, the summer floods yet to be met; perhaps, he now thought, he had been overfair in emphasizing the arguments for the head-gate. For the hundred feet were now a thousand feet—yet he had spoken of that to Marshall: "Calculate for yourself the difference in expense since the flood widened the break. It is a vastly different problem now. Disaster Island, which they figured on for anchor, is a mere pit of corroding sugar in the channel. An infant Colorado could wash it away. However, a lot of work has already been done, and a lot of money spent. There is a fighting chance. Perhaps the bad year is all Indian talk."

A guess, at best, whatever they did! It was pure gamble what the tricky Colorado would do. Anyway, he had given the whole situation to Marshall.

In his box at the hotel was a telegram which had been sent over from the office; from Tod Marshall. "Take the fighting chance. But remember to speak more respectfully of Indians!"

"Marshall all over," laughed his subordinate. "Now, it's a case of hustle! But dollars to doughnuts, as Junior says, we don't do it!"

CHAPTER XIV

HARDIN'S LUCK

TWO days later, there was a shock of earthquake, so slight that the lapping of the water in Rickard's bath was his intimation of the earth's uneasiness. In the dining-room, later, he found every one discussing it. "Who could remember an earthquake in that desert?" "The first shake!"

"The Indians might have something to say about that," thought Rickard.

His pompadoured waitress was ready to fall into hysteria. "Several dishes fell off the pantry shelves. Give me a Kansas cyclone to an earthquake, I say, every time. For there is always a cyclone cellar. But the earth under your feet! Me for Kansas, every time!"

After he had placed his breakfast order, while waiting for his eggs—"Ten minutes in boiling water, off the stove, mind!"—Rickard got the Crossing on the telephone. Matt Hamlin answered the call. He insisted on describing the exact place he had stood when the shock came. It wasn't anything of a quake. A baby to the shake of '67. No harm done out there. While he was on the line, Rickard heard the sound of other voices. "It's Silent just in from the Heading." "Hello, there," cried Rickard. "Don't hang up. Ask him about the gate. Any damage done?"

Silent, himself, came on the wire. The gate was all right. "That was nothing of a quake." Rickard then got Grant's Heading. The temblor had been felt more there, but no serious damage had been done. Rickard went back to his boiled eggs. The earthquake was forgotten.

During the morning, unfathered, as rumors are born, the whisper of disaster somewhere spread. Their own slight shock was the edge of the convulsion which had been serious elsewhere, no one knew quite where, or why they knew it at all. The men who were shoveling earth on the levee began to talk of San Francisco. Some one said, that morning, that the city was badly hurt. No one could confirm the rumor, but it grew with the day.

Rickard met it at the office late in the afternoon. The word was growing in definiteness. There was trouble up North. A terrible disaster; people had been killed; towns were burning. There was a report of a tidal wave which had swept San Francisco. Another quoted that San Jose had telegraphed all the wires from San Francisco down; that San Francisco was burning. He went direct to the telegraph operator's desk.

"Get Los Angeles, the O. P. office. And be quick about it."

In ten minutes, he was talking to Babcock. That human clock confirmed some of the ugly rumors. The wires between San Francisco and the rest of the world *were* down; impossible to get any word from there.

"Any relative there?" he inquired with sympathy on tap. Such messages had been coming in all day.

"Oh, no. How much do you know? How do you know it?" persisted Rickard.

Babcock said that the damage by earthquake to that

HARDIN'S LUCK

city was not known, but it was afire. San Jose had confirmed it. Oakland had reported the flames creeping up the residence hills of that gay western city. Cinders were already falling in the transbay town.

Rickard dropped the receiver. "Where's Hardin?"

Tom Hardin emerged from a knot of men who were talking in a corner by the door.

"Where's that machinery?"

"What machinery?"

Rickard saw the answer to his question in the other's face.

"The dredge machinery. Did you attend to that? Did you send for it?"

"Oh, yes, that's all right. It's all right."

"Is it here?"

Hardin attempted jocularity. "I didn't know as you wanted it here. I ordered it sent to Yuma."

"Is it at Yuma?"

Hardin admitted that it was not yet at Yuma; it would be there soon; he had written; oh, it was all right.

"When did you write?"

Hardin reddened under the catechism of questions. He resented being held up before his men. The others felt the electricity in the air. Hardin and his successor were glaring at each other like belligerents.

"I asked when did you write?"

"Yesterday."

"Yesterday!" Rickard ripped out an oath. "Yesterday. Why at all, I'd like to know? Did you understand that you were ordered to get that here? Now, it's gone."

"Gone?" The others crowded up.

"San Francisco's burning." He walked into his inner

office, mad clear through. The group around Hardin were tearing his wisp of news. San Francisco on fire. The city of their fun gone.

He was not thinking of the ruin of the gay young city; not a thought yet did he have of the human tragedies enacting there; of homes, lives, fortunes swept into that huge bonfire. As it affected the work at the river, the first block to his campaign, the catastrophe came home to him. He had a picture of tortured, twisted iron, of ruined machinery, the machinery for his dredge. He saw it lying like a spent Laocoön, writhing in its last struggle. He blamed himself for leaving even such a small detail as the hastening of the parts to Hardin's care, for Hardin wasn't fit to be trusted for anything. No one could tell him now the man was unlucky; he was a fool. A month wasted, and days were precious. A month? Months. Hardin's luck. Oh, hell!

Then he began to speculate, as he cooled, over the trouble up yonder. A whole city burning? They would surely get it under control. He began to think of the isolation; the telegraph wires all down. That might happen anywhere! He walked to the door and looked thoughtfully at the company's big water-tower. That wasn't such a bad idea! He picked up his hat, and went out.

CHAPTER XV

THE WRONG MAN

MRS. Hardin heard from every source but the right one that Rickard had returned. Each time her telephone rang, it was his voice she expected to hear. She began to read a meaning into his silence. She could think of nothing else than the strange coincidence that had brought their lives again close. Or *was* it a coincidence? That idea sent her thoughts far afield.

She was thinking too much of him, for peace of mind, those days of waiting, but the return of the old lover had made a wonderful break in her life. Her eyes were brighter; her smile was less forced. She spent most of her days at the sewing-machine. A lot of lace was whipped on to lingerie frocks of pale colors. She was a disciple of an eastern esthete. "Women," he had said, "should buy lace, not by the yard, but by the mile."

She had attended his lectures while in New York, acquiring a distaste for all her possessions. He had taught her to disdain golden-oak, to fear bric-à-brac, to forswear all vivid colors. She could see no charm in the tailor-made girl, in Innes' trig shirt-waists and well-cut skirts. The yellow khakis always outraged her sense of beauty. The girl's ideas on fitness would have shocked and wounded her.

As her fingers worked among the laces and soft mulls,

her mind roved down avenues that should have been closed to her, a wife. She would have protested, had any one accused her of infidelity in those days, yet day by day, she was straying farther from her husband's side. She convinced herself that Tom's gibes and ill-humor were getting harder to endure.

It was inevitable that the woman of harem training should relive the Lawrence days. The enmity of those two men, both her lovers, was pregnant with romantic suggestion. The drama of desert and river centered now in the story of Gerty Hardin. Rickard, who had never married! The deduction, once unveiled, lost all its shyness. And every one saw that he disliked her husband!

She knew now that she had never loved Tom. She had turned to him in those days of pride when Rickard's anger still held him aloof. How many times had she gone over those unreal hours! Who could have known that his anger would last? That hour in the honeysuckles; his kisses! None of Hardin's rougher kisses had swept her memory of her exquisite delight—delirious as was her joy, there was room for triumph. She had seen herself clear of the noisy boarding-house. Herself, Gerty Holmes, the wife of a professor; able to have the things she craved, to have them openly; no longer having to scheme for them.

It was through Rickard's eyes that she had seen the shortcomings of the college boarding-house. She had acquired a keen consciousness of those quizzical eyes. When they had isolated her, at last, appealing to her sympathy or amusement, separating her from all those boisterous students, her dream of bliss had begun.

In those days, she had seen Hardin through the eyes of the young instructor, younger by several years than his pupil. Her thud of disappointed anger, of dislike, when the face of Hardin peered through the leafy screen! To have waited, prayed for that moment, and to have it spoiled like that! There had been days when she had wept because she had not shown her anger! How could she know that everything would end there; end, just beginning! Her boarding-house training had taught her to be civil. It was still vivid to her, her anxiety, her tremulousness—with Hardin talking forever of a play he had just seen; Rickard growing stiffer, angrier, refusing to look at those lips still warm with his kisses!

And the next day, still angry with her. Ah, the puzzled desolation of those weeks before she had salved her hurt; with pride, and then with love! Those days of misery before she could convince herself that she had been in love with love, not with her fleeing lover! Hardin was there, eager to be noticed. That affair, she could see now, had lacked finesse.

Rickard had certainly loved her, or why had he never married? Why had he left so abruptly his boarding-house, in mid-term? Doesn't jealousy confess love? Some day, he would tell her; what a hideous mistake hers had been! She ought not to have rushed into that marriage. She knew now it had always been the other. But life was not finished, yet!

The date set for her summer "widowhood" had come, but she lingered. Various reasons, splendid and sacrificial, were given out. There was much to be done.

"I wish she would be definite," Innes' thoughts complained. She was restless to make her own plans. It had not yet occurred to her that Gerty would stay in all summer. For she never had so martyrized herself. "Some one must be with Tom. It may spoil my trip. But Gerty never thinks of that." She believed it to be a simple matter of clothes. It always took her weeks to get ready to go anywhere.

"But I won't wait any longer than next week. If she does not go then, I will. Absurd for us both to be here." It was already fiercely hot.

Gerty, meanwhile, had been wondering how she could suggest to her sister-in-law that her trip be taken first. Without arousing suspicions! Terribly loud in her ears sounded her thoughts those days.

Her husband flung a letter on the table one evening. "A letter to you from—Casey."

She tried to make the fingers that closed over the letter move casually. She could feel them tremble. What would she say if Tom asked to see it?

It was addressed to her in her husband's care. Hardin had found it at the office in his mail. And she going each day to the post-office to prevent it from falling into his hands! She gave it a quick offhand glance.

"About the drive, of course. Supper's getting cold. Look at that omelet. Don't wait to wash up. It will be like leather."

When she had finished her meal, she read her letter with a fine show of indifference. "He sets a date for the drive." She put the letter carelessly into her pocket before her husband could stretch out his hand. It would never do for jealous Tom to read that: "Your letter was received two weeks ago. Pardon me for appearing to have forgotten your kindness."

"The nerve," growled Tom again, his mouth full of Gerty's omelet. "To take you up on an invitation like that. I call that pretty raw."

"You must remember we are such old friends," urged his wife. "He knew I meant it seriously."

"Just the same, it's nerve," grumbled Hardin, helping himself to more of the omelet, now a flat ruin in the center of the Canton platter. His resentment had taken on an edge of hatred since the episode of the dredge machinery. "To write to any one in my house! He knows what I think of him; an ineffectual ass, that's what he is. Blundering around with his little levees, and his fool work on the water-tower."

"The water-tower?" demanded his sister. "What's he doing with that?"

"Oh, I don't know," rejoined Tom largely, his lips protruding. He had been itching to ask some one what Rickard was up to. Twice, he had seen him go up, with MacLean and Estrada. Once, there a large flare of light. But he wouldn't ask! Some of his fool tinkering!

His sister's gaze rested on him with concern. He had too little to do. She guessed that his title, consulting engineer, was a mocking one, that his chief, at least, did not consult him. Was it true, what she had heard, that he had made a fluke about the machinery? He was looking seedy. He had been letting his clothes go. He looked like a man who has lost grip; who has been shelved.

She knew he was sleeping badly. Every morning now she found the couch rumpled. Not much pretense of marital congeniality. Things were going badly, there—

"Everybody has accepted," Gerty was saying. "They have been waiting for me to set the date."

"And you cater to him, let him dangle you all. I wonder why you do it, unless it's to hurt me."

"Hurt you, Tom," cried his wife, her deep blue eyes

wide with dismay. "How can you say such a thing? But if it is given for him, how can I do anything else than let him arrange the day to suit himself? It would be funny for the guest of honor not to be present, wouldn't it?"

"I don't see why you want to make him a guest of honor," he retreated, covering his position.

Gently, Gerty expressed her belief that she was doing the best thing for her husband in getting up a public affair for his successor. She did think that Tom would see that it showed they had no feeling.

"I think it a fine idea," agreed Innes heartily. "I'm sure Tom will, too, when he thinks about it." But she did not give him any chance to express himself. "How are you going to manage it, Gerty? You said it was going to be progressive?"

"We shall draw for partners," said Mrs. Hardin. "And change every half a mile. The first lap will be two miles; that will give some excitement in cutting for partners." Easy, being the hostess, to withhold any slip she pleased, easy to make it seem accidental!

"When is this circus coming off?" inquired her husband.

"Mr. Rickard says he will be back on the first; that he'll be free on the second."

Hardin scraped his chair over the pine board floor which Gerty had helped Sam to treat until it looked "hard." Each alternate strip had been stained dark, the whole waxed and rubbed until it almost gave a shadow, the housekeeper's idea of elegance.

"For half an hour, I'll listen to Mrs. Youngberg tell me how hard it is to have to do without servants, as she's never done it in her life before. For another half-mile, Mrs. Hatfield will flirt with me, and Mrs. Middleton will tell me all about 'her dear little kiddies.' Sounds cheerful. Why didn't you choose cards? No one has to talk then."

There was an interval when his wife appeared to be balancing his suggestion. "No, I think it will have to be a drive; for I've told every one about it."

"Well," remarked her husband, "I only hope something will happen to prevent it."

"Tom!" exclaimed Gerty Hardin. "What a dreadful thing to say. That sounds like a curse. You make my blood run cold."

"Shu!" said Hardin, picking up his hat. "That was no curse. You wouldn't go if it rained, would you?"

"Oh, rain!" She shrugged at that possibility.

"Well, you wouldn't go if the wind blows!" retorted Hardin, leaving the room.

A minute later he stuck his head through the door.

"Mrs. Youngberg's outside."

"Mrs. Youngberg!" cried Gerty, pleasantly fluttered. She ran out into the street without waiting to pick up a hat. "For I'll make her come in this time," she thought. "I won't stand craning my neck and squinting up at her as if she were the great high executioner."

Mrs. Youngberg leaned out from the box buggy, and kissed her. "How are you these days?" Her voice was solicitous.

"Oh, splendid!" Gerty smiled gaily toward the occupant of the buggy, but the desert sun deflected the smile into a grimace. "Won't you come in to-day? Do tie up, and have a little visit."

"Oh, I can't this morning. I have a hundred errands to attend to, and I must get back in time to get lunch for my family. I lost my maid; isn't it terrible down here? You can't keep a girl for a week. I don't mind cooking for my husband, but I do draw the line at being cook for the hired men. And the coarse things they like! You can't always cook a double meal. And I lost one of the best workers we ever had, that was when we first came here, because he didn't like the food I gave him. Stuffed eggs, and Waldorf salad. What do you think of that? It's quantity they want, and that man went off and said I'd starved him."

"Do come in," urged Gerty, squinting at the sun.

"I can't. I'd like to, but I can't. My husband likes his meal prompt, and the men simply come in and sit down, and watch you until it's ready."

"Yes, I know," interposed the other, half-blinded. "But surely you can stay a minute. I have so many things to tell you."

"I, too. I want to have the ladies of the Improvement Club in to tea before I go out; I think it will be Friday. After I sound the ladies a little, I'll let you know."

"Last year, she would have had *me* set the day." Gerty was on the outlook for stings; she felt that she had lost her position in the valley set.

"Of course, that includes Miss Hardin," added Mrs. Youngberg, drawing up the reins.

"I wanted to talk to you about the drive," cried Mrs. Hardin. "It is to be on the second. Will you take this as the invitation, or must I write to you?"

"Please, don't write." And Mrs. Youngberg was driving off when a thought seemed to strike her.

"I saw the levee as I was driving past. What in the world is that for? Does Mr. Hardin think there will be bigger floods than we've had already? Isn't the New River deep enough to carry all the flood waters?"

Mrs. Hardin had never had her tact so completely taxed. She balanced her answer carefully, with apprehension. Almost anything would sound wrong quoted as from her. She was Hardin's wife; his success or failure must still involve her. She could hear her answer quoted to Mr. Rickard. "Mr. Hardin hoped it would not be necessary." And then warmly she praised Rickard's foresight in case anything did happen!

She went into the house, flushed and blinking and uncomfortable, revolving a better, more diplomatic answer. She was convinced that that last question had been the object of the visit. These top-buggy visits, as Innes called them, annoyed her. It was an irritation to all the women of the towns, for Mrs. Youngberg never had time to get out; she always would keep them standing restive under the glare of desert sun. From the wife of Youngberg, they would never have endured it. Senator Graves made the situation a trifle delicate.

CHAPTER XVI

THE BEST LAID SCHEMES

IT was the forenoon of the second. Several times during the morning Gerty left her preparations to take forecasts of the weather. It was not so hot as it had been and there was a moon. She congratulated herself; it would be a fine night.

Her tent door was locked all morning. A new variety of salad was on the way, the latest New York idea. For hours, Gerty's fingers were shredding the skins from muscat grapes which were to be chilled, and served with French dressing on crisp desert lettuce. The grapes, too, were desert bred. It was a long task, and while her fingers worked, her mind ran ahead nervously to the few name-cards that had to be finished, white cards with a design of the palo verde, the characteristic tree of the region. The color scheme was pastel green and white. Pistachio ice-cream and vanilla had been ordered from Los Angeles, and Gerty herself had colored the cream peppermints. Innes had suggested using the yellow blossoms of the mesquit, but Mrs. Hardin hated yellow; it was too "positive."

Her eyes watched the clock hands. Eleven o'clock, and those candle-shades not done! More time than she had reckoned on had gone into the building of the white mull lingerie dress; it had pressed her with the shades and cards. And she had no time to work at night, for the Hardins were always around then. Not that there was any reason why she should not occupy herself indeed just as she chose, but she hated interference. If there was anything she resented more than another, it was interference. Rather than explain why she wanted namecards, or must have paper shades for the candles, or moreover why it was necessary to have a frock that had not been seen before, she preferred to lock her doors and work "like mad." Tom's ridicule was so stupid, and his sister was getting to be like him; not that she said much, but she had such a scornful look!

The clock hands were flying. She stopped to count the grapes already peeled and seeded. "At least fifteen to each plate," she had calculated. "And twenty guests, twenty times fifteen—three hundred." She counted them again. "Only two hundred!" The clock hands ticked away another half-hour. Her fingers began to go wild; several finished grapes fell to the floor. "I'll wash them off," she thought.

She was peeling the two hundred and fiftieth, when there was a sound of wheels. A clear "Oo-hoo" summoned her.

"It is Mrs. Youngberg." She was horrified. "And she wasn't to come until after lunch." She slipped off her gingham apron and ran out breathless to the sidewalk.

"Hope you don't mind my coming early," called Mrs. Youngberg. "It was now or never. Can you come with me?" She waved to the greens in the box buggy. "And are these enough?"

"Oh, yes," responded Gerty absently. She was wondering what in the world she would do about the unpeeled grapes, and the unfinished shades and the name-cards. Perhaps she could do with eleven. Innes had offered to help; she supposed she could put her to work at the grapes. But she hated to have people help, people who looked scornful and superior. She could hear her say: "Why all this fuss? Why not a simpler salad?" If worse came to worse, she could put a plain card at her husband's place, and her own. She needed Mrs. Youngberg's help with the table—

"I'm afraid I'm putting you out," her friend was taking note of the discomfiture. "You are not ready?"

Mrs. Hardin hastened to deny that. "Oh, yes! I was just thinking what I'd take along. Will you come in?" For once, she was grateful to the Youngberg habit of the buggy. She took the answer for granted, and the tent door mangled the response of the niece of Senator Graves.

When she came out, her arms were overflowing with bundles. A large hat box surmounted the smaller ones, held in place by her chin. The top bulged open. As she reached the sidewalk, her progress grew precarious, for a slight wind was blowing. She had not closed the hat box in fear of her precious shades.

"Give me something," cried Mrs. Youngberg. She caught the band-box. A gust of evil wind raised the top; one of the shades blew out, and Gerty, helpless with crockery in her hands, watched it tumble toward the irrigation ditch. It danced, the pretty thing of pastel green and white, on the surface of the muddy stream.

"You can save it," cried Mrs. Youngberg. "Oh, what a pity!" For as she spoke it collided with a floating branch. Mud-splashed and ruined, it sailed down the street.

"Oh, never mind that," protested Gerty with magnificence. She forced a cheery smile as she clambered over her parcels into the buggy.

"And I was one short already!" she remembered as they drove down the main street, the buggy heaped high with boxes holding the treasured shades, the cards and napkins, and a few choice plates. The supper was to be at the hotel, but Gerty planned to use her own dishes and cutlery—to give it a home-like feeling! Coulter's two clerks gaped at them from the store as they passed; the buggy trailing long willow branches, and Gerty with her boxes obscuring her vision.

In front of Fred Egger's store the usual group of Indians lounged, the squaws careening in many ruffles, the bucks brave in paint and shirts, heavy with beads. Young Morton bowed to them from the bank windows on which a man was laboriously working. He had already finished a faint black outline, The Desert Bank, and was beginning to fill in the first letter with gold-leaf. The festive buggy made quite a stir in the desert town; every one had heard of the progressive drive.

"The ditch is running very high this morning," observed Mrs. Youngberg, noting its muddy flow.

"Somebody is irrigating his melons." Mrs. Hardin's observation was a trifle absent. She liked the attention they were attracting. How she would love to be in a position where she could use her social talents!

Mrs. Youngberg was reining up in front of the Desert Hotel. Half a dozen men jumped forward to tie the mare, and to help the ladies with their bundles. Gerty declared she would not let them carry the packages; she would send the boy after them. She felt the importance of a leader of society.

"You don't mind if I do a few errands first," called Mrs. Youngberg after her. Gerty whirled, her cheeks red, her eyes seeing not Mrs. Youngberg but a vision of the kitchen at home; the unpeeled grapes, the candle-shades, the waiting name-cards.

"Why, I thought you were going to help me," she cried, her consternation shrilling her voice.

"I shall be right back," reassured her friend. "You may rely on me. Mr. Youngberg could not come in this morning; he gave me a list a yard long. And I must see Mrs. Blinn about the Improvement Club; it can't be put off. I'm not going to fail you. You may rely on me."

It was really too provoking. The whole morning had gone wrong. Mrs. Hardin marched into the hotel, her color high. She might have guessed that Mrs. Youngberg would fall down; she always did. She should have relied on some one else, that homely Towne girl who is always so good-natured!

Already ruffled, she found everything to be exasperating in the Desert Hotel. She had taken it for granted when Patton had promised her the use of the dining-room weeks before that she could arrange the table as she would use it at eleven. He upset all her plans by telling her he needed the space; he had not intended to give her that impression. She had said, he reminded her, that she needed the room for an eleven o'clock supper.

She was convinced that she detected a difference in his manner to her. "He would never have treated me so last year. We are nobodies, now!"

The very best he could do, Mr. Patton assured her, was to let her arrange the table in the drummers' sample room whence it could be carried "all set" into the dining-room after it was properly cleared. "I have

THE BEST LAID SCHEMES

to consider my girls," he said. "If I ask them to do anything extra, they would throw the whole waitresses' union in my face."

"Give me a soda lemonade, Mr. Patton," ordered Gerty, moving to the white and silver counter. "I'll think it over."

When she returned to the attack, he was still obstinately fearful to antagonize the maids. "Servants are not servants in California!" He led the way to the drummers' room, where she had an inspiration.

"Let me have this room, Mr. Patton," she urged. "It will be so much cozier, and we can move the piano in, and have music without it being so public as it is in the hall."

"I'm sorry, Mrs. Hardin, I'd like to accommodate you, but there's always drummers coming in here. There's sure to be one or more on that six o'clock train. It's right after supper they spread their samples."

"Then they'd ruin my table!" cried Gerty.

"Oh, no, I'll give them another table, Mrs. Hardin," protested Patton. "It's the best I can do. I can't afford to lose their custom. You see, they pass it about, from one place to the other, and if anything they don't like happens, the first thing your custom has fallen off."

Haughtily, Gerty had to succumb. She found her next block when she wished to bank the willow greens in the dining-room. It lacked a few minutes to twelve. The doors of the dining-room would be thrown open to the patrons of the hotel; she compromised on vases. They brought her a few small affairs which refused to stand when filled with the top-heavy branches.

"I've got some crockery jugs in the kitchen," Patton volunteered. "I'll have them washed and sent in to you."

"And I'm waiting for the cloth, Mr. Patton. None of mine was long enough."

Patton confessed that his were too short for the long drummers' table, but she could use two. No one would ever see where they doubled in the center.

"Oh, very well," cried Gerty Hardin. Her nerves were on edge with the delay. She busied herself with unpacking her bundles, listening for the sound of Mrs. Youngberg's buggy wheels. The table was fully set, the candle-shades placed, the name-cards adjusted, even the willows arranged as best she could in the gray crockery jugs before Mrs. Youngberg returned.

She professed herself entranced with everything. And where had she got the idea of those darling shades? The green blotting-paper cut out stencil-wise in the design of water lilies, the white paper lining making the petals, was altogether charming and original. Would Mrs. Hardin mind if she copied them?

Mrs. Hardin's answer was a little strained. "Of course, I do not mind." Mrs. Youngberg decided to use pink and green when she made her copies; the white *was* a little insipid! She was taking keen note of the arrangement of the guests, of her husband's name and Mrs. Hatfield's, side by side.

"Is it all right?" inquired Mrs. Hardin, watching her face. "It's the hardest thing to place people, I think."

Not for the world would Mrs. Youngberg have suggested her annoyance. Every one put her husband next to Mrs. Hatfield. He did not like that incorrigible coquette! Every one knew by this time that rightfully she was a grandmother. Her divorced husband was in a remote background with the children and grandchildren. The second husband was a minus, negative enough to maintain the tie which Mrs. Hatfield's coquetry must put under severe strain.

"Admirable," said Mrs. Youngberg. She wondered if Mrs. Hardin knew that a wind was rising? She would not tell her. "Admirable," she repeated.

Gerty's eye casually observed every corner of the hall as the two women made their way out. She wanted to look at the register to see if Rickard's name were there, but her self-consciousness withheld her. He might see her. Not until it was too late did she reflect that she might have announced a curiosity as to new arrivals. The street reached, she stared blankly at the wind-struck town; then at Mrs. Youngberg.

"Isn't it a shame?" murmured her friend. "I hated to tell you."

Ready to cry was Gerty. Even the wind sided against her party. It was blowing down the main street like a baby hurricane with the colic. Her hat was wrenched from its moorings.

"It's not so bad as it used to be," shrieked Mrs. Youngberg, clambering into the buggy. "Before the alfalfa was planted!"

The loungers had left the sidewalk. Up-stairs, the disheveled chambermaids were making the beds in the overhanging bird-cage. The street was deserted, save for the Cocopahs who flanked the door of Eggers' store like bronze inscrutable sentinels. Two squaws came out to watch the progress of the wind-blown buggy. Their wide ruffled skirts were blown into balloons. Large colored handkerchiefs, sewn together into a cloak, bellied with the breeze. They watched the two white women incuriously, steadily. Mrs. Youngberg was hanging on to her Mexican sombrero with her left gauntleted hand.

Gerty was grabbing her pretty sun hat with her tired fingers.

As they passed the bank, the workman was leaving his job; the day was not propitious for gold-leaf. Two words were completed, "The Desert." The rest of the letters were inconspicuous skeletons.

Gerty jumped out at her tent door. She would not risk asking Mrs. Youngberg in. The unexpected might happen.

"You are going just the same?" called Mrs. Youngberg, her mouth full of dust.

Mrs. Hardin nodded. "Sure." She ran in to her wilting grapes.

CHAPTER XVII

THE DRAGON TAKES A HAND

THE company's automobile honked outside. Hardin frowned across the table at his wife. "You're surely not going such a night as this?"

Gerty gave one of her light, elusive shrugs. No need to answer Tom when he was in one of his black moods. This was the first word he had spoken since he had entered the tent. She had warned Innes by a lifted eyebrow—they must be careful not to provoke him. Something had gone wrong at the office, of course! How much longer could she stand his humors, these ghastly silent dinners?

"The river on a rampage, and we go for a drive!" jeered Hardin.

The flood was not serious—yet! Tom loved to cry "Wolf!" No one was alarmed in town—Patton, Mrs. Youngberg, would have told her. Of course, one never knew what that dreadful river would do next, but if one had to wait always to see what the river's next prank would be, one would never get anywhere!

Innes was leaving the table. "Well, I suppose I should be lashing on my hat!" Gerty's pretty lips hardened as the girl left the tent. These Hardins always loved to spoil her enjoyment. They would like her to be a nun, a cloistered nun!

At the opening of the door, the wind tore the pictures from the piano, wrenching the faded green mandarin skirt which Gerty had brought from San Francisco. Her sketches were flung to the floor. Gerty ran into her room, shutting herself in against further argument. Tom fastened the outer door, replacing the sketches that stood for the sum and height of his wife's several flights, her separate career.

He was still staring through them, when his wife came back into the room, powdered and heavily veiled against the wind. A heavy winter ulster covered the new mull gown which she had not worn at supper, though Innes could have helped her with the hooks! But there was always so much talk about everything!

They had to face the gale as the machine swept down the wind-crazed street. "Never saw such a blow in all the time I've been here," yelled Wooster over his wheel to Hardin.

"Where's Mr. MacLean?" Gerty leaned over from the back seat where she had been huddling. She felt awkwardly conscious of not having invited Wooster. She did not have any other reason for excluding him, except that she did not meet him at the other houses. Still, if Rickard were not coming—they would be short a man.

"He had some work to finish—he asked me to take out the machine," called Wooster without turning. The dust was blinding him.

"He's probably coming later!" cried Gerty to Innes, and then she huddled in her corner again. It was easier not to talk; one had to scream to be heard.

It was too bad to have a night like this! And all her work—Tom and his sister would have it go for nothing! She was made of stubborner stuff than that. Life had been dealing out mean hands to her, but she would not drop out of the game, acknowledge herself beaten—luck would turn, she would get better cards. To-night she was tired. It had been a hard scrambling day. Several times she could have cried. Sam was so stupid, she could not make him understand where he was to leave things at the hotel—if anything happened to those shades, or to that salad!

In the hall of the Desert Hotel, the party was assembling. Mr. and Mrs. Blinn were already the center of a group, flinging matrimonial volleys. Innes could hear Blinn's loud voice as she entered the door: "That was before we were married. Now, it's very different. That's what matrimony does." Every one knew they covered their devotion with chronic jeers. She steered toward another corner where the Wilsons held court.

"Too bad, isn't it?" Mrs. Youngberg advanced toward Gerty, who was looking for Rickard. She did not like to ask if he had come.

Howard Blinn broke off to greet his hostess. "You saved our lives by being a little late," he exclaimed. "Our dinner was late. It's always late, since the Improvement Club was organized!"

Mrs. Hardin's roving eye scoured the hall. Rickard was not there. Patton called her from the desk. Some one wanted her at the telephone. It was Rickard, of course, at the office; to say he had been detained. The fear which had been chilling her passed by.

It was not Rickard on the wire, but Mrs. Hatfield, loquacious and coquettish. She urged a frightful neuralgia, and hoped that she was not putting her hostess to any inconvenience at this last moment. She wanted to prolong the conversation—had the guests all come?

Were they *really* going? Then she must be getting old, for a night like this dismayed her! Gerty felt her good night was rudely abrupt. But was she to stand there gabbling all night, her guests waiting?

She prayed that Rickard would be there when she returned. What a travesty if the guest of honor should disappoint her! Though he was not among the different groups, her confidence in his punctiliousness reassured her. She must hold them a little longer. She flitted gaily from one standing group to another; she outtalked the jolly Blinns. Her eyes constantly questioned the clock.

"How long are you going to wait for Mrs. Hatfield?" Her husband came up, protesting.

"Mrs. Hatfield," she explained distantly, "is not coming. We are waiting for Mr. Rickard."

"He didn't come in on that train; he's at the Heading." Hardin added something about trouble at the intake, but Gerty did not heed. Tom had known and had not told her when there was yet time to call it off!

"A pretty time to tell me!" Had he been looking at her, he would have been left no illusions. Her blue eyes flashed hate.

"I did not know it until we got here. There was a message from MacLean at the desk, waiting."

MacLean was not there, either!

"Quarreling?" cried Blinn, drawing nearer. "I must separate husband and wife. Depend upon me to take your part, Mrs. Hardin."

A heroic smile answered him. A joke, that!

"We are all ready," she cried. "Mrs. Hatfield and Mr. Rickard can not come." Not for worlds would she give in to her desire to call the whole grim affair off; let them think she was disappointed, not she. Though the world blew away, she would go.

She found herself distributing slips of mangled quotations. The white slips went to the women; the green bits of pasteboard to the men. She held a certain green card in her glove: "Leads on to fortune." Rickard might come dashing in at the last moment, the ideal man's way; a special, perhaps; it did not seem credible that he would deliberately stay away without sending her word.

"I've drawn my own wife!" cried Blinn, with exaggerated ruefulness.

Youngberg was moving through the groups. He could not find his half-quotation. "Who has the rest of this?" he was demanding.

Gerty read it over his shoulder. "Gang aft a-gley. Oh, the best laid schemes. That's Miss Wilson."

In a burst of laughter, the company discovered then that the guest of honor was also absent. Mrs. Hardin hurried them out to the waiting buggies.

When she had seated the chattering crowd, Gerty discovered that Tom had drawn Mrs. Hatfield, and was planning a desertion. Blankly, they faced each other. "Well, let's get it over." His words sounded brutal to his wife, whose nerves were flayed by the day's vexations. Drearily, they drove together down the flying street. The wind was at their backs, but it tore at their hats, pulled at their tempers. Their eyes were full of street dust. Through the gloom, they could see the two finished words gleaming from the plate-glass windows of the bank: "The Desert." Even dull imaginations could get that prophecy—the town blotted out by flying sand; The Desert come again into its own.

A flash of light as they were leaving town brightened the thick dust clouds. "What was that?" cried Gerty. She was ready for any calamity now. "Not lightning?" Again, the queer light flashed across the obscured sky. Tom roused himself to growl that he hadn't seen anything. And the dreary farce went on.

Innes' partner was young Sutcliffe, the English zanjero. He was in the quicksand of a comparison between English and American women, Innes mischievously coaxing him into deeper waters, when there was a blockade of buggies ahead of them.

"The A B C ranch," cried Innes, peering through the veil of dust at the queer unreal outlines of fences and trees. "It's our first stop."

"Oh, I say, that's too bad," began Sutcliffe. Innes was already on the road, her skirts whipped by the wind into clinging drapery.

Gerty's party found itself disorganized. Partners were trying to find or lose each other. "Get in here!" Innes heard the voice of Estrada behind her. He had a top buggy. She hailed a refuge.

"Splendid!" she cried. "What a relief!" Climbing in, she said: "I hope this isn't upsetting Gerty's arrangement."

"Arrangement! Look at them!" The women were hastening out of the dust swirl into any haven that offered. With little screams of dismay, they ran like rabbits to cover.

Gerty found herself with Blinn. At the next stop, there was a block of buggies. "No use changing again!" She acknowledged herself beaten. "Let's go on. What are they stopping for?" Dismal farce it all was!

She was pushing back her disheartened curls when

the beat of horses' hoofs back of them brought the blood back into her wind-chilled cheeks. "Rickard!" she thought. "He must have come in a special!" The gloom suddenly disgorged MacLean.

"Hardin! Where is he?"

"What's up?" yelled Blinn. "Is it the river?" MacLean's face answered him. His ranch scoured again—"God Almighty!"

"The river!" screamed the women. The men were surrounding MacLean, whose horse was prancing as if with the importance of having carried a Revere. "The levee!" called MacLean. "Where's Hardin?" He spurred his mare toward Hardin, who was blacker than Napoleon at Austerlitz.

"You're needed. They're all needed." The other voices broke in, the men pressing up. This threatened them all. Blinn's ranch lay in the ravaged sixth district. Nothing would save him. Youngberg belonged to Water Company Number One; their ditches would go. Hollister and Wilson, of the Palo Verde, saw ruin ahead of them. Each man was visualizing the mad onward sweep of that destroying power. Like ghosts, the women huddled in the dust-blown road.

"Where is it now?" demanded Blinn.

"It's here, right on us. You're all needed at the levee," bawled MacLean.

The levee! There was a dash for buggies, a scraping of wheels, the whinnying of frightened horses. Some one recalled the flashes of light they had seen on leaving town. "What were those lights—signals?"

"From the water-tower." MacLean's voice split the wind. "The wires are all down between the Crossing and the towns. Coronel was on the tower—he got the signal from the Heading—he's been there each night for a week!" This was a great night—for his chief, Rickard!

Gerty Hardin caught the thrill of his hero-worship. How splendid, how triumphant!

Innes found herself in her brother's buggy. His horse, under the whip, dashed forward. Suddenly he pulled it back on its haunches, narrowly averting a jam. "Where's MacLean?"

The boy rode back. "Who's calling me?"

"Give me your horse," demanded Hardin. "You take my sister home."

Gerty Hardin's party was torn like a bow of useless finery. Facing the wind now, no one could talk; no one wanted to talk. Each was threshing out his own thoughts; personal ruin stared them in the face. Every man was remembering that reckless exposed cut of Hardin's; pinning their hope to that ridiculed levee. The horses broke into a reckless gallop, the buggies lurching wildly as they dodged one another. The axles creaked and strained. The wind tore away the hats of the women, rent their pretty chiffon veils.

The dusty road was peopled with dark formless shapes. The signals had spread the alarm; the desert world was flocking to the gorge of the New River, to the levee. Gerty was swept past the stores which had gaped at her in the morning. Coulter's was deserted. At Fred Eggers', a candle flickered behind a green curtain. Gerty could see the half finished sign on the plate-glass windows of the bank. "The Desert" shone wanly at her.

The women were dumped without ceremony on the sidewalk, under the screened bird-cage of the Desert Hotel. Shivering, her pretty teeth chattering, Gerty Hardin ushered them into the deserted hall. The Chinese

CHAPTER XVIII

ON THE LEVEE

HARDIN did not go home that night. He was feeling to the quick the irony of his position; his duty now to protect the levee he'd ridiculed; now the only hope of the towns! The integrity of the man never faltered, though his thoughts ran wild. Like the relentless hounds of Actæon, they pursued him, barking at his vanity.

He started the anxious ranchers at sacking sand. Bodefeldt ran up to tell him that there was a hill of filled sacks over in Mexicali. "Rickard had a bunch of Indians working for a week."

The confusion of the shy fellow did not escape Hardin. Oh, he knew what Bodefeldt was thinking, what every one was saying! They were all laughing at him. The coincidence of this extraordinary flood had upheld Rickard's wild guess, haloed his judgment. It was all a piece of his infernal luck. Sickening, that's what it was! His orders scattered. He ran up and down the levee, giving orders; recalling them when he found he was repeating Rickard's.

This new humiliation, coming on the heels of the dredge fiasco, put him in execrable temper. He shouted his orders over the noises of the night. He rated the men, bullied them. No one did anything right! Lord, what he had to put up with! The other men, the ranchers and engineers, saw in his excitement certainty of the valley's doom.

The wind and the darkness contributed to the confusion. Eager shovels were tossing up earth before any one could tell where the danger point would be. The water was not yet high enough to determine the place of battle. Sacked sand was being brought over from Mexicali. Fifty pair of hands made short work of Rickard's "Hill." Lanterns were flashing through the darkness like restless fireflies. The wind and rushing water deadened the sound of the voices. It was a battle of giants against pygmies. In the darkness, the giants threatened to conquer.

At three in the morning, a horseman rode in from Fassett's, one of the big ranches to the north, cut by the New River.

"The river is cutting back," he called through the din, "cutting back toward the towns."

A turn in the gorge, a careless dump-pit had pulled the river like a mad horse back on its haunches. It was kicking back.

"They are short-handed up there. They need help."

"Dynamite," cried Silent and Hardin antiphonally. They happened to be standing near.

"We must have dynamite," bawled Hardin. "Are the wires down between here and Brawley? We must get a wire somehow to Los Angeles, to rush it down here this morning."

"It's here. There is a carload on the siding," yelled Silent.

Hardin did not need to ask by whose orders it was there. An angry scowl spoiled his face.

"Put some on the machine." He was turning away.

Silent called after him. Did Mr. Hardin think it was safe? There was no road between the towns and Fassett's. The night, the explosive,—should they not wait till morning? The question threw his late chief into a rage.

"Did I ask you to take it?" It was the opening for his fury. "Safe! Will the towns be safe if the river cuts back here? The channel has got to be widened, and you talk of your own precious skin! Wait till I ask you to take it. Get out the machine. I'll take it to Fassett's myself."

Silent left the levee, smarting. As he fumbled for the lanterns hanging in the shed where the machine was stalled, he lived over those last few years; with Hardin in the desert. When had he ever hesitated over a risk of life? When had he thought of his own safety? But this was a foolhardy thing, no matter who took the machine. Daylight would be here in a few hours. The way to Fassett's, through the ravaged country, was scarred by other floods. There was a half-mile of levee to be covered; a ticklish thing by day to carry a machine over the narrow mound, scraping bottom all the time. By night—with dynamite in the bumping tonneau it was a gamble—and the wind blowing like this. But he wouldn't let Hardin take it, he would show Hardin what he meant by "safe"!

By the pale flicker of the single lantern he got out the long gray car, nosed like a hound, filled the tank with oil, the canteens with water from a filter in the adjoining shop. He backed the machine out of the shed and sped through the darkness toward Mexicali, where the car of explosives was isolated.

He went over his grievance while he handled the dangerous stuff. The boss was taking chances; that was what he meant. He was not afraid of danger. Afraid!

Hardin, buttoned up to the ears, his soft hat pulled tight over his forehead, was waiting impatiently. Here was something to be done; he coveted the activity.

"I thought you were never coming," he grumbled.

"Let me take it!" pleaded the engineer.

"Nonsense, there is no danger." Hardin saw personal affection in the plea. He put his hand affectionately on the man's shoulder.

"But you are needed here."

"The trouble is not here; it won't be either, if we blow out the channel. Here, jump out."

"I want to go." Silent kept a stubborn hold on the steering gear. He felt Hardin's place was at the levee.

"You go home and catch a nap; this is my job." He was standing on the step. "Crank her."

There was nothing for Silent to do but to get out. Hardin pointed the long nose of the car into the darkness. She was off like the greyhound she suggested, missing a telegraph pole by half an inch.

"Just like him," mused Silent. "The slimmest margins, the biggest chances, that's Tom Hardin." The touch on the shoulder had dispelled his grouch.

"Just like Hardin to insist on carrying the dynamite to Fassett's." Spectacular, maybe, like all of his impulses, but splendid and fearless as the man himself. "He never knows when he is beaten," glowed the engineer. "If this valley ever comes into its own, it will be because of Tom Hardin."

"Who is in charge here?" a woman's voice was piercing the racket of wind and wave.

The dawn was breaking. Down the New River he could see the wind whipping the water into whitecapped fury. "Vicious," he muttered. "Those heavy waves play the Old Harry with the levee."

"Where is my brother?"

"Miss Hardin!" cried Silent.

"Where is he?" demanded Innes. Her hair streamed away from her face. Her cheeks were blanched. Her yellow eyes, peering into the dusk, looked owlish. Her wind-spanked skirts clung to her limbs. To Silent she looked boyish, as though clipped and trousered. "Where is my brother?" she repeated.

Silent told her without reservations where he had gone and why. There was no feminine foolishness about that sister of Hardin's. A chip of the old block. Funny, the men all thought of her as Hardin's daughter on account of the difference of age. As to a comrade, proudly, he bragged of the taking of the dynamite over that roadless waste.

"Whom did he leave in his place?" She did not see him shake his head. "I want George Whitaker to be sent home. He is coughing his head off down the levee, he is wet to the skin; he was being doctored for pneumonia a week ago."

Silent knew, only, that he himself was not in charge! Hardin had ordered him to bed.

"Maybe Mr. Estrada?" she hazarded.

"He is not here, he went down the road to look after the track. Hardin went off in such a hurry, I guess he told nobody," chuckled the engineer, still glowing.

"Then I'm it!" cried Innes Hardin. "Will you take my orders, Silent?"

"Sure," he chuckled again.

"Send George Whitaker home. And not to report till to-morrow morning. Say Hardin said so. You needn't say which Hardin."

She pinned up her blown hair, the wind fighting her. Her thoughts would accuse Tom! Perhaps the apparent confusion was all well ordered; perhaps this was the way men worked when the need was desperate, when homes were at stake! Yet, there was Tom racing across the country when a lieutenant would have done as well. Was he losing his grip? The earthquake episode had frightened her. She knew he lacked discipline, of school, and gentle home-training. The struggle with the wilderness had absorbed his parents. She knew he was oversanguine, careless of details, careless of the means to his ends. Perhaps it was because she was a woman, and fearful, and saw things in a womanish way. Perhaps all strong men, men who achieved great results, attacked them as Tom did. The daring chance, for Tom always. A corner to be turned, he must always take the sharpest curve. If he were as reckless with other people's lives as he was with his own—

The voice of Silent was in her ear. "He is gone. I've sent him home."

The yellow eyes gleamed prankishly in the half light. "Will you take more orders from me, Silent?"

"You're the captain!"

"I saw Mr. Dowker down there. His wife is sick. Send him home, say Hardin said so."

She called after him; "Parrish, too, if you can find him!"

She watched the whitecapped waves break into harmless spray against the levee. A little higher, and those waves would not be harmless. If the wind kept up, if those waters rose—ah, these men would be needing their strength to-night!

The dawn was creeping in like a laggard culprit. The whitecaps caught the light, scattering it as foam. The flashing lanterns grew pale; Innes could discern some of the faces. She saw Coronel wrapped in a gray blanket, squatting on the newly-raised bank. His unbound hair slapped his old weathered mask. "The map of the desert furrowed on his face," Captain Brandon had once said. She wrapped her coat around her head.

Silent came back. "Dowker's gone, I couldn't find Parrish." He cut his words off with a click, for through the rush of the wind and water came the whistle of a locomotive.

"A special!" cried Silent. Hardin's sister and his friend looked at each other, the same thought in mind: Rickard, in from the Heading!

On her face Silent saw the same spectacular impulse which had flashed over Hardin's features a short time before.

She put her hand on his arm. "Silent, you're his friend. Straighten this out. We can't have him come back—spying—and find this." She waved her hand toward the disorganized groups.

"I'd take more orders," suggested the engineer.

"Then send a third of them home, tell them to come back to-night at six. Send away the other third, tell them to come back at noon. Keep the other shift. Say you'll have coffee sent from the hotel, tell them Hardin says to stop wasting stuff. Tell them, oh, tell them anything you can think of, Silent, before he comes." Her breakdown was girlish.

She could hear the signal of the locomotive; coming

closer. Then she could hear the pant of the engine as it worked up the grade. It was a steady gentle climb all the way from the Junction, two hundred feet below sea-level, to the towns resting at the level of the sea. It quickened her thought of the power of the river. Nothing between it and the tracks at Salton. Nothing to stop its flow into that spectacular new sea whose basin did not need a drop of the precious misguided flow. She could hear the bells; now the train was coming into the station; she would not wait for Silent. She did not want to meet Rickard.

No one saw her as she left the levee. She passed Silent, who was issuing orders. She heard him say, "The boss says so."

She took the road by the railroad sheds, to avoid the dismissed shifts, moving townward. At full speed, she collided with a man, rounding the sheds' corner. It was Rickard. Her veil had slipped to her shoulders and he saw her face.

"Miss Hardin!" he exclaimed. "Whatever are you doing here?"

"I was looking for my brother."

"You ought not to be out at night alone here."

"It's morning!"

"With every Indian in the country coming in. I'll send Parrish with you."

She recognized Parrish behind him. She tried to tell him that she knew every Indian in Mexicali, every Mexican in the twin towns, but he would not listen to her. "I'm not going to let you go home alone."

She blinked rebellion at the supplanter of her brother. But she found herself following Parrish. She took a deep pride in her independence, her fearlessness. Tom let her go where she liked. She had an impulse to dismiss Parrish; every man was needed, but he would obey Rickard's orders. MacLean had told her that! "They don't like him, but they mind him!"

Rickard made his way down to the levee. "Where is Hardin?" he asked of every one he met. The answer came pointing in the direction where Innes had stood.

He made a swift inspection. It was not so bad as he had feared. Orders had scattered in the night; but it might have been worse.

Silent came up to explain that Hardin had gone up to Fassett's just a few minutes ago to carry dynamite. The river was cutting back there. "Good," cried Rickard, "that's bully!"

"He left me in charge," glibly lied the friend of Hardin. "Any orders, sir?"

"Things are going all right?" began the manager. He stopped. From above came a dull roar.

"Dynamite!" cried Rickard.

The friend of Hardin had nothing to say. "I thought you said he went only a few minutes ago?" demanded his chief.

There was another detonation. Down the river came the booming of the second charge.

"That's dynamite for sure," evaded Silent.

"Not a minute too soon!" declared Rickard, going back to his inspection.

CHAPTER XIX

THE WHITE REFUGE

THE town woke to a matter-of-fact day. The sensational aspect of the runaway river had passed with the night. The word spread that the flood waters were under control; that the men had gone home to sleep, so the women got breakfast as usual, and tidied their homes. The Colorado was always breaking out, like a naughty child from school. Never would the cry of "The river!" fail to drag the blood from their cheeks. But relief always came; the threatened danger was always averted, and these pioneer women had acquired the habit of swift reaction.

That afternoon, Mrs. Youngberg was to entertain at the A B C ranch the ladies of the Improvement Club. It was a self-glorification meeting, to celebrate the planting of trees in the streets of Calexico, and to plan the campaign of their planting. Mrs. Blinn drove into town to get Gerty Hardin. Neither woman had seen her husband since the interrupted drive the night before.

"I don't know whether I should go," Mrs. Hardin hesitated, her face turned toward the A B C ranch. "Perhaps there is something we could do."

"I have just come from the levee." Mrs. Blinn's jolly face had lost its apprehension. "The water has not risen an inch since breakfast. Most of the men have been sent home. When Howard didn't come home to lunch, I grew anxious. But Mr. Rickard says he sent him to Fassett's with more dynamite."

"Dynamite!" shuddered Gerty. "Aren't you terribly afraid?" So Rickard was in town! Her breath fluttered. Strange, how her spirits rose!

Mrs. Blinn wondered if the wife was the only person in the town who had not heard of Hardin's melodramatic ride that morning. She decided that the story had been purposely withheld. She would not be the one to inform her.

"Would you mind—" Gerty laid a well-kept hand on her friend's knee. "Would you mind turning back? I'd be more *comfortable* if I could see Tom or Mr. Rickard; hear what they think about it."

"But Mr. Rickard told me," began Mrs. Blinn.

"I'm worried about Tom," cried Gerty, flushing. Danger to Tom was a new thought. With Rickard in town the levee beckoned irresistibly. Were it Mrs. Youngberg, with her sharp eyes, or Innes, she would not dare, but Mrs. Blinn was dull; she would never suspect anything!

Mrs. Blinn's devotion to her husband, who was the butt of her fond ridicule, and the center of her universe, made her believe all women like herself. Gerty's high color, she thought, meant anxiety.

"Of course we'll turn back."

"There he is," thrilled Gerty.

Mrs. Blinn's eye swept the street. "Where? Your husband?"

"No, Mr. Rickard. Passing the bank. There, he's stopped. I wonder if he is going in? You call him, Mrs. Blinn."

Obediently her friend hailed Rickard. He turned back

to the windy street. He felt boyish: the crisis was giving him mercurial feet. He loved the modern battle. Elements to pit one's brains against, wits against force!

Gerty Hardin's face was flushing and paling. "The river," she faltered. "Should we be alarmed, Mr. Rickard?"

Smiling, he assured her she should not be alarmed; the levees would protect the towns.

She found it hard to meet his eyes; they had always made her conscious in the old Lawrence days. They suggested controlled amusement, a critical detachment. She used to hunt for the cause. Now she was experienced, yet his smile still gave her that old hampered sense of embarrassment.

"She is anxious about her husband," Mrs. Blinn had to explain. Gerty bit her lip. What a parrot Mrs. Blinn was!

"Mr. Hardin is up at Fassett's ranch, he will be coming back to-day. I told your husband, Mrs. Blinn, to catch a nap and then relieve Mr. Hardin."

Gerty found a significance in his words, he had said "Mr. Hardin," and "your husband, Mrs. Blinn." It was enough to weave dreams around.

"A nap," exclaimed Mrs. Blinn, "why, he didn't come home."

"I think I saw him go into the men's quarters." Distinctly Rickard had heard Blinn's jolly voice as he had left the levee: "If I'm to catch a nap, I'll not go home. No sleeping there!"

"We can't do anything, Mr. Rickard, to help?" urged Gerty Hardin, her voice tremulous.

"I hope we won't have to call on you at all."

There was no excuse to linger. Gerty threw a wistful little smile at parting.

The brown mare's head was turned toward the country. Rickard turned back to the bank.

He looked again at the plate-glass windows. Two words were finished, The Desert, brilliant in gold-leaf. The rest of the sign still stood in its dim skeleton! Boyish mischievous blood raced in his veins that morning. He went in.

"Mr. Petrie in?" he asked the cashier. Young Oliver said he was not. "He is tying vines to-day."

"When are you going to finish that window?"

"Why, after this flood, I guess, Mr. Rickard." The question was unexpected. Every one knew Casey now by sight. The cashier glanced at his tie. Casey had forgotten his pin that morning.

"That's the way it looked to me. There is too much desert in this town, *Desert* Hotel, *Desert* Reclamation Company, and now this—The Desert! If you would only put *"bank"* on it! It looks as though you thought you were going to be washed out, as if you were saving your gold-leaf. A bank has got to keep up a bold front, if it's only plate-glass, Mr. Cashier."

"Hold on!" called young Oliver. "Wait a minute, Mr. Rickard. I guess you did not understand what I meant. There is no one to finish this lettering! The man who was doing it owns a ranch over in Wistaria. He is the only man who can do it. He is down at the river, fighting to save his crop."

"Then I'd finish it myself," said Rickard, "or get some one down from Los Angeles who could," and left the bank.

A sign hanging from a neighboring door, "For Sail," caught his eye.

The owner of the store peered out at the group of giggling Indians. "Fried Eggs," as the irreverent young engineers had dubbed him, waved them away from an empty crate. It was not a bad simile, thought Rickard, smiling at the orange-colored mop which crowned the albumen-like whiteness of the house-bleached face of Fred Eggers. He stopped to watch the man's queer antics. From shelf to counter he bounced, an anxious eye on his open crate on the platform where the group of covetous squaws and bucks encroached. Rickard was vastly amused. Eggers waddled out of the door, obscured by his bales of brilliant calico. He waved back the Indians. He threw his bundle into the crate, and sidled into the store for another load, his eyes still challenging the Indians. His distress was comical. They were his best customers; he must not drive them away, but he could not trust them. He snatched up a bolt of blue and white gingham, and was back on the platform. "Stand back, stand back," he urged. "Don't you see that you are in my way?"

They giggled maddeningly.

The man's distress was maudlin. He jumped sidewise into his store, picking up his scattered stock by finger sense only, his eyes riveted on the squaws. Haste, concern, were written all over the corpulent unwieldy body, in the unlined pasty face of "Fried Eggs."

"Moving away, Mr. Eggers?" Rickard called out to him.

It had been a long time since he had been dignified by that name. He turned to answer, and in that instant a swarthy Amazon snatched a small roll of turkey red

THE WHITE REFUGE

calico, and hid it under her amply ruffled skirt. He did not see his loss.

"I'm getting ready to move if I have to. The river don't look good to me, that's sure." He shot a quick glance of suspicion at the blank-faced Indians, snickering by the door. The bucks had brilliant bandannas wound around their mud-crusted heads. The black stiff hair of the women streamed in the wind which puffed their skirts into balloons.

"It cost me three thousand, the lot, the shop and the stock. I'd take a thousand."

"I'd give you that," Rickard began roguishly.

"Done!" cried Fred Eggers.

"*But*," objected the newcomer, "it would be taking a mean advantage of you. You're playing sure to lose."

Eggers sat on the edge of his crate and looked at the man who had said he would give him a thousand for his goods.

"If you stay and the river ruins your stock you will probably save your store; you'll surely keep your lot." Eggers shook his head. "You'll probably lose nothing, the water is not coming up here. If you sell to me, for a thousand, or to any one else you're fixed to lose two. Oh, stay and bluff it, Eggers."

So it was only a joke, then. "You won't buy it," the house-whitened face was crestfallen.

"You won't sell, if you take time to think it over," called Rickard, moving on.

Eggers felt something moving behind him. A squaw drew back from the crate. One hand was lost under her flowing cloak of gaudy colored handkerchiefs.

"Stop that," he yelled. "Here you Indians, vamose. D'ye hear me? Vamose."

The group of Indians drew back but only a few steps, giggling. The sidling motion began again. Rickard, laughing, looked over his shoulder at Eggers' absurd dilemma.

On the morning-glory-covered veranda of the adobe offices of the Desert Reclamation Company, Ogilvie was waiting.

"I've been looking everywhere for you, Mr. Rickard." His tone was sepulchral and foreboding.

"It's a big place, the towns. Hard to find any one, unless it's an accident." He made for his office, followed by Ogilvie. Rickard, who had had two hours of sleep, felt refreshed and rollicking. This was some fun! These dismal fearful citizens! He and Marshall would show them what a railroad force could do!

He threw himself into his swivel chair and looked up at the expert accountant whose blue-veined hands were describing circles with his straw hat.

"I think," plunged Ogilvie, "that this is no place for the papers of the company."

"No?"

"They ought to be in Los Angeles," stammered the accountant, forgetting his speech.

"If I'm not mistaken, you persuaded them contrarily a few months ago!"

Ogilvie squirmed. "Oh, but the flood,"—his pallid skin showed a flexibility that almost suggested animation. "That alters everything."

"The flood? Why, I think we can fix that."

"I may go?"

"No, I did not say you might go. I agree with you that the papers belong here, where we may have easy access to them instead of having to go to Los Angeles every time we want to have a question of history or authority answered."

The man whose woozling had come to nothing cleared his throat. "This office is not safe—"

"I said I'd fix that."

"I'd like to write to Los Angeles, telling them about the flood. The wires are down—"

"You don't need authority from Los Angeles. I'll fix you up. You know that rise, east of the town? Back of the school? I'll have a tent rigged up there—"

"The wind," objected the accountant.

"The wind won't hurt the papers. I'll send up a safe and a bed."

"A safe suggests money, valuables—the Indians!" murmured Ogilvie.

"I'll give you a gun." Rickard was enjoying himself. The fellow was a driveling coward. MacLean's word fitted him like a glove: woozling!

That afternoon Rickard was not too busy to order a tent stretched on the rise back of the schoolhouse. It was not all mischief! The office building might go! A safe was lugged across town. Ogilvie dismally bossed the proceedings. The platform must be tight; he mentioned snakes. He wanted a spider, but there was neither lumber nor men to spare; he spoke of wind-storms. He wanted double doors, one of screen wire; he had a good deal to say about flies.

Toward evening an iron bed was hauled to the tent which the younger engineers, fresh from their day's rest, had spied and already christened the White Refuge. Ogilvie showed the two impassive Mexicans why it should be placed so that his feet pointed north; he explained thoroughly about magnetic currents. There, they left him, with his papers.

The disappointed tenant of the White Refuge sat down on the foot of his bed, and dismally reviewed the situation. The hurried platform of the tent was creaking ominously. The canvas walls sagged and strained against the wind. He rehearsed the situation.

The burning of San Francisco had flooded the southern part of the state with clerks and accountants; to Los Angeles they had come in droves. He could not leave the towns, defying Rickard, and expect to find another place with the Overland Pacific Company. He wished, in deep gloom, that he had not bought those hundred shares in the smaller organization. It had appeared to him as a crowning bit of diplomacy, and put him, he thought, on the same basis as the directors, Hardin, Gifford and the others. But it had left him strapped. He had had to borrow to make up the hundred shares. He had only just paid that debt. The Desert Bank held less than fifty dollars to his credit. That sum between him and poverty! He decided to brave it out, though physical discomfort hurt him like pain.

He listened to the rising of the wind. The worst storm, old-timers had told him, in fifteen years.

"What was that?" He bounced up from his bed. Hardin's cannonading shook his frail tent. He sat down again. He remembered a performance given by Edwin Booth in Boston. *Lear,* it was. He had insisted that the storm scene was grotesquely exaggerated. He could not hear the actors' voices over the storm! Now, he revised his criticism. The man who had staged that play had been in the desert; that desert. It was a fearful night.

He decided that it was not safe to undress, so he threw himself across his painted bed. Every few minutes the deep detonations of Hardin's charges up at Fassett's ranch jarred the platform.

Down at the levee, the night-shifts were piling brush, dragging it to threatened points where the lapping waves broke over the levee; sacking sand, piling it in heaps. On the other side of the gorge, Rickard was blowing out the west channel to let the increasing flood waters through. Up the gorge, but below Fassett's ranch now, following the retreating platoons of the river, Hardin was toiling, directing his men. He had refused to listen to Blinn. Sleep, with the river cutting back like that, hazarding the valley? Rest? He couldn't rest with that noise in his ears. Why, man, this spells ruin!

The wind rose to a gale. Ogilvie's tent bellied and swelled. The waves were blowing over the levee. At midnight, the alarm was sounded. The sleeping shifts scrambled out of their beds, full dressed, and rode or ran down to the river. The bells of the two churches kept ringing. Pale women and children followed the men down to the embankment. There was work for every one that night. Men were hustling like mad to raise the levee an inch above the rising fury of the river. The women rushed back to their homes, bringing baskets, old tins, coal-oil cans, anything to scoop or carry earth. They dragged down worn-out clothes, bags of scraps, fire-wood; they were fighting now for their future.

Men stood a few feet apart measuring each white-foamed wave to be ready when it should strike the bank.

Wired with hog-fencing on the river side, the long timbers chained in place to take the blows of the waves, the levee threatened to melt before each rush of the river. Shovels stood at attention to throw earth on each new break; to raise the levee an inch above the lapping waters. Earth could not now be wasted. The women were cautioned to conserve their ammunition. Teams from the ranches brought in hay; wagon-loads of brush for the dikes.

Down the stream rushed masses of débris; logs, sections of fence, railroad ties. Every eye on the bank followed their course. Where would that floating wreckage lodge? Long poles jumped to shove off into the stream the drift which must not be allowed to lodge, to impede that stream for an instant. Swift eyes, swift hands, needed that night! And all night long into the gray of the morning, over the roar of the rushing water, and the whistling of the demons of the wind, boomed the dynamite at Fassett's. In the White Refuge, Ogilvie miserably slept.

CHAPTER XX

OPPOSITION

THE second night of the flood, the women of the towns dragged brush and filled sacks for the men to carry. It was past midnight when Innes Hardin left the levee. While her feet and fingers had toiled, her mind had been fretting over Tom. Two nights, and no rest! It was told by men who came down the river how Hardin was heroically laboring. She yearned to go to him; perhaps he would stop for a few hours to her entreaty. But an uncertain trail across country, with the dust-laden wind in her face? She decided to wait for the dawn. A snatched sleep first, but who would call her? She would sleep for hours, so weary every muscle. Her mind fixed on Sam as the only man in town who had time to saddle a horse for a woman.

She went in search of him. She found that the long adobe office building had already taken on the look of defeat, of ruin. The casements had been torn from the partitions; the doors and windows were out. The furniture had been hauled up to the White Refuge for safety. She went hunting through the ghoulish gloom for the darky, turning her lantern in every dark corner. She knew that she would find him sleeping.

Then she heard steps on the veranda. She ran toward them, expecting to see Sam. She swung her lantern full on two figures mounting the shallow steps. Rickard was with her sister-in-law.

"Oh, excuse me!" she blurted blunderingly. Of course Gerty would take a wrong intention from the stupid words!

The blue eyes met those of Innes with defiance. It was as though she had spoken: "Well, think what you will of it, you Hardins! I don't care what you think of me!"

What indeed did she think of it? Why should she feel like the culprit before these two, her words deserting her? It was Gerty's look that made her feel guilty, as though she had been spying. To meet them together, here at midnight, why should not *they* feel ashamed? She had done nothing wrong. And Tom down yonder fighting—and they make his absence a cover for their rendezvous—

"I'm looking for Sam!" The effort behind the words turned them into an oratorical challenge.

"So are we. I want to send him home with Mrs. Hardin. She's worn out."

"She can go home with me. I am going directly. As soon as I give a message to Sam." She instantly regretted her words, abruptly halting. It came to her that Rickard would insist upon delivering her message. Of course, he would oppose her going. Some petty reason or other. She knew from the men that he was oppositional, that he liked to show his power. Not safe, he would say, or the horse was needed, or Sam too busy to wait on her!

"You can not go home alone, you two. The town is full of strange Indians. Give me your lantern, Miss Hardin; I'll rout out that darky."

Rebelliously she gave him the lantern. The light turned full on her averted angry eyes.

A haughty Thusnelda followed him.

Sam was discovered asleep in the only room where the windows had not yet been attacked. His head rested on a bundle of sacked trees which the ladies of the Improvement Club had planned to plant the next day. Deep snores betrayed his refuge.

"Here, Sam! I want you to take these ladies home. Chase yourself. They've been working while you've slept. I thought you'd have all these windows out by now."

Gerty had to supply the courtesy for two. She told Mr. Rickard in her appealing way that he had been very kind; that she "would have been frightened to death to go home alone."

Innes had to say something! "Good night!" The words had an insulting ring.

The wind covered a passionate silence, as the two women, followed by Sam, yawning and stretching, made their way down the shrieking street. "It was true," Innes was thinking. She had at last stumbled on the rout, but it was not a matter of personal, but moral untidiness; not a carelessness of pins or plates, of tapes or dishes. It was far worse; a slackness of ethics. It meant more unhappiness for Tom.

As she put her foot on the step leading to her tent, it discovered something, bulky, resistant.

"Sam," she cried. "Come back!"

Both Sam and Mrs. Hardin came running from different directions. An Indian, dead-drunk, lay sprawling across her steps.

"Oh, suppose we had come alone?" moaned Gerty.

"Well, we didn't," retorted her sister with intentional rudeness. "What can you do with him, Sam?"

It was a half-hour before Sam could get the reeling Cocopah started toward Mexicali.

"Don't forget to call me at five!" cried Innes after him.

Her aching muscles told her that she could not have slept four hours when the darky was back, knocking at her door.

"All right," she pulled herself together. "I'll be out in a minute."

"I'll have to hold him, Miss Innes," came the negro voice through the screen door. "He'll get all tangled up in the rope. The winds got him all skittish."

She came out, rubbing her eyes; her khaki suit creased where she had lain in it. She asked him if he had seen her brother.

Sam, whom sleep had been occupying, answered evasively. "I'm not looking for him yet-a-way, Miss Innes! The river's cuttin' back, mighty fas', they say. A third of a mile in twenty-fo' hours. If it keeps up that-away, it'll be on us right soon. Mr. Hardin he's not a-comin' back so long's he's got that there river to fight."

"I'm going after him. He's got to stop for me. Don't tell any one, Sam, where I've gone."

"You oughtn't to be goin' alone, Miss Innes," he called after her loping horse. "The new boss wouldn't like it. He's mighty careful about womenfolk!"

She sent a mocking grimace over her shoulder. "Pff!"

Sam grinned. "If she ain't jes' the spit of her brother!" His pace lagged. It had been a hard night's work!

Innes' horse loped through the silent streets.

"I'll run past the levee; perhaps Tom has come back." It occurred to her that there might be a message at the hotel. She pulled on her left rein, and swept past the deserted adobe.

The gorge of the New River was but a rod or so now from the west side. Sam was right. If the scouring out of the channel could not be kept to the farther bank, the towns must go. The levee wouldn't help them then.

She knew the danger; she had heard the engineers talk with Tom. The gradient from Yuma to the Basin was four feet to the mile, in land which corroded like sugar. The very thing which had helped them in their initial labor of canal building would militate against the safety of the valley now, with the marauding Dragon at large.

As she reined in her horse, Rickard stepped out on the sidewalk. He, too, was heavy-eyed from a snatched nap.

"Were you looking for me?"

The scorn in the girl's face told him that his question was stupid. For *him!*

"Has my brother come back?"

He said he did not know. "You can see, I have been dreaming!" She would not smile back at him, but rode off toward the levee. Rickard stood watching her.

Down the street, Fred Eggers was opening his store. She could see two Indians peering in through the open door.

Was this the river? West of the levee, a sea of muddy water spread over the land. There was yet a chance to save the towns, the *town,* she corrected herself, as her eye fell on the Mexican village across the ditch. For Mexicali was doomed. Some of the mudhuts had already fallen; the water was running close to the station-house.

She saw Wooster standing near, calculating the distance, the time, perhaps, before the new station would go. Over the door, in freshly painted letters, were the words —"Ferro Carril de Baja California." To the east, a few feet only away, was one of the monuments of the series placed by the engineers of the Gadsen survey. They marched from Yuma to the sea in the path of the old Santa Fe trail, marking on the way the grave of many a gold-seeker.

She hailed Wooster. Ruin was presaged in the lines of his forehead.

"Pretty bad?" she cried.

He shook his head.

"Is Tom back?"

"He's over there, now. Fighting like all possessed. He'll work till he drops." Wooster was proud of that method.

"We all know Tom!" Her pride sprang up. "But he's got to stop for a while. I'm going up after him."

"Not if my name's Wooster. I'll go. He'll mind me." What if he were dropping, himself, with sleep and fatigue? It was a chance to serve Hardin; to bring a smile of gratitude to the eyes of this little comrade of the desert, whom the engineers adored in their several fashions. Wooster's worship was louder than the others; the younger men shyer, but more fervent. Wooster found her calm boyish eyes beautiful, but not disturbing. But she was a Hardin; and a pretty one. Wooster would serve a Hardin, or a pretty woman, were his last hour come.

"Can you?" she cried; meaning—"Would you be so good?"

"Can I? He'll mind me," bragged Wooster. His small bright eyes snapped over some recollections. "I've made him rest before when he didn't want to. I can do it again."

"It's terribly good of you, but I mean, can you get away?"

"I'm through here." He omitted to say that he was to report at six in the evening. "I'll send him back to you, Miss Hardin."

"You're terribly good," she repeated.

She watched the flowing river, swollen with wreckage. She saw, with comprehension, a section of a fence; somebody's crop gone. There was a railway tie, another! The river was eating up Estrada's new road-bed? A cry broke from her as a mesquit on the coffee-colored tide caught on a buried snag. The current swirled dangerously around it. Instantly, the water rose toward the top of the levee. Men came running to pry away the tree. A minute later, it was dancing down the stream. They raised the bank against the pressing lapping waves. There, the tree had stuck again. They ran down the levee with their long poles. Each time that happened, unless the obstruction were swiftly dislodged, she knew it meant an artificial fall somewhere, a quick scouring out of the channel. The men were working like silent parts of a big machine; the confusion of the first night was gone. From their faces one would not guess that their fortunes, their homes, hung on the subduing of that indomitable force which had not yet known defeat, which had turned back explorer and conquistador. Ah, there was the lurking fear of it! Victory still lay to its credit; the other column was blank.

"Mr. Parrish," she called.

A man on the bank paused, shovel in hand.

She spurred her horse abreast of him.

"How is your wife?"

"Pretty bad. I had to leave her at midnight. I couldn't get no one to stay with her. The women have to mind the ranches these days. She had a spell of her neuralgia. She couldn't have come with me any way." He was torn between his duty and his fears.

"When do you go back?"

"I don't know. We are all needed here. Mexicali's going. I'll be lucky if I get sent back to-night."

"It's going down the Wistaria?"

"Enough to scare her. The ranch's as good as gone already. What good's the land if we can't get water up to it?"

"I know," murmured Innes.

"I'm not blaming any one, Miss Hardin. Unless it's myself. I ought never to have brought her here. Not until the river's settled. The wind's the worst to her; she's that scared of the wind."

"I'll go and bring her home with me. You'll feel better to have her near town," she suggested.

"That's first-class." His relief was pathetic. His dull fidelity, his love for that nervous wreck of a woman, rose that instant to the dignity of a romance. She thought of the purple flannel waist, the untidy home, the smell of burning rice, of scorched codfish, the loving struggle of the woman who dared life in the desert beside her mate, lacking the strength to make it tolerable to either.

"I'll bring her home with me," she repeated.

She did not wait for his gratitude. Her horse was turned back to town. She saw Wooster coming toward her. His snapping black eyes shot out sparks of anger.

"He won't let me go."

"Who won't let you?" But she knew.

"Casey. Says he'll send some one else. I said as nobody else'd make Hardin stop. He said as that was up to Hardin."

Of course, he wouldn't let Wooster go! Her offer to Parrish suddenly shackled her.

"Orders me to bed," spat Wooster. "Wonder why he didn't order gruel, too. It's spite, antagonism to Hardin, that's what it is!" She believed that, too. Tom was right. Rickard did take advantage of his authority.

She did not see Rickard until he stood by her side.

"I'm sorry not to spare Wooster, Miss Hardin. But there's stiff work ahead. He's got to be ready for a call. If Hardin insists on spoiling one good soldier, that's his affair. I can't let him spoil two."

Wooster shrugged, and left them. "Spoiling good soldiers!"

"I've taken Bodefeldt off duty. I told him to relieve Hardin."

Bodefeldt who blushed when any one looked at him! He would be about as persuasive to Tom as a veil to a desert wind! She turned away, but not before Rickard saw again that transforming anger. Her eyes shone like topazes in sunlight. She would not trust herself to speak. Wooster was waiting for her. Rickard could hear the man repeat. "I'm sorry, Miss Hardin. It's an outrage. That's what it is."

Queer, they couldn't see that it was Hardin's fault;

Hardin, who was up the river fighting like a melodramatic hero; fighting without caution or reserve, demoralizing discipline; he couldn't help admiring the bulldog energy, himself. That was what all these men adored. He'd clenched the girl's antagonism, now, for sure! How her eyes had flashed at him!

Hello! There was a tree floating down toward the station-house . . .

"Bring your poles!" he yelled.

CHAPTER XXI

A MORNING RIDE

INNES was loping toward the Wistaria, the wind in her face till she turned west by the canal. It occurred to her then, that she did not know how she was going to cross the river; it cut the canal; that was the cut which was threatening that district. She had not thought to ask Parrish whether they boated it across, or if there was a cable across the stream. She would not turn back, she would meet some one.

She was a part of a fleeing universe; the wind, the dust-clouds, the victorious racing river, her good horse loping free—herself on the edge of the mad wild world! Because she was young, and life was dramatic to her, the wind took possession of her spirit, which spread its wings toward the broad sweep of moving plains, to the sharp jagged line of dust-obscured mountain. The conflict of Titans called to her; it was a great music drama; the wind had its own wild rôle; the river, the fervid lover, and the desert a lean, brown Indian maid resisting his ardor. The Valkyrie's call burst from her. She was riding to it; she threw the five splendid notes against the shriek of the elemental battle.

Desperate pygmies, all of them; ants, protecting their little ant-hill against Titans—Ogilvie in his tent, Eggers a prisoner to fear—the women planting their little trees, the men defending their toy levee against the Dragon and the strength of its ravished mate; absurd, impotent the weak human effort! Had she caught Estrada's feeling? She had taxed him often with skepticism. True, he has not answered her, except with those truthful, melancholy eyes of his!

Queer, that reserve—with her, when she knew what she knew! What had given her the conviction that he did not want to tell her that he cared? Why did he guard his lips, when his eyes, his mind cried out to her, not only when she was with him, but in the night, when all the world slept, and he miles from her, his need wakening her, chaining, was it imagination, or was this—Love? His affection deeper than all the others, and he the only one she did not have to remind,—continually remind!—of their soldiery.

Good soldiers!

Had she been too quick to take offense that morning? Could she expect that he—Mr. Rickard—could not see the failings she herself feared? Tom was splendid, heroic, yes, but a good soldier? The other had taken a soldier's drilling—Eduardo had told her of Wyoming, and the Mexican barrancas—Tom was unjust in that— unjust to Marshall. Rickard was not a bookman. Even if she did not like him—!

She saw Busby, who was driving away from the Wistaria.

She hailed him. "Tell me," she called. "How do you get over?"

"They've strung a cable. Looking for Mrs. Parrish?"

His wagon was heaped high with household loot, tins and frying-pans, brooms and a battered graphophone.

Something had happened! The wind drowned her words, but her hands challenged his cargo.

"Her tent blew down! She's over at my house." He drove abreast of her.

"*Her* tent!"

That it should be her tent to go! She thought to ask if Mrs. Parrish had been hurt, but Busby did not hear the question.

"I've just been over to see what I could save. The Indians would be carrying these away. A woman sets a store by her pots and pans and dishes. The dishes, well, they're gone, of course; splinters!"

"Then there is no use going there—I'll go over to your place."

"Go back by Jones' ranch," shouted Busby over his shoulder. "It's quicker than the road ahorseback."

Her pagan joy was quenched. Her pace was now a sober one. He had not said if Mrs. Parrish was hurt.

The tidy farm of the Busbys looked wind-blown and dispirited. The young orange trees had torn from their stakes; they curved away from the castigating wind. The alfalfa fields had withstood the blight, and the young willows which fringed the ditch, doubling to the breeze, sprang back like elastic when it passed.

Mrs. Busby came out on the porch to meet her. Innes was tying her horse. "How is she?" she demanded.

"Asleep, I think. Tie him fast. This wind makes the beasts restless. Come right in."

Not even a desert storm would be allowed to meddle with that interior. The room Innes entered was freshly dusted. It was glaringly ugly; neat and comfortable. Tiers of labeled boxes rose from a pine shelf; a motley collection of calico bags hung from hooks beneath.

"How did you get her here? How did you know?" demanded Innes.

"She told us herself. She must have *crawled here.*"

"Crawled! She *was* hurt, then!"

"Who told you? Where'd you hear it?"

"I met Mr. Busby. *Was* she hurt?"

"Did he find anything? Was he goin' there or was he comin' away? I guess there wasn't much left with that roof fallin' in."

There was a sound from the room beyond. Mrs. Busby disappeared. A minute later, she beckoned from the darkened chamber. Innes crept in fearfully.

It was a terrible face that looked up from the pillow. A red gash had mutilated the cheek; the nose was scraped. Worse to Innes was the motion of the features —the eyelids, the lips, the chin were twitching the face into a horror. From the staring eyeballs, a crazed appeal shot up.

"She's anxious as you shan't tell her husband. He's got his work to do. She sent word by Busby as she's all right."

"I shan't tell him," said Innes pitifully.

A hand that looked like a claw picked at the coarse white spread. The jerking mouth was trying to tell her something. Mrs. Busby leaned over the bed.

"She's worrying about Mrs. Dowker. Now, if that doesn't beat all! I'm tellin' her you'll go and see if they're all right. The boy is sick." An open wink disavowed the obligation.

"Of course, I'll go," cried Innes, not heeding the signal. "Is—is her arm broken?"

Mrs. Busby was silent. The woman on the bed had to answer that question.

"It—fell on me. I—always—knew it would. I got under the bed. A beam struck my arm."

Innes pointed to the skilful bandage.

"Who set it?"

"I did." Mrs. Busby showed embarrassment. Frontier skill and her new faith were not yet in harmony. "It wasn't no time to argue."

The morning was gone when Innes turned from the Dowker tent. She was despondently comparing life to a vise, "that is, woman's life!" How much easier to be a man, to fight the big fight, than the eternal wrestle with dirt and disorder! No, a woman's life is a river, she changed her comparison whimsically, a shallow stream ending in a—sink! Small wonder that the sad asylums were full of women, women from the farms. Tom's work would help that, the Hardins, the Estradas; she had heard Captain Brandon tell of the deliverance promised by the gospel of irrigation! The women on the farms of to-morrow would not have isolation or pioneer toil for their portion. But these were the real pioneers, these women! Theirs was the sacrifice.

Gerty called to her from the neighboring tent as she was entering her own.

"Do you mind cleaning up for me to-day? Tom may come home. I left the dishes last night, and I've got one of my terrible headaches."

Soon she had the hot water waiting for the tray of scraped dishes. She had planned to go back to the river. "A shallow stream ending in a sink!" she chirped to a rueful reflection from one of Gerty's new tins. "Oh, smile, Innes Hardin! You look just like a Gingg!"

CHAPTER XXII

THE PASSING OF THE WATERS

BABCOCK came rushing down from Los Angeles that morning to see what in thunder it was all about. He asked every one he met why some one didn't get busy and stop the cutting back of that river? There was no one at the offices of the company to report to him! Why, the building was deserted! Ogilvie's letters had prophesied ruin. It all looked wrong to him. Going on to the levee, he met MacLean, Jr., who was coming away. The boy told him vaguely that he would find Rickard around there, somewhere.

"I'll hunt him up for you."

"Why, they are letting it get ahead of them!" Babcock's manner suggested that he was aggrieved that such carelessness to his revered company should go unpunished. Something, he told MacLean, might have been done before the situation got as bad as this!

His excited stride carried him across the dividing ditch, which now was carrying no water, into Mexicali. MacLean had to lengthen his step to keep pace with him. The havoc done to the Mexican village excited Babcock still more.

Estrada, just in from his submerged tracks, was lounging against an adobe wall. His pensive gaze was turned up-stream. The posture of exhaustion suggested laziness to Babcock, who was on the hunt for responsibility. He was more than ever convinced that the right thing was not being done.

"Estrada!"

Estrada took his eyes from the river. Babcock looked like a snapping terrier taking the ditch at a bound. MacLean, Jr., a lithe greyhound, followed.

"What the devil are you doing to stop this?" A nervous hand indicated the Mexican station gleaming in its fresh coat of paint; to the muddy water undermining its foundation.

Estrada drew a cigarette out of his pocket; lighted it before answering.

"Not a God damn thing. What do you suggest?"

A big wave struck the bank. The car on the siding trembled.

"Another wave like that and that car'll go over," cried Babcock, jumping, mad. "Why don't you do something? Why don't you hustle—all of you?" He would report this incompetency.

Down the stream came a mass of débris, broken timbers, ravaged brush, a wrenched fence post, a chicken coop. A red hen, clinging to its swaying ship, took the rapids.

"Hustle—what?" murmured Estrada.

Babcock glared at him, then at the river. His eye caught the approaching wreckage. Men came running with their poles. The caving bank was too far gone. The instant the drifting mass struck it, there was a shudder of falling earth, the car toppled toward the flood waters, the waves breaking into clouds of spray.

Human responsibility fell to a cipher. The river's might was magnificent. Even Babcock, come to carp, caught the excitement. "Come, MacLean," he cried. "Watch this! The station's going!" He joined Estrada by the adobe wall.

"Have a cigarette?" murmured Eduardo.

His eyes glued to the lurching station-house, Babcock took a brown-paper-rolled cigarette from the proffered box.

"Look," he cried. "There, she'll go. See that—"

There was a splash of splintering timber; a Niagara of spray as the building fell into the flood. A minute later, a wreckage of painted boards was floating down-stream.

At table Babcock resumed his campaign. "The trouble with you all, you have cold feet. You're all scared off too soon."

Wooster, up from his nap, looked across the table. "Cold feet? So you'd have if you had been up for nights, wetting your feet on the levee, as some of us have, as Hardin has. Mine are cold all right." He lifted an amazed foot. "Cold! Look here, boys, they're wet!" The men looked to find the water creeping in—Babcock climbed on his chair.

"This means the station," cried Wooster. Every man jumped. If the waters had got to *them,* it wouldn't be long before they were reaching the O. P. depot! The tracks would go— They were piling out of the door when the telephone caught them. It was a message from Rickard. A car was to be rigged up, papers, tickets and express matter taken from the station. The river was cutting close to the track. The car would be the terminal, a half-mile from town.

The situation looked black. Coulter, Eggers, began to pack their stock. The levee, it was said, would not hold— Half of Mexicali was gone. Calexico would go next.

THE PASSING OF THE WATERS

Rickard's Indians were kept stolidly piling brush and stuffed sacks on the levee. This, the word ran, would be the fierce night—no one expected to sleep.

They were preparing for the big battle, the final struggle, when the grade recession passed the town. Spectacular as was its coming, there was an anticlimax in its retreat. The water reached the platform of the depot, and halted. The town held its breath. There was some sleep that night.

The next day, the nerves of the valley relaxed. The river was not cutting back. The men at the levee dropped their shovels, and went back to the discussion of their lawsuits. Their crops were ruined; too much water, or too little. Whatever way they had been hurt, the company would have to pay for it!

A small shift guarded the river. Rickard, in his room at the Desert Hotel, and Hardin up the river, slept a day and a night without waking. The chair-tilters picked up their argument where they had left it: was the railroad reaping a harvest of damage suits when they should be thanked instead? Faraday, the newspapers reported, was trying to shift his responsibility; he had appealed to the president. Their correspondence was published. The government was in no hurry to take the burden. A telegraphic sermon, preaching duty, distributing blame, was sent from Washington. Perhaps not Faraday himself was more disturbed than the debaters of the Desert Hotel.

"The railroad's no infant in arms! It wasn't asleep when it took over the affairs of the D. R." Here spoke the majority. "A benefaction! It was self-interest! When the river is harnessed, who'll profit the most from the valley prosperity? It can afford to pay the obligations; that is, it could. It will find a way," the ravens croaked, "of shaking the Desert Reclamation Company's debts; of evading the damage suits. Look how Hardin was treated!"

The feeling ran higher. For many of the ranchers were ruined; there was no money to put in the next year's crop unless the promises of the irrigation company were kept. A few landowners, and others who had not completed their contracts, distrusting the good faith of the company, or its ability to pay, had "quit" in disgust, to begin again somewhere else. Parrish, and Dowker, and others of the "Sixth" scoured district had secured the promise of employment at the Heading. Work, it was expected, would be begun at once now that the danger to Calexico had passed.

MacLean and Estrada met outside the water-tower.

"Have you been up?" Estrada nodded toward the platform that carried the great tank. "Come up with me. They say it's worth seeing."

"Can't." MacLean was plunging toward the office, his boyish face indicating the enjoyment of his importance. "Too much work. The office work is all piled up. The office, itself, looks like the day after a fire! They're putting back the windows. Casey and I have a desk between us. We're requisitioning quarries, and scraping the country with a fine comb for labor. Jinks, but it's great!"

Estrada climbed alone the steep inner staircase of the water-tower. He was thinking of the young American, vaguely envying him. There was something the other had that he wanted. He himself could work as hard for the river; but shout for it? That was where he stopped. He lacked, he could admit it to himself, the quality of enthusiasm. A son of Guillermo Estrada,—lacking enthusiasm!

From the platform he looked down over the submerged country. To the west, the muddy waters spread out over the land. Eleven miles, he had heard it said, were covered. His sympathy was seeing, not a drowned country, but submerged hopes. The pain of it, the histories beneath it, tugged at his heart. Distantly, he could see the ravaged district of the Wistaria, spoiled for this year surely, perhaps forever made useless. Not until the waters withdrew, would they know the extent of the ruin. From the north, between Fassett's and the towns, steadily advancing, Hardin's gang was still serenading; the boom of his drums came clearly through the still air.

Below him lay the valley of his father's vision. The story of that desert journey had been told him so vividly, so variously that he had made himself one of the party. Coronel was there, the general, and Bliss—dead soon after; Hardin, Silent. Out of a clear morning, following the storm, flashed the mirage which came to Estrada as prophecy,—the city vision which summoned him to fulfil the Fremont-Powell dream. "That barren land, and a rich river flowing over yonder!" His father's vibrant voice returned to his memory; how often had he heard him cry: "The young men pressing in from the congested cities to get their living out of that unworked soil; a clean living, Eduardo!" And Silent had told him how the general had looked like a prophet of ancient Israel that mystic morning when he turned from the mirage of spires and turrets and tender colored walls, exclaiming, "God! If I were young like you, Silent, I'd build that city! that city that we see!"

And now, the cities, embryonic, were there, but would they stay? Built like the parabled city upon sand—sand without water!—would they not crumble and melt away, even as the mirage had faded? He forced himself to translate his conviction into material reasons. The desert was convincing. With its past defying history, its future appealed to the imagination as unchanging, eternal. Even now, those houses down yonder, in their ugly concreteness, were less real than the idea of the desert surrounding the little patch of civilization. Brandon's words, from his monograph on desert soils, recurred to him. "The desert is a condition, not a fact." To him, the desert was a fact.

Eduardo was conscious that he was thinking with the surface of his mind. He was withholding the belief in the negative sense which told him that he would never see that river subdued to service. A skeptic, Innes had called him! He made himself argue it out as a matter of temperament; his father's had been optimistic, fervid; his was detached and analytical. The general had been militant; he was a dreamer. To him, this was a drama of form and color, a picture, a panorama—Parrish, Hardin, each in his place.

Had he but the dynamic energy which had swept his father through his vivid, versatile life! Once, under the spell of the general's magnetism, he had been able to force that zeal, that enthusiasm, to recharge his own weakened batteries; but later, while flinging, perhaps, a track across a waste of sands, and a squaw's bright skirt against a cloud-free sky, or a buck's striped breast rising from a clump of creosote, would make his work a grind again. He had misplaced himself. What else, then, should he be doing?

Often, and now, looking down on that chocolate-colored land, it would come to him that his was the yearning, the wistfulness of the painter. Those purple mountains flushing to rosy points against a clear blue sky, that rushing water, what did it rouse in him? A sense of militancy, as with Rickard and Hardin, MacLean, all of them? It pricked instead, an irritation, a feeling of incompleteness. He wanted something; could a man be homesick for what he never had?

It was not the valley scheme alone, which made of his mind a battle-ground. Did he not meet life so, with a ready hand and a lagging spirit? That girl down there! Had he the blood of his father in his veins, would he not take her of the steady boyish gaze, match her sweetness with just loving? What was it that told him it would never be? Why did he keep guard over lips and eyes? She looked at others with the same level, straightforward frankness she gave to him; the game was, perhaps, yet to him who ran! If it were going to be, there would be a spring of joy within his heart. It was not going to be. He had asked before, and it had answered.

Whose was the answer, that came to him, sometimes at call, often unbidden? Intangible as moonlight, real as the voice of a friend? Can you see a voice? No substance to a voice? Let it come to again, let it tell him of that river; should he see it, the vision of his father, of the others, he, Eduardo?

Standing in the wash of clear sunlight, his arms outstretched to the land his father's vision had peopled, he sent out his call that he should see that dream fulfilled, the river conquered. Give him back his belief! Give him back the courage that would make him one with the folk down there!

Out of that land of silence came, as a wave of darkness, a mist shutting out the sun, separating him from his fellows, the answer. No need to question that! Had it ever erred? Slowly, as a dream-walker, he went down the tower steps, and mingled with men again.

A week later, he was standing on the same platform. The sky was still fleckless; the painted flat mountains made sharp points into the vivid blue of the sky. The heat was holding off. The desert was spelling out her siren lure. But her lover had retreated to his gipsy bed; her brown lean breast was no longer pillowing him.

In the gorge west of the town, the water was now confined. The recession of the waters disclosed the ravaged Palo Verde, its shattered vineyard set in a square of eucalyptus trees, young giants of three years' planting. Northward, Estrada caught the gleam of sunshine on broad barley-fields; he saw the glistening foliage of the orange orchards, Busby's and the others. Between him and the eastern range spread miles of sweet-smelling alfalfa. Young willow growth checker-boarded the country, marking the canal system. All that in a few years; the miracle of irrigation. He had seen virgin desert, as this had been when his father had crossed with Bliss and Hardin; six years before, when he had first seen it, it was still desert, such as he was flinging a track across, of creosote bush, and tough mesquit roots, and here and there, the arrow-weed. Who could tell of the next six years? Perhaps, the rest would be vanquished, and the river yet a meek water-carrier? But he knew!

On the veranda of the office, an hour later, he met Rickard, carrying his Gladstone.

"I'm off!" The American halted, poised, as if for the next step of a dance, so it appeared to Estrada. His eyes were glowing, as though a boy springing toward vacation.

"The Heading? Have you had word yet?"

"They're still passing the buck to each other! But I'll be there when it comes. You'll see that Dragon scotched yet, Estrada!"

He carried the look of victory. But so also, had Tom Hardin! So once had the general! And the river still running to the sea!

CHAPTER XXIII

MORE ORATORY

FOUR men sat at a small table in a corner of the crowded hotel dining-room, in El Centro. Their names made their corner the psychological center of the room. Marshall was always a target of speculation. MacLean, straight and soldierly in his mustard-colored clothes, was, as usual, the man of distinction. Black started the whisper going that the dark stranger was General de la Vega, the Mexican commissioner.

What was he doing in that group? Babcock completed a combination which encouraged speculations and head-shakings. The room was jammed with valley men. The meeting of the ranchers and the several water companies had been called for that afternoon, the summons signed by Faraday himself. Nothing else had been talked of for a fortnight.

It was known throughout the valley that the work at the intake was not yet begun; that Rickard was waiting there for orders; that Faraday and the president of the United States were involved in correspondence as to the responsibility for the future control of the river. Faraday's eagerness to shift his burden was looked upon as suspicious. It was in the air that the officers of the Overland Pacific would demand a recall of the damage suits before they would complete the protective works at the Heading. The men of long vision, members of the water companies, and Brandon, through the valley *Star,* were pointing out that the valley's salvation depended on the immediate control of the river; that the railroad, only, had power to effect it. These conservatives were counseling caution. Only that morning, the *Star* had issued an extra, a special edition pleading for cooperation. "If the river breaks out again," warned Brandon's editorial, "without immediate force to restrain it, reclamation for that valley is a dream that is done. And the only force equal to that emergency is the railroad. Why deliberately antagonize the railroad? The Desert Reclamation Company, it is well known, is bankrupt. For the instant, the railroad has assumed the responsibilities of the smaller organization. Apply the same situation to individuals. Suppose a private citizen is in straits, and another comes forward to help him. Must every creditor assume that the Samaritan should pay the crushed citizen's bills? In the present issue, self-interest should urge consideration. Better a small loss to-day that to-morrow may amply refund, than total ruin in the future."

"Subsidized by the O. P.!" With the whisper ran a wink. The advice of all the conservatives was believed to be business policy. Black and others were inflaming public spirit. During the week that followed Faraday's call, there had been meetings of the various water companies; incendiary excitement had demoralized the discussions. "The pledges of the Desert Reclamation should be kept."

Hardin, from his morose unshared table, could see the anxious curiosity setting toward the railroad group. Over glasses, heads were close together. Near him, the talk ran high. Scraps of inflammable speeches blew his way from Barton's party.

Hardin's mouth wore a set sneer. "Water company talk!" Black was haranguing his comrades. "Stand out against them. Don't let them bluff you. Marshall will try to bluff you. Stand together!" Barton's resonant organ broke through the clatter. "Marshall is not going to bluff us." Grace and Black began to talk at once. Hardin's lip grew rougher. Where had they all been if it had not been for him? Why, he'd pulled them from their little farms back East, where they were toiling —where they'd be toiling yet. They'd had the vision of sudden wealth—they hadn't the grit to work for it, to wait for it! How many years had he been struggling? He was a young man when he'd gone into this thing, and he was old now.

His eyes fell on Hollister from the Palo Verde, with Youngberg and his wife, who in pale gray cloth looked as though she were on her way to a reception. He scowled at the leveling of gold lorgnettes in Morton's group—the eastern swells there for a possible sensation! And Senator Graves had thought it important enough to come down from Los Angeles? The tall duffer with him, his head gleaming like a billiard ball, was probably the New York lawyer who was dickering for the A B C ranch. He had read of it in the Los Angeles papers; a big syndicate thought this the time to get in cheap, when confidence was at a low ebb. "It's high-water mark with Graves, or nothing," scowled Hardin. "He's no spring chicken. They'll all make money out of this valley, but me. I haven't tried to make money; I've made the valley! And is there a more hated man in this room? Sickening!"

Coffee and cigars had been reached of the midday

dinner. Babcock was nervously consulting his watch. "Shouldn't we arrange the meeting?" he asked for the third time. The social and casual air of the meeting had teased him. What had the political situation in Mexico to do with the important session confronting them? His fussy soul had no polite salons; office rooms every one of them. MacLean looked to Tod Marshall to answer.

"I think it will arrange itself," his voice was silken. "It is to be a discussion, a conference. You can't slate that."

"We could program," began Babcock, looking at his watch again.

"I don't think we'll have to." Marshall smiled across the table. "You'll find this meeting will run itself. There is not a man here who is not burning to speak. Look at them now! Drop a paper in that crowd, and see the blaze you'd get! You can open the meeting, Mr. Babcock, and I would suggest that you call on Mr. de la Vega first."

"And next?" Babcock's nervous pencil hovered over his note-book.

"The rest will resolve itself." Marshall's eyes were twinkling. "We'll find our cue. I'll kick you under the table when I want to talk. You can't program against passions, Babcock."

"But we ought to be starting." Fussily Babcock marshaled them from their leisurely cigars. "It is getting late."

The eyes of the dining-room followed the party as they filed past the buzzing tables. Faraday was not in town; Marshall represented that power. As he walked out, bowing right and left, his right hand occasionally extended in his well-known oratorical, courteous gesture.

His black tie was stringing down his shirt-front; his black clothes were the worse for his lunch. But no one, save the eastern girls, saw spots or tie. The future of that valley lay in that man's hand, no matter how Black or Grace might harangue. In five minutes, the dining-room was emptied.

The main street was lined with groups of ranchers, who had driven in to the advertised meeting. On some of the wagons, men were finishing their basket lunches. The sun was mild; the sky clear.

Hardin overheard bits of eager argument as he threaded the crowded street, his head down, avoiding recognition.

"The Service'll try to get in." "The O. P.'s got a good thing." "I tell you, the railroad's in a hole." "Faraday's a fathead."

As snow gently falling, had gathered the first damage suits of the ranchers. The last flood had precipitated a temperamental storm. Men were suing for the possible values of their farms, impossible values of crops. Not alone the companies had been blanketed with the accusing papers, but against Mexico the white drifts had piled up. Mexico! No one knew better than Hardin how absurd it was to accuse the sister country of responsibility. A pretty pickle they were in! Where was it all going to end?

The town teemed with importance. In the whole valley, this was the one place which could house the expected crowd. The spectacular new city, which had sprung full grown from the head of its Jovian promoter, Petrie, whose outlying lands must be brought into value, had justified itself. It had offered its theater. Toward that white-painted building, fresh as crude wine, the groups were turning. To Hardin, borne along with the stream which overflowed from the narrow walks, came the memory of a forgotten tale: a palace raised in a single night was scarcely more spectacular than this town of a year's growth. A theater, a steam-laundry, an ice-plant, and his eyes included two new book-stores, new at least to him. Where would all this have been if it had not been for him? And what was he? An outcast in their midst, no one speaking to him! But they'd need him yet; they'd be turning to him. It would be all right, somehow! He'd make Gert proud of him!

Groups of men were standing around the entrance to the Valley Theater, where the lithographed bill-boards were still proclaiming five weeks of grand and comic opera. One week of successful programs, the preceding spring, and the roistering singers had disbanded to form a melon company. They had rented a tract, some tents, and had gone in pursuit of swift money. After the harvesting of their crops, the heat of the summer and the clink of the dollars in their pockets had discouraged the completion of the engagement. Abandoning their intention, the genial troupe had swept out of the steaming valley to tell their merry story on the Rialto.

In the lobby, Hardin ran up against Brandon, who was following a news scent. Through the valley it was being rumored that subscriptions were to be asked for the completion of the work. If this were the intention, there would be a hot meeting, worth sending to the *Sun*. The war-horse was treading battle-ground.

"You are going on the platform?" assumed the newspaper man. "No? Then will you sit with me?"

"If you will sit up-stairs," scowled Hardin, "I don't want to be dragged on to the platform."

He led the way up the dusty dark steps to the balcony, and on to the rear where the ceiling sharply slanted. They established themselves in seats by the wall. The air had a dry smell of old tobacco and stale perfumes; of face powders. Brandon had a minute of coughing.

When they had entered, only a few seats were occupied. That instant, the crowd crushed in. Men and women jostled one another in the narrow aisles; the chairs filled up; some of the younger men jumped over chair-backs, as sheep over rocks. Hardin and Brandon leaned over to see the inrush. They saw Barton's shriveled body and leonine head borne in by his friends. Senator Graves was entering a proscenium box with his companion.

"That's Hawkins, who represents the Eastern syndicate that's bargaining for the A B C," informed Brandon.

"I could have got that land for ten cents an acre when I began this work, if I'd looked out for myself! It would have been better if I had looked out for myself; what thanks do I get for only working for the valley?" grouched Hardin. "What's Graves holding out for?"

"One thousand an acre, and he'll get it," answered Brandon. "That soil is as rich as gold dust. Hello, there's Watts, of Water Company Number Two; and John Francis, and Green and Ford. They've not sent representatives from the water companies, Hardin! They've come as a body!"

His excitement communicated itself speedily to his companion.

"Something's going to drop, sure!"

"And Wilson, with Petrie. I didn't know *he* was in any of the water companies."

MORE ORATORY 221

"Is there anything in the valley he's not in?" All of them with the idea of making money; all but himself!

Down in the orchestra, Black from the Wistaria was haranguing a group of gesticulating ranchers. Phrases climbed to the men on the balcony seats. "Keep their pledges. Promise makers. Let them look at our crops!"

"Every man thinking of himself, of his own precious skin!" sneered Hardin.

Hollister and the Youngbergs were seen taking their seats near the orchestra stand, behind the bickering merry Blinns. Morton was filling the other proscenium with his eastern guests.

Brandon had to surrender to an attack of coughing. He leaned, spent, against the wall. "That audience," he gasped, "represents several million dollars—of dissatisfaction." The phrase had come to him in his paroxysm. He would use it in his story for the *Sun*. If there was a story.

"If Marshall expects to coerce those men, I lose my guess. Then he's no judge of men," cried Hardin. "Look at those faces." The floor was a sea of impassioned features.

"Something's going to drop," echoed Brandon.

From the wings, Babcock's inquisitive glasses were seen to sweep the house. Hardin could catch the summons of an excited forefinger to the group unseen. There was a minute of delay. Then Babcock's nervous toddle carried him on to the stage which had been set for *Robin Hood,* the scenery deserted when the singers had rushed out of the valley. Babcock's striped, modern trousers looked absurdly anachronistic against the background of old England. There was a titter from Morton's proscenium box where the lorgnettes were flashing.

De la Vega followed Babcock. There was a hush of curiosity. The house did not know who he was. Behind him, soldierly, stiff, stalked MacLean. Marshall's entrance released the tongues. There was an interval of confusion on the stage. Babcock, like a restless terrier, was snapping at the heels of the party. At last, they were all fussily seated. De la Vega was given the place of honor. Marshall, Babcock put on his left, MacLean on the right.

Babcock raised his staccate gavel. A hush fell on the house. His words were clipped and sharp.

"You have left your plowing to come here. You are anxious to hear what we have to say to you. You can not afford to be indifferent to it. You acknowledge, by your presence, a dependence, a correlation which you would like to deny. Irrigation means cooperation, suffering together, struggling together, succeeding together. You prefer the old individual way, each man for himself. I tell you it won't do. You belong in other countries, the countries of old-fashioned rain. You want to hear what we have to say to you, the company who saved the valley, the company you are suing. But you have also suits against Mexico. There is a gentleman here who has a message from Mexico about those suits. I have the honor, gentlemen, to introduce, Señor de la Vega."

There was a gentle stir of released hazards. The Spaniard approached the footlights, his survey sweeping the house.

"That wasn't bad," murmured Brandon, opening his note-book.

"Ladies," bowed the Mexican. "Gentlemen, Mr. Chairman. It is with an appreciation of the honor that I accepted for to-day the invitation of Mr. Marshall to speak before you, to speak *to* you; I must tell you first my thought as I sat there and looked at you, the youth, the flower of the American people. A few years ago, we were calling this the great Colorado Desert; now, the world calls it the hothouse of America. This theater is built over the bones of gold-seekers, who dared death in this dreaded desert to find what was buried in those mountains beyond. The man, I say, who crossed this desert, took the hazard of death. It was a countryman of mine who piloted, fifteen years ago, a little band of men, across the desert. Perhaps he camped on this very spot. It is not impossible! It is here, perhaps, that he got his inspiration. He saw a wonderful territory; he dreamed to quicken it with the useless waters of the Colorado. You will all agree that it was Guillermo Estrada who dreamed the dream that has come true; that it was through him that some of your countrymen secured their privilege to reclaim this land. Later, when one of your countrymen found he could not fulfil his promise to you, the promise to deliver water to your ranches, he came to my nation and got permission to cut into the river on our territory. Most gladly did Porfirio Diaz grant that privilege. For that, to-day, you are suing him. This, I am told, is your complaint."

His abrupt pause betrayed a confused murmur of voices. De la Vega's polite ear tried to differentiate the phrases. There was a jumble of sound. De la Vega looked inquiringly at Babcock, who waved him on.

"It has nothing to do with the history, but I would like to say in passing that so assured were your people of our friendly feeling toward you that they did not wait to receive permission from Mexico to make the cut. Your people were in a hurry. Your crops were in danger. First the lack of water, then too much water damaged your valley. A few acres—"

A voice from the crowd cried out, "A few acres? Thousands of acres." Instantly others were on their feet. "Thousands of acres. Ruin." One man was shouting himself apoplectic.

Babcock's gavel sounded a sharp staccato on the table. "Thousands of acres." De le Vega was unruffled. "And more than that. The valley, it must be remembered, does not stop at the line. Mexican lands, too, have been scoured by the action, the result of the action of your irrigation company. It was a mutual," he paused, and a quaint word came to his need. "A mutual bereavement. It did not occur to us to accuse you of our troubles. Your damage suits pained and astonished us. But they gave us also a suggestion."

The rustling and the murmurs suddenly ceased. A prescient hush waited on De la Vega. "You have been advised to sue us. To sue us for giving you that concession. Therefore, the only answer is for us to withdraw that concession! You accuse us, for giving it to you. That concession is valuable. What else *can* we do? Before your damage suits were filed, we were approached by others for the same privilege. If you do not withdraw your suits, my nation sends word to you that you may not take water from the Colorado River through Mexican soil. You will not be without water probably long; I have said that concession is valuable! Other arrangements will probably be made so that the valley will be given water. I would like to take your answer to my government."

It was several seconds before the house got its breath.

The import of the diplomat's words was astounding. Barton got to his feet, yelling with his great bass voice, "Betrayed!" His shrunken finger indicated a youth with "R. S." in black letters on his collar. "The valley has been betrayed."

In the balcony, the uproar was deafening. Around Hardin and Brandon words were thudding like bullets. "Reclamation Service." "That's their game." "The concession!" "They won't get it." "Betrayed. We are betrayed."

Down-stairs, Babcock's gavel rapped unheard. Behind the excited figure wielding the stick, sat Marshall, his unreadable, sweet smile on his face. His eyes were on Babcock, who was vainly clamoring for order. "Program that meeting?"

Hollister was trying to make himself heard to Barton over two rows of seats, but his voice was like a child's on an ocean beach. Barton was surrounded by eager anxious men. The audience had split into circles of haranguing centers. It was impossible to get attention. Hardin could see Marshall pull Babcock by the tails of his coat. Unwillingly, he could see Babcock allow the crowd five minutes by his consulted watch. Then again, the gavel danced on the table. Marshall was still smiling. Babcock's shrill voice split the din. "Order." The ocean of voices swallowed him again.

"We won't let them in," Grace was bellowing, "the valley won't stand for it."

"Take your medicine," thundered the big organ of Barton. "I warned you, Imperial Valley."

"Betrayal," groaned the crowd.

"A pretty international block." Brandon was smiling, too. This was better than he had expected. A rattling good story the *Sun* would have. Bertha would read it over her breakfast rolls. "This is history."

Down in the orchestra, Barton was holding a hurry-up meeting of the water companies. De la Vega had stepped back and was consulting with Tod Marshall.

Babcock pulled out his watch, his gavel calling for attention. This time he was heard.

De la Vega approached the footlights, a questioning look on his face.

"We ask for a little time," began Barton. Instantly the house was on its feet. "Withdraw the suits. Give him your answer. Give him our answer. We don't want the Service. The valley don't want the Service. Withdraw the suits."

Barton's moon face looked troubled. "We can't answer for all the ranchers."

"Yes, you can," screamed Grace, jumping up and down like a baboon. "If you don't, I'll answer for them. Don't you see, it's a trick? It's a trick. I see the hand of the O. P. in this." Friendly hands pulled him down into his seat.

The audience was chanting. "Withdraw the suits. Take your medicine.—Don't lose the concession.—Lord, the Service!—Give them the answer, now."

Barton held up a withered hand. The undeveloped body was dignified by the splendid head. "Don't withdraw your concession. I think I can say that Mexico will not be sued."

Again, the shout went up. "Answer like a man. Think! Good lord! Say we withdraw the suits!"

"We withdraw the claims against Mexico." Barton sat down to a sudden hush. The first blood had been let.

MORE ORATORY

Once more Babcock's glasses swept the house. He rapped the table.

"That's not all. We've got more to say to you. Gentlemen, Mr. Marshall."

Marshall stepped forward to a silence which was a variety of tribute.

He bowed. "I will be brief. Mr. Faraday has asked me to take his place here this afternoon. It's only fair. If it were not for my interference, he would not be involved in this situation. I think you will grant that it is Mr. Faraday's company which can save the valley?"

"To save its own tracks!" yelled a voice from the balcony.

Marshall sent a soft smile heavenward. "Incidentally. And its traffic. Why don't you say it? We don't deny that. The Overland Pacific's no altruist."

There was a jeer which rose into a chorus. "Altruist! Octopus. That's what it is."

Marshall's hand went up. "If you want to hear me?" He waved away Babcock's descending gavel. "I was told it would cost two hundred thousand dollars to close that break of yours. Do you want the actual figures? It has eaten already a million, and the work is not yet done. You know the history of the undertaking. The Desert Reclamation Company was in straits. Faraday promised his help on the condition that the affairs of the Desert Reclamation Company would be controlled by his company. He took the control. He inherited— what? Not good will. Threats, damage suits. Do you think that snow-slide of complaints is going to encourage him to go on? This is what I came here to talk to you about. You ranchers don't want to cut your own throat.

Now, there's a good deal going on about which you are in the dark. Faraday's got a right to feel he's shouldered an old man of the sea. He's been trying to dislodge it. He's appealed to the president. Ever since we came into this, the cry from Washington has been, 'Do this the way we like, or we'll not take it off your hands.'" A murmur of angry voices started somewhere, swelling toward the balcony.

"We don't want the government—" began the rising voices. Marshall's voice rang out:

"But the government wants—you! Unless you will help save your own homes, the government will have to, in time. It's got to. Up there at Laguna, have you seen it? There's nothing going on. They're watching us. That's a useless toy if our works are washed out. Faraday says *this* to you—" Not a sound in the stilled house. "Unless you withdraw your damage suits, he won't advance another damned cent."

Sharply he sat down before the audience realized that his message was finished. The house had not found its voice, when Babcock's gavel was pounding again for attention. The question, he felt, had not been put to them completely. Perhaps, they did not gather the full import of Mr. Marshall's message. Mr. MacLean would follow Mr. Marshall.

MacLean's superb figure rose from a tree-paneled background.

"He should sing *Brown October Ale*," suggested Brandon to Hardin humorously.

Hardin's eyes were on MacLean. What did he know about it? What could he tell those men that they did not know? MacLean was a figurehead in the reorganized irrigation company. Why hadn't they called on him,

Hardin? He knew more about the involved history of the two companies than the whole bunch on the stage down yonder. He could have told them, he could have called on their justice, their memory—

MacLean was speaking.

"Mr. Marshall has likened the river project to the old man of the sea. He has it on his back, while it is busily kicking him in the shins!

"Mr. Marshall has given you Mr. Faraday's message. He has asked you to dismiss your damage suits. I ask you to do more than that. Put your hands in your pockets! Come out and help us. You don't want the government. I am told that is the sentiment of the valley. When you called to them, they wouldn't help you; they wouldn't give you an adequate price. Congress will soon be adjourning. What is Mr. Faraday to say to Washington? Is he going to close that break? That depends on you. Withdraw your suits. Do more. Stop fighting against us. Fight *with* us—"

The audience stirred ominously, angrily. Before MacLean was done, a voice screamed from the balcony. "You can't quit. That's a threat. You're in too deep. You can't fool us. You've got to save yourself. You've got to go on. Tell Faraday to tell that to Washington."

The uproar was released. Black, from the Wistaria, jumped on his chair. "I am speaking for the valley. We can't help. You know it. We're stripped. We're ruined. You think to threaten us with the government—if we wait for the government to decide, the valley is gone—and the railroad's money with it. I tell you, your bluff won't go. We want justice. We are going to have justice."

"Justice!" came from the surging ranchers.

"Fair play," yelled Black. "You can't trick us. We were not born yesterday. We have rights. The company brought us here. What did we give our money for? Desert land? What good is this land without water? We bought water—we were pledged water. Give us back the money we've put in—that's what we're asking for. We won't be scared out of our rights."

There was a growling accompaniment from the back rows, herding together.

"Order," cried Babcock, thumping his gavel. "Let Mr. Black have the floor."

Black had not stopped. Wildly his hands cut the air. His speech, though high-pitched, had a prepared sound; it worked toward a climax. He gave individual instances of ruin. "Grace, Willard Grace, his crop gone, his place cut in two. Hollister and Wilson, of the Palo Verde, the ranch a screaming horror. Scores of others." He would not mention his own case; and then he itemized his misfortunes. Parrish, his place scoured beyond all future usefulness. What had they come into the valley for? Who had urged them? There were pledges of the D. R., water pledges. That was all those ruined men were pleading, the redemption of those pledges. Individual ruin, what did it mean? A curtailing of luxuries, of personal indulgence. "I tell you, it means food, bread, potatoes; milk for the babies; or starvation."

Black had touched the deep note. This was the answer. This was what they wanted to say.

"You ask us to help you, us, we who are taxed already to our breaking point. You say your company won't go any further. What does that help mean to you? Poverty? A few thousands, a million to the O. P., a corporation, what does a loss mean to them? Poverty!

I tell you, no. A smaller dividend, maybe, to whom? Yes, to whom? To the men who live in Fifth Avenue, whose wives are dragged about in limousines. Withdraw their suits? Help Faraday, and ruin men like Parrish? Men of the valley, what is your answer to Faraday?"

The crowd was on its feet, swaying and pushing. The air was fetid with breaths. Wilson's crowd had forgotten its lorgnettes. "No," yelled the ranchers. "We say, no."

A boy made his way from the wings, a yellow envelope in his hand.

Babcock waved him on to Marshall. The audience was crying itself hoarse. Babcock lost control of the meeting in that minute of turning. Hollister, of the Palo Verde, was striving to be heard; Babcock's hammer sounded in vain. But Marshall's eye had caught a spark from the yellow sheet. He sprang forward, throwing the despatch toward MacLean. His excitement caught the eye of the crowd. "The river!" There was a sudden hush. "The river's out again!" A groan swept through the house, there was a break toward the doors.

Marshall's voice halted them. "Men of the valley." The audience, swayed again, listened. "Hear me. The river's running away again down yonder. This is a message from Rickard. It's broken through the levee. It's started for the valley. Now, who's going to stop it? Who can stop it? Can you? Where's your force, your equipment? Who can rush to that call but the company you are hounding? I gave you Faraday's message. His hand's on the table. Not another cent from him unless you withdraw those suits. You say you have given me your answer, Black's answer. Now the river plays a trick. It calls your bluff. Shall we stop the river, men of the valley? We can. Will you withdraw your suits? You can. What is your answer now, Imperial Valley?"

The scene broke into bedlam. Men jumped to their chairs, to the velvet rim of the boxes, all talking, screaming, gesticulating at once. The *Yellow Dragon* was never so fearfully visualized. Out of the chaos of men's voices came a woman's shriek, "For God's sake, save our homes." It pitched the panic note. "Save the valley! Stop the river!"

Marshall's Indian eyes were reading that mass of scared faces as though it were a sheet of typed paper. "Barton," he called through the din. "Where's Barton?"

Two men lifted Barton's puny figure upon their shoulders. His vibrant voice rolled above the shouting. "The valley withdraws its suits against the company."

"Then the company," yelled Marshall's oratory, "the company withdraws the river from the valley!" Pandemonium was loose. There were cheers, and the sound of women sobbing. Barton was carried out on the shoulders of his henchmen. Black led a crowd out, haranguing to the street. Morton's party waited for the house to empty. De la Vega, from the wings, watched the scene with polite curiosity.

Picking their way past a painted side shift of merry England, MacLean and Babcock followed Marshall from the stage.

On the street, Marshall fell back to MacLean. "That was a neat trick the river threw in our hands." His voice had dropped from oratory; the declaiming fire was gone from the black eyes. "It's only a break in the levee. Rickard says he can control it; estimates two weeks or so. It may cost the O. P. a few thousand dollars, but it saved them half a million. Now we'll have that game of poker, MacLean!"

In the balcony, Hardin was staring at Brandon.

"If that wasn't the devil's own luck!"

CHAPTER XXIV

A SOFT NOOK

INNES traveled, gleefully, in a caboose, from Hamlin Junction to the Heading. She could not stay away a day longer! Never before had Los Angeles been a discipline. Her surprise was still fresh over the change in her friends, two girls who had been her comrades during her unfinished college course. She had left, in the spirit of self-sacrifice, to look after Tom. They had finished, but their two years of wifehood had made a wider gap than her break. Their plans of individual accomplishment all merged into new curtains for the guest chamber, and surprise dishes for Tom and Harry! Why had it fretted her, made her restless, homesick? Then she had discovered the reason; history was going on down yonder. Going on, without her. She knew that that was what was pulling her; that only!

The exodus of engineers had started riverward in July. Gerty went with Tom, and she had made it distinctly clear that it was not necessary for Innes to follow them. Ridiculous for two women to coddle a Tom Hardin! Unless Innes had a special interest!

Her pride had kept her away. But Tom did not write; Gerty's letters were social and unsatisfactory; the newspaper reports inflamed her. The day before she had wired Tom that she was coming. She had to be there at the end!

There was no one to meet her. Tom was down on the levee work; the camp was deserted. She found her way to the Hardin tents, helped by the Chinese cook whom she found installed behind a clump of mesquits.

Gerty welcomed her stiffly. Assuming a conscientious hostess-ship, she caught fire at her waning enthusiasms. The arrangement of the tent, of the simple furniture, did not Innes find it sweet? That smaller tent to the west of theirs had been added that morning. A Mexican was even then carrying in a wash-stand and an iron bed. Outside, in a hand-cart, were a couple of chairs, a basin and pitcher of gray enamel.

"If we had known you were coming, we would have been ready for you," suggested Gerty.

Innes' gaze had been turning outward to the lines of canvas, making a white glitter on the alkali floor of the encampment, trapezium in shape. Stark in outline, vivid in color, she saw the desert again as a savage; her terms, brutal, uncompromising. But were they taking her on her terms, these intruders? They were making her over to their wishes, as a man makes unto his liking the wife of his satisfied choice? She was following a thought born of her late visit. Strange, the zeal which would remake the sweetheart, thought peerless! Her mouth curved with ironic tenderness. Gerty's treble notes fell around her ears. She was listening to her own musing, and watching the dripping arm of the dredge as it dug a trap for the Colorado.

The prattle grew insistent, interrogative. She had to look at shelves, at cupboards, at a clever ramada which was both pergola and porch. Returning to the outer tent, she went back to the door, her Hardin pulse leaping to the implication of that dredge arm swinging low in the river.

"Isn't it all cozy?" Gerty's eyes shone on her contrivances. "It all means work. It has taken two whole months to get it to look like this. Every piece of lumber had to be coaxed for, and you'd think the carpenter was a ward boss, he's that haughty."

Gerty looked younger and prettier. Her flush accented her childish features which were smiling down her annoyance over this uninvited visit.

"I had the ramada put up after the shed; an afterthought. They gave me a tent for a kitchen at first—as if I could cook in a tent! We eat in the ramada. The flies ate us up, so I sent for screen wire, and had it enclosed. It isn't perfect, but it's much better than it was. The flies will get through that roof. It keeps one busy to remember to have fresh brush piled over it. It dries so quickly in this sun. Isn't it hot here? Hotter than the towns ever were; don't you think so?"

Innes said she had not been there long enough yet to tell!

"We have all the home comforts, haven't we?" Innes' gaze swept the disguised tent with its home-made sketches and cushions and *art-nouveau* lamp-shades—even the green mandarin skirt had found a place on the center-table made of rough pine. "Why shouldn't we be comfortable when we are to be here for months? I'm going to brave it out—to the bitter end, even if I bake. It is my duty—" She would make her intention perfectly clear! "There ought to be at least one cozy place, one soft nook that suggests a woman's presence. We have tea here in the afternoon, sometimes. Mr. Rickard drops in." The last was a delicate stroke.

"Afternoon tea? At the Front? Is this modern warfare?" The girl draped her irony with a smile.

"Warfare? What do you mean?" Gerty turned from the new chafing-dish and percolator she had intended showing to Innes.

"I thought this was a battle."

"All the more reason for having a pleasant corner to rest in," triumphed Mrs. Hardin. "And the comfort the men take in it, the Service men especially! By the way, Innes, I met Mr. Estrada on the *Delta* last evening and told him you were coming. I asked him to take you over the encampment. He was perfectly willing to do it, although it's an old story to all of them, now. You've no idea how many newspaper men have been down here. It's been quite exciting." She caught herself in time to add: "Though it has been unendurably hot! This is a model camp, as you will see. That's why Mr. Rickard can get such work out of his men; he has made them so comfortable."

"You need not have gone to so much trouble—" Innes told herself that she was perverse. Just peevishness to dislike plans being made for her! Gerty's polite sentences had a way of ruffling her. She ought not to suspect deviousness.

Gerty was stealing a pleased survey in the mirror through the rough door that opened into the division called her bedroom. The sunburned, unconscious profile of Innes was close to her own. Pink and golden the head by the dark one. She looked younger even than Innes! Good humor returned to her.

"We are going to dine on the *Delta* to-night." She pinned up a "scolding lock," an ugly misnomer for her sunny clinging curls! The mirror was requisitioned again. "That's the name of the new dredge. It was christened three weeks ago, in champagne brought from Yuma."

"You christened it?" Innes, following a surmise, stumbled on a grievance.

"No!" sharply. Then a minute later, "They'd asked Mrs. Silent, old man Hamlin's daughter. I suppose Mr. Rickard thought he had to. Mr. Hamlin's the pioneer here, he's such a dreadful old man. Besides, they're always asking the men up to dinner. They can get a real *meal* there,— Mrs. Silent has a stove, and they keep chickens." She frowned toward the chafing-dish and percolator; stern limitations theirs!

"You said *dine* on the *Delta*. Do you mean they have meals there?"

"You should see it," cooed Gerty. "It's simply elegant. It's a floating hotel, has every convenience. Some of the young engineers have a sort of club there, they have brought in their own cook from Los Angeles. The camp cook, Ling, has his hands full. He does very well, but it must be very rough. The *Delta* has worked things up here."

"Going to wear that?" They were standing now by the door of Gerty's dressing tent. Over the bed a white lingerie gown was spread.

"I live in them. It's so hot," shrugged Mrs. Hardin.

"However do you manage to get them washed?"

Mrs. Hardin did not think it necessary to relate her struggles, nor her chagrin to find that no one thought important the delivery of her weekly wash to Yuma.

A SOFT NOOK

Only because she would resent possible comment did she refrain from recounting her trials with Indian washerwomen. She recalled some tattered experiments that she had made—

"I'll look like your maid, Gerty!" Innes' exclamation was rueful. "I didn't bring anything but khakis."

"If that isn't just like you, Innes Hardin!"

"Why, I thought of you as living in the most primitive way; as roughing it! Oh, yes! I remember throwing in, the last minute, two piqués to fill up space. But I never dreamed I'd need them."

"Why, we have dances on the *Delta,* and Sunday evening concerts; you'll be surprised how gay we are. You knew the work at Laguna Dam is being held up? The government men of the Reclamation Service are down here all the time. But it's time to be getting ready."

"You'll be ashamed of your sister. Tom's going, of course?"

"There's no 'of course' about Tom, he does just as he feels like."

Later, Tom flatly refused to accompany them.

"I thought as much." Gerty shrugged an airy irresponsibility. Innes could detect no regret.

"Where will you get your dinner?" His sister was uncertain how far she might venture into this domestic situation.

"Oh, anywhere," brusked Tom.

"At the mess table, the regular eating tent. He usually goes there when there is a dinner at the *Delta.* He doesn't dance, you know."

They passed a cot outside the tent. "Who sleeps there?"

"Tom." The eyes of the two women did not meet. Innes made no comment.

"He finds the tent stuffy." Gerty's lips were prim with reserve. They walked toward the river in silence. As they reached the encampment, Gerty recovered her vivacity.

"That's Mr. Rickard's office, that ramada. Isn't it quaint? And that's his tent; no, the other one. MacLean's is next; we all call him Junior now. The kitchen's behind those mesquit trees. They gave the only shade in the camp to the cook!" She made a grimace men would have found adorable, lost quite on Innes Hardin.

"There's Junior, now," dimpled Gerty Hardin.

But his eyes were too full of Innes to see mature dimples. His boyishness lacked tact. It was nearly three months since he had seen her; a desert of days, those! The difference in the quality of his greetings smote Gerty like a blow. Until her mirror told her differently she would feel youthful. And she had never considered Tom's sister attractive, as a possible rival. Yet, after a handshake, she saw that to MacLean, Jr., she did not exist.

A boat was anchored to a pile on the muddy stream. MacLean jumped in. "I'll hold it steady."

Innes scrambled past his waiting hand, and steadied herself toward the stern. "I'll steer."

Mrs. Hardin and her lace ruffles were placed carefully in the bow.

"Can you climb up that ladder?" MacLean asked Innes.

"Climb? I'm a cat! Didn't you know it?"

A group of welcoming faces was bending over the rail as they drew up in the shadow of the dredge. Innes was on the ladder before MacLean could secure the boat. She had disappeared with the welcoming young engineers who had much to show her, before Mrs. Hardin and her lace ruffles were over the side.

Gerty was deeply piqued. Until now, the field had been hers, divided distantly by the Silent kitchen. She might perhaps have to change her opinion of Tom's sister. Boys, she had to concede, the younger men, might find her attractive, boyishly congenial; older men would fail to see a charm!

The arrangement at table annoyed Gerty. The boss, MacLean explained gaily, would not be there for dinner. He had been called down the levee, taking Irish with him. He might come in later. Two men from the Reclamation Service tried to entertain Mrs. Hardin.

"Did you get Jose Cordoza?" demanded Bodefeldt under cover of a rush of voices, and then crimsoned because every one stopped to listen to him.

"He promised to bring his guitar, and to get a friend who has a mandolin, if the strings are not broken!" laughed Crothers of the railroad.

"Cordoza plays wonderfully!" cried Mrs. Hardin. "If I were eighty, I could dance to his waltzes!"

"The deck's ripping," cried MacLean, his eyes still full of Innes Hardin, "and in the moonlight it's a pippin!"

"It isn't a battle." Innes looked around the gay rectangle. "It's play!"

The thought followed her that evening. Outside, where the moonlight was silvering the deck, and the quiet river lapped the sides of the dredge, Jose's strings, and his *"amigo's"* throbbing from a dark corner, made the illusion of peace convincing. This was no battle.

Breck, of the Reclamation Service, was dancing with her. The modern complexity of the situation fell away from her; the purpose of the *Delta,* of the gathering army of laborers, of the pile-drivers in the river, was obscured. The concentrating struggle against the marauding Dragon of the Colorado delta, that was the illusion. It was easy to believe herself again at Mare Island, or Annapolis—the *Delta* a cruiser, and young Breck one of Uncle Sam's sailors.

Later, Gerty passed her, two-stepping divinely. Before her partner turned his head, Innes recognized the stiff back and straight poised head and dancing step of Rickard. Every muscle in control; it was the distinction of the man. She admitted he had distinction, grudgingly. She could not think of him except comparatively; always antithetically, balanced against her Tom. She wished Tom would not slouch so. Tom had all the big virtues, none of his faults was petty. But he was being nagged into unloveliness.

"I'm tired; let's rest here." She drew into the shadow of the great arm of the dredge. They watched the dancers as they passed, MacLean playing the woman in "Pete's" arms, Gerty with Rickard, two other masculine couples. The Hardins were the only women aboard.

It was because of Tom that Innes felt resentment when the uplifted appealing chin, the lace ruffles fluttered by. Tom, lying outside an unfriendly tent!

"Don't they dance superbly?" Breck's eyes were following the couple, too.

"Come on, let's dance." She pretended not to hear him.

It was easy, in that uncertain light, to avoid Rickard's glance of recognition. Estrada, who had come aboard with the manager, sought her out, and then Crothers, of the O. P. Again, she saw Rickard dancing with the lingerie gown. There seemed to be no attempt to cover Gerty's preference; for Rickard, she was the only woman there! Because she was Tom's sister, she had a right to resent it, to refuse to meet his eye. Small wonder Tom did not come to the *Delta!*

Going in with MacLean, Jr., to the mess room for a glass of water, she met Rickard, on his way out. She managed to avoid shaking hands with him. She wondered why she had consented to give him the next waltz.

"He'll not find me," she determined. Whatever had made her assent? Easy in that womanless group to plead engagements. She led MacLean into innocent but eager conspiracy. He followed her gladly to the dark corner of the deck where Jose's guitar was then syncopating an accompaniment to his *"amigo's"* voice.

> *"A donde ira veloz y fatigada,*
> *La golondrina que de aqui se va?"*

"How beautiful!" cried Innes. "But how sad." She had picked up some Spanish in the towns. "I have never heard that before." She leaned over and asked Jose if he would not write it out for her. Unblushingly, Jose said he would; "Mañana."

"Dollars to doughnuts, he can't write even his own name!" whispered Junior. "But I'll see that you get it mañana!" he added. He would type it for; anything she wanted, he would get for her!

To her surprise, Rickard penetrated her curtain of shadows.

"Our dance, Miss Hardin? Give us *Sobr' Las Olas,* again, Jose."

The hand that barely touched his arm was stiff with antagonism. He stepped off at once to the music; they had no points of contact, these two. No eager threads of talk to be picked up and turned into a pattern. She told herself that he had to dance with her—politeness, conventionality, demanded it. But, instantly, she forgot her resentment, and forgot their awkward relation. It was his dancing, not Gerty's, then, that was "superb." Anybody could find skill under the leadership of that irresistible step. She was just an ordinary dancer, yet she felt as though she had acquired grace and skill. And then the motion claimed her. She thought of nothing; they moved as one to the liquid falling beat. She passed Estrada, just arrived. His smile fell past her. He stood watching them. The girl was not talking. He could not make out the still fixity of her face.

The music dropped them suddenly, isolating them at the stern of the deck. The silence was complete. It was a moment of unreality, the rhythmic blood still in motion, the wistfulness of the moonlight falling on peaceful waters. Rickard broke it to ask her what she thought of the camp.

Her resentments were recalled. She blundered through her impression of the lightness, the gaiety.

"So you think we ought to be solemn?" His tone teased her. The eyes that always confused Gerty were on her. She again tried to be vocal.

"It does not suggest a battle-ground, I mean. The talk to-night at table, the dancing, the fun! It does not seem like a battle camp—"

"You've been in a battle camp, Miss Hardin?"

She would not be flouted. "The atmosphere—it's a camp vacation."

"A work camp does not have to be solemn. You'll find all the grimness you want if you look beneath the surface." She thought, later, of what she might have said to him, but then she stood silent, feeling like a silly child under his light mockery.

The guitars were tuning up. "Shall I take you back? I have this dance with your sister."

She thought of Tom—on his lonely cot outside his tent. She forgot that she had been asked a question. He was dancing again with Gerty! If that silly little woman had no scruples, no fine feeling, this man should at least guard her. If he had been her lover, he should be careful; he must see that people were talking of them. She had seen the glances that evening! The business relation between the two men should suggest tact, if not decency! It was outrageous.

Rickard stood waiting to be dismissed; puzzled. Through the uncertain light, her anger came to him. She looked taller, older; there was a flame of accusing passion in her eyes.

It was his minute of revelation. So that was what the camp thought! The wife of Hardin—Hardin! Why, he'd been only polite to her—they were old friends. What had he said to call down this sudden scorn? "Dancing— again—" Had he been all kinds of an ass?

"My turn, Miss Innes!" demanded MacLean, Jr.

"Oh, yes," she cried, relief in her tone.

Rickard did not claim his dance with Mrs. Hardin. He stood where the girl had left him, thinking. A few minutes later, Gerty swept by in the arms of Breck. Her light laughter, the laughter that had made the Lawrence table endurable, came to him in his unseen corner. Later, came Innes with Junior; the two, thinking themselves unseen, romping through a two-step like two young children. He was never shown that side of her. Gay as a young kitten, chatting merrily with MacLean! Should her eyes discover him, she would be again the haughty young woman!

He'd gone out of his way to be polite to the wife of Hardin. What did he care what they thought? He'd finish his job, and get out.

The sound of oars came to him; the splashing of waves against the dredge. He leaned over. A boat was tying by the ladder.

"Hi, below!" called Rickard.

"Come for Mr. Crothers," the voice from the shadows answered. "He told me to come for him at ten o'clock."

"Hold on!" Rickard was clambering over the side. "I'm Rickard. I've got to get back to camp. You can come again for Crothers."

A minute later, he was being rowed back to camp.

CHAPTER XXV

THE STOKERS

"COMPLETE, isn't it?" Estrada was leading Innes Hardin through the engineers' quarters.

"Yes, it's *complete!*"

Her brother had told her at breakfast that morning how grandly they had been wasting time! She would not let herself admire the precision of the arrangements, the showers back of the white men's quarters, the mesquit-shaded kitchen. Gerty's elaborate settling was of a piece, it would seem, with the new management. Housekeeping, not fighting, then, the new order of things!

Tom was afire to get his gate done. She knew what it meant to him; to the valley. The flood waters had to be controlled. That depended, Tom had proved to her, on the gate. And the men dance and play house, as if they were children, and every day counting!

She thought she was keeping her accusations to herself, but Estrada was watching her face.

"We are here, you know, for a siege. There are months of work ahead, hot months, hard months. The men have got to be kept well and contented. We can't lose any time by sickness"— He wanted to add "and dissensions." The split camp was painful to him, an

Estrada. "Even after we finish the gate, if we do finish it—"

She wheeled on him, her eyes gleaming like deep yellow jewels. "You've never thought we could finish it!"

Estrada hesitated over his answer.

"You are a friend of Tom's, Mr. Estrada?"

"Surely! But I am also an admirer of Mr. Rickard, I mean of his methods. I can never forget the levee."

She had to acknowledge that Rickard had scored there. And the burning of the machinery had left a wound that she still must salve.

"You have no confidence in the gate?"

"The conditions have changed," urged Estrada. "You've seen the mess-tent? As it was planned, it was all right, a hurry-up defense. Marshall all along intended the concrete gate for the permanent intake. Have you seen the gap the Hardin gate is to close? Have you heard what the last floods did to it? It's now twenty-six hundred feet, and Disaster Island, which your brother planned to anchor to, swept away! If it can be done, it will, you can rest assured, with Rickard—" he saw the Hardin mouth then!—"and your brother's zeal, and the strength of the railroad back of them. I haven't shown you the office yet. Can you stand this glare? You ought to have smoked glasses."

"I have. I forgot them." She pulled her wide Mexican brim low over her eyes.

The camp formed a hollow trapezium; the Hardins' tents, and Mrs. Dowker's, were isolated on the short parallel. Rickard's ramada and his tent were huddled with the engineers'. Across, toward the river, behind Ling's mesquits, began another polygon, the camp of foremen and white labor. Some of these tents were empty.

"Is this Mexico, or the states?" asked Innes.

"Mexico." She wondered why he halted so abruptly. She did not see, for the glare in her eyes, a woman's skirt in the ramada they approached.

Estrada marched on.

Outside the ramada, the two women met. Gerty's step carried her past like a high-bred horse. Her high heels cut into the hard sand. There was a suggestion of prance in her mien. She waved her hand gaily at the two, cried, "How hot it is!" and passed on.

Innes saw Rickard at his long pine table used for a desk.

"I can see it all from here." Not for money would the sister of Tom Hardin go in!

Estrada saw by her face that the hope of conciliating the ex-manager by the sister was a false trail. She threw a curt nod to MacLean whom her glance just caught.

"Where are we going now?"

"I'm planning a trip to Arizona!" he returned. "You think this is all play. Now I'm going to show you the 'stokers.'"

A few minutes later, he called out to her: "Step high!"

She looked at the ground, and then inquiringly at him. The ground was as flat as a hardwood floor.

"You are crossing the line," he announced. "You are now in Arizona."

"I thought the Indian camp was in Mexico, too?"

"No, across the river to avoid custom's duty. See those roofs of boughs?"

He was making for a knoll from whence they could get a view of the river, and of the Hardin gate.

Her memory isolated a word of his. "The stokers—who are they?"

"We call them that. The brush-cutters. They look for all the world like the poor wretches in the ship's engine-room."

"Indians?"

"I wish they were. No, Mexicans. Rickard couldn't get enough Indians, and Mexicans can't stand this."

Beyond them stretched the river of yellow waters, dividing like the letter Y, the east branch the dry bed of the Colorado. From a distance they could see the great arm of the dredge drop into the mud of the new channel, by which the water was to be diverted through the Hardin gate. Innes watched the bucket rise, dripping with soft silt, saw the elbow crook as the arm swung slowly toward the bank.

"That's where you danced last night," he observed.

"I thought I was on a cruiser!"

"A cruiser's also a battle-ship!"

A hot sweet smell rose from the bank. She thought her sudden sway of faintness was from the sun.

"It's too much for you. That's the arrow-weed."

"I've smelt arrow-weed before. This is different."

"Not in quantity before, Miss Hardin. I shouldn't have brought you here. We will go back."

"Is this what they are cutting?"

"They're the stokers."

"I don't see them." Her eyes questioned the mat of undergrowth.

"You can't."

She could not detect a human figure moving in the

clot of branches. Then she caught the gleam of a machete. A face peered from an opening, blackened and strangling. Her cry sounded like pain.

"Oh, did you see him?" Dripping with sweat, gasping, it made a horrid sight.

"It's not all play!" he observed.

"Look what he is doing, no, not that one." From the tangle came running a dripping human. He tossed his hands, staring up at the burning bowl of a sky. No help there! The sun-baked sands, glittering like brass, gave no escape. He raised his hands, and they could see him take the poise of diver; like a projectile he shot into the pool of living green beneath.

"He thinks it's water," whispered Innes.

"*He's* got it," cried Estrada, caught with excitement. "It's a madness. One man died yesterday."

"Died!"

"Why, no white man, for they're white, those Mexican, can stand that hole. It's an inferno. There have been two deaths already. If another goes, they'll walk out. I've told Rickard; he knows. They're superstitious as niggers—the third death—they're boiling with discontent already. Then where'll we be, where'll the gate be?" The graceful indolence of the Cardenas was gone; he was all Estrada now, vehement and impassioned.

"He may die?"

"I shouldn't have brought you here!"

He tried to get her away. Her eyes would not leave that pool of living green, the hole that the poor wretch had thought was cooling waters. The smell of cut arrow-weed, sickly sweet, smote against her nostrils. Then she saw a movement in the undergrowth. A group of men were pulling him out—she saw his face, distorted, livid. His lips were chattering; he screamed like a raucous ape.

"Did you see him?" she breathed.

"I saw *them*," his answer was grim. He watched them, their composite expression foreboding, as they bore to camp the struggling madman.

"Is he really mad? Do they get over it?"

"They get over it!" He did not tell her how! To divert her, he told her that these were the men for whom Porter had been scouring Zacatecas.

"Mexicans don't take kindly to a contract when it means arrow-weed. Rickard's Indians haven't come yet, the men Forestier's promised; he's the Indian agent. The hoboes are still wandering in, but not in the numbers we expected. Rickard was right. You can't count on that sort of labor."

Rickard was right? She glanced sharply at the beautiful face of her companion. Then who was wrong? She was growing sensitive, ready for a slight to hit her brother.

"If they go, I wouldn't swap places with Rickard." The Mexican was moody.

For the first time, she forgot to notice the incongruity of his speech. His years at an American college had given him a vocabulary which belied his nationality. She was resenting his concern. Every one thinking of Rickard! What responsibility was his? He was here to direct the work, but if it failed, was the stigma not all her brother's? She flamed into speech.

"It's a snap for him, for Mr. Rickard," she cried. "All the pioneering, the breaking of earth has been *done!*

Your father, Mr. Estrada, and my brother paved the way for him. With the entire equipment of a great organization like the O. P. behind him—money, men, everything, it isn't fair. He'll walk in and win, and the world will think he did it."

"You wouldn't like it to fail, would you? And it's not so easy as you think, Miss Hardin." He was carefully picking his way. "He's told he has a free hand, but he hasn't. The work's stopped up there at Laguna; there's no use going on with that until we make good. If we can't control the river here, their quicksand works go, but you know that?"

She nodded. Tom had told her all that.

"Those men are swarming in here like bees to honey. They've been told to help, and then they are curious. They have all got ideas of their own. And they're talking and writing to the higher-ups. It all gets back to Rickard, sooner or later."

"He doesn't have to please them," murmured the girl.

"Not directly. But the O. P. didn't go into this forever! The road was the most deeply interested corporation with power. Marshall got Faraday to promise to put up the money. He promised to make it good with his own money if he couldn't stop the river. I heard this on the inside! But he wanted it stopped his way. He wanted his own men in, men who would take his orders—" he pulled himself away from thin ice. "The O. P. did not expect to get in as they have. Now, they can't get out! The work's got to please the Service men, or it won't be recommended to the government. That's what's tying Rickard up—that, and other things."

It sounded new to her.

"And some of these fellows are yelling so, you can hear them in Washington." She stole an amused look at him. How American he was!

They were back at the encampment. Slowly, they walked across the open space, which was glittering in the sun. Innes was acknowledging, silently, a headache. The trip, she said to herself, had depressed her.

When they reached the Hardin tents, she felt obliged to offer hospitality. "Won't you come in, Mr. Estrada? My sister would love to make a cup of tea for you." She knew her invitation lacked cordiality. Her temples were bursting. "It's an eye headache," she told herself. "I should have had my glasses."

She tried to forget it as she thanked him for "her trip into Mexico," and renewed her invitation to tea.

He said he had to go, but he lingered. He said good-by, and stayed. His look held hers for that instant, the look she could never fathom. Then he turned away. She watched him out of sight.

At table, that evening, her family heard with surprise Gerty's announcement that they were to eat in the messtent with the men. It was too hot to cook any longer; this had been one of the hottest days in the year.

"Let me cook!" urged Innes. "It's only fair. And I want to do something to justify my being here." Her words recurred to Gerty later.

"Sometimes the autumn heat is the worst. Besides, it is all arranged. We begin to-morrow. You heard too, then, what Mr. Rickard said about not wanting women in camp?"

"No, I did not! But to be here without doing anything, just being one more mouth to feed, and head to cover—I'd feel more comfortable," she added.

"He gave it out in the towns that he did not want men's wives or families following them to the Heading. He made an exception for Mrs. Parrish—she was too timid to leave, and Mrs. Dowker, and, of course, it was different with me."

Innes felt uncomfortable.

"It's all right being with Tom," she began.

"Why is it all right? Who am I?" He lifted his eyes from his plate. It came home to Innes that it was not his camp any longer. She thought, then, that she would go back to Los Angeles the next week.

She expected to hear a protest to the new arrangement from Tom. She was to see a new development—sullen resignation. If he would accept it, she must not argue. Both sister and brother knew why it was too warm to cook any longer. Gerty found them both dull.

"That poor Mexican." She remembered Estrada's concern. "The one who went mad? Have you heard how he was?"

"Dead. The peons are all stampeding."

"Who's stampeding?" Gerty came back from a deep reverie. Lavender, it had just been decided, was to be the color of the next frock. It was cool and not too positive. She must remember to send out for samples that day. She could not recall having heard Rickard express himself about colors. She wondered if he had preferences or aversions to shades. He must like green; she remembered he had admired that mandarin skirt. "And if the lavender fades, I can rinse it in purple ink."

Innes was telling Tom of the tragedy of the afternoon.

"Oh, don't," cried Gerty, pushing away her plate. "I can't hear of such things." They saw that her pretty eyes were full of tears. "You know I can't."

CHAPTER XXVI

THE WHITE OLEANDER

MRS. Hardin's descent on the office that afternoon was successful, but not satisfactory. She had found the manager brief to curtness. She was given no excuse to linger. She traced Rickard's manner to the presence of MacLean, and snatched at her cue. She, too, could be businesslike and brief. Her errand was of business; her manner should recommend her!

Rickard had seen her making straight toward the ramada. It was not the first time; her efforts to line her nest had involved them all and often. But to-day, he was in a bad humor.

"For the lord's sake," he groaned to MacLean as she approached. "More shelves! I wonder if she thinks the carpenters have nothing to do but rig up her kitchen for her?"

MacLean's grin covered relief. He had never heard Rickard express himself on the subject before. Could he believe, he speculated, that her frequent appeals for assistance were serious? "The dead-set Hardin's wife was making at Casey," was the choice gossip and speculation of the young engineers on the *Delta*.

MacLean had a bet up on the outcome. He grinned more securely.

"I am not going to spare any more carpenters," growled

THE WHITE OLEANDER

Rickard. It was an inauspicious day for Mrs. Hardin's visit. Things had gone wrong. Vexations were piling up. A tilt with Hardin that morning, a telegram from Marshall; he was feeling sore. Porter's men had marched out, carrying their dead. Desperately they needed labor. Wooster had just reported, venomously, it appeared to Rickard's spleen, increasing drunkenness among the Indians.

Gerty's ruffles swept in. Her dress, the blue mull with the lace medallions, accented the hue of her eyes, and looked deliciously cool that glaring desert day. Her parasol, of pongee, was lined with the same baby hue. Her dainty fairness and childish affability should have made an oasis in that strenuous day, but Rickard's disintegration of temper was too complete. He rose stiffly to meet her, and his manner demanded her errand.

She told it to him, plaintively. It was getting so hot! Her kitchen was a veritable Turkish bath these days. At noon, it was terrific. Her eyes were appealing, infantile.

"It's not shelves." MacLean's grin sobered.

Would it be too much to ask, would Mr. Rickard mind in the least, he must be perfectly frank and tell her if they would be in the way at all, but while this hot spell lasted, could they, the three of them, eat in the mess-tent with the men?

"Surely!" Rickard met it heartily. She would find it rough, but if she could stand it, yes, he thought it a good idea. His eagerness suggested relief to one listener. The Hardins' meals had been a severe drain on that office. The new arrangement offered a cessation of petty problems.

Her point so easily gained, she knew she must go. She

acknowledged interrupting business, but there was one thing more. Would Mr. Rickard tell her how to trace a lost bundle? If she were at home, of course, she would not have to ask any one, but here, so far away from express offices! A package had been sent to her from Chicago, it must be months ago. It reached the towns shortly after she left. She had written casually there to forward it; it had not yet come. She really did not know how to begin.

"Make a note of that, MacLean," Rickard volunteered. He was still standing. "He'll send a tracer out after it, Mrs. Hardin."

And then there was nothing for her to do but go. Her retreat was graceful, without haste, dignified. There was a womanly suggestion of business decorum. She smiled a farewell at MacLean, who was watching the approach of Innes Hardin and Estrada. The neglected smile passed on to Rickard, accented. He did not see the aborted entrance of Hardin's sister and the young Mexican. He was itching to be at his work.

He let out a growl when Mrs. Hardin was out of ear-shot.

"What in thunder did she want all those shelves for? And cupboards and a cooling closet? Every week since she came, she had to have a carpenter, and I couldn't refuse; you know what they'd think, that I was trying to show my power. Shucks! What in Halifax do women come to a place like this for? There's Hardin—brings in two women to cook for him, and now, please may they all eat with the men?"

His secretary subdued a chuckle. He was visualizing a procession of boxes of choice Havanas—from Bodefeldt, Hamlin and the rest of the gang. He need not buy a smoke for a year.

"Must think this is a summer resort!"

Rickard threw himself back in his chair. "Take this letter, MacLean. To Marshall." Then his worry diverted him. "Who in thunder is selling liquor to my Indians?"

"Just that way?" quizzed MacLean.

"Hold on; that letter can wait. You get the horses up, MacLean, and we'll ride down to Maldonado's. He'll have to get busy, and clear up this thing, or I'll know why. I'll threaten to report him for laziness. It's his place to stop this liquor business, not mine."

A few hours later, they were approaching the adobe walls of Maldonado. They found the gate locked. A woman, whose beauty had faded into a tragic whisper, a ghastly twilight of suggestion, came to their knock, and unbarred the gate for the white strangers. She left them by the white oleander whose trunk was like that of a tree. MacLean sniffed like a young terrier. "What's the matter with the place?"

Mystery hung over the enclosure like a pall. Their voices fell inevitably to a whisper. Once, it had been a garden; now, only the oleander defied the desert. Dry ditches told the story of decadence. Once, the river had wandered by, a stone's throw away. Maldonado had turned some of its flow into his adobe court. But the river channel was dry, and a dead vine clung to the house walls; fell, shrinking in the breeze, from the roof.

The woman came out to say that Maldonado would follow in *"un momento."* To Rickard she looked like the dried vine quivering from the wind. She asked the señors would they sit? The house was not fit; she was cleaning.

Maldonado, his face creased from his nap, came out, but not in *"un momento."* He had been busy—"some wretched fellows!" Rickard knew the man was lying. He had been asleep. The woman had interrupted his siesta. His eyes were almost lost; he blinked; he said it was the sun. The day was so hot. *Dios mio,* why did she stand there and not take pity on the señors, dying of thirst as they must be. A glass of water. It was his shame that he might not offer them wine—but he was a poor man—with wife and children. His eyes shifted from Rickard to MacLean.

The woman quivered away from the group. She disappeared in the house.

"Glasses," called Maldonado after her.

Her *"Si"* sounded like a hiss.

Rickard told his errand. Maldonado sputtered and swore. By the mother of Mary the Virgin, that thing would be stopped. It would be looked into, the rascal would be caught. He pulled back his cotton coat, mussed with sleep as was his face. He showed to the señors, with pride, his badge. He was a rurale; he was there to uphold the law. If the señors would but follow him, they would see that he did not sleep at his post. He had caught some of those drunken Indians on the road. He had brought them here.

They followed him around the house, through the wrecked garden. Maldonado shrugged at the stumps as they passed, ruins that had once been roses. MacLean felt his mouth pucker with repulsion as he watched the figure in striped cotton, the eyes lost in their sleepy folds of flesh, the cruel evil mouth. He was drawing from the pocket of his cotton pantaloons a bunch of iron keys, tied with a dirty string. They were approaching a shed, a cattle shed, it appeared to the guests. Maldonado unlocked a gate of bars.

"Would the señors look in there?"

On a bed of old straw, three inert figures sprawled; theirs complete oblivion.

Maldonado, kicked one of the figures with his feet. "Drunken swine." He locked the door with majesty. He had proved his services, his ruraleship.

"But where do they get it?" demanded Rickard, turning back into the sunshine.

"Certainly," the man evaded, "there is an 'oasis' somewhere. Perhaps, the señor remembers, I told him before, back in the sand-hills, 'somewhere.'"

"Why don't you find it?"

Maldonado was going to find it, surely! The señor must have patience. His hands were so full. He remembered the bunch of iron keys that he dropped in his pocket. Every action of the man was surreptitious, Rickard was noting. Maldonado would stand watching! "I'm doing my duty, señor."

"If you are so busy, Señor Maldonado," suggested Rickard, "I can help you. I'll send down a few men to help search. How many would you like?"

He expected a minute's hesitation, but there was none. Oh, it was not necessary. Later, maybe, he would call on señor but it chanced that next week, or the next, a squad of rurales was to be there for that very purpose sent for by Maldonado. Oh, he was awake to his duty! The señor would be satisfied. There would be no more drunken Indians.

"Slick," thought Rickard.

The woman was waiting by the oleander with glasses. She filled them from an olla hanging in the shade of the tree. It was cold as if iced.

Rickard saw her shrink every time she had to pass Maldonado. Obviously, the fellow was a brute. She was aware of his displeasure. She winced at a word from him.

Both men were glad to go. Rickard left a piece of silver in the woman's hand. He hoped Maldonado had not observed him.

They were riding away when a cry broke the stillness of the air. "Hark, what was that?" MacLean turned a shocked face toward Rickard. "A woman?"

It was anguished, strangled almost at birth. The men waited, but there was silence in the patio.

"He got that money all right," speculated Rickard. "Struck her!"

"Or kicked her. That fellow is a brute."

"Aren't you going back?"

"Going back? What would we get for our pains? Make it all the worse for the woman. You noticed he called her his *wife?* The rurales are not supposed to marry. It's their unwritten law. But if she is, do you know what that means? She's his goods, his chattel; his horse, his ox, his anything. You're not in the states. We can't do anything."

There is perhaps no more absorbing topic than "wife" to the man who has not yet acquired one. Rickard and MacLean let an unrecorded silence fall between them. The word had sent them both traveling down secret trails. MacLean was thinking of the girl he intended to marry, when he was grown, of a girl with yellow eyes; Rickard of a mistake he had once nearly made. His wife, if ever he had one, must be steadier than that; she must not carry her sex like a gay flag to the breeze. His instinct of flight, distaste had justified itself at camp. She was a light little woman. He was beginning to feel a little sorry for Hardin!

"I'll race you into camp, MacLean!"

Their horses, released, sprang toward the Heading.

CHAPTER XXVII

A WHITE WOMAN AND A BROWN

FOR a few weeks, Mrs. Hardin found the mess-tent diverting. Before the *Delta* had expanded the capacity of the camp, her soft nook had been overtaxed, her hospitality strained. The men of the Reclamation Service, thrown into temporary inactivity, were eager to accept the opportunity created for another. Failing that other, her zeal had flagged. Events were moving quickly at the break; Rickard was absorbed. Mrs. Hardin told herself that it was the heat she wished to escape; not to her own ear did she whisper that she was following Rickard, nor that the percolator and chafing-dish, her shelves and toy kitchen were a wasted effort. As inevitably as a diamond finds a setting, so did Gerty Hardin. She would return to it later, gathering luster from its suggestion of womanliness. Sometime, the pretty play would be resumed. All this subconsciously, for she hung a veil between her processes. She kept on good terms with herself by ignoring self-confidences. She would have called morbidness the self-analysis of those who dig deep into their psychology for roots of motives, who question each trailing vine.

Rickard, the discovery unfolded slowly, took his meals irregularly. His breakfast was gulped down before the women appeared; his dinners where he found them.

"No wonder!" reflected Gerty Hardin. "Ling's cooking is so bad." Discontentedly, she pictured Rickard as finding solace in the Hamlin kitchen; reveling in Mrs. Silent's chickens and eggs. The camp butter was shocking. She found Ling's large quantities unpalatable.

There came a butterless epoch; a horrid gap. Ling did not *manage* right. Butterless toast and broiled chicory! Small wonder the manager foraged for his meals. Somehow, the thought of Rickard living as did Hardin in times of stress, as the bird of the air, did not occur to the woman who thought of Rickard as different, a gentleman who required luxury. She had created a man from her own imaginings; she was evolving a woman to meet the approbation of her creation.

A dinner of pale oily beans, followed by a dessert of prunes swimming in a pallid sirup, gave her a morning of reflection. The Hamlin kitchen was giving her uneasiness. Her own abilities, unoccupied, were ironic. She worked out a mission as she lay across her bed that hot afternoon.

"To justify my being here." A phrase of Innes recurred to her; it became now her own.

Her duty became so clear that she could no longer lie still. Immediately, she must retrieve her weeks of idleness; what must Rickard think of her? In spite of the scorching space that lay between her tent and the ramada, of the sun beating down like burning hail on the glittering sand, she must dress and seek out Rickard.

She buttoned herself thoughtfully into a frock of pale colored muslin, cream slipping toward canary. White was too glaring on a red-hot day like this. Pink was too hot, blue too definite. Pity the lavender dress was still a fabric of dreams! A parasol of pastel green, and she looked like a sprig of fragrant mignonette. The exertion of dressing brought the perspiration to her face. It had to be carefully dusted with powder. Strange, how she used to think the summers of the desert insupportable. After a torrid season of New York in her toy apartment, that humid sticky heat, that shut-oven of smells, this was to be borne. Already, the desert was improving; for she herself had not changed, of course.

It was the ice! She decided that any place could be endured once ice is procurable. Even bad butter is disguised when frozen into bricks. Her thoughts rounded the circle, brought her back to her grievances. Ling certainly needed help.

She found the open space of the trapezium swarming with strange dark faces. So silent their coming, she had not heard the arrival of the tribes. Over by Ling's coveted mesquits gathered an increasing group of bucks with their pinto ponies which had carried them across a country of glaring distances. She isolated the Cocopahs, stately as bronze statues, their long hair streaming, or wound, mud-caked under brilliant head-cloths. Foregathering with them were men of other tribes; these must be the Yumas and Deguinos, the men needed on the river. Tom had told her that the long-haired tribes were famous for their water-craft. These were the men who were to work on the rafts, weave the great mattresses. A squad of short-haired Pimas with their squaws and babies and their gaudy bundles, gaped at the fair-haired woman as she passed. They were dazed and dizzy from their first long railroad ride. The central space was filling up with Pimas and Maricopas, Papagoes, too; she knew them collectively by their short hair. These were the brush-cutters to replace the stampeding peons. This, then, meant the beginning of real activity. Tom would at last be satisfied. He would no longer sulk and rage alternately at the hold-up of the work.

It began to look dramatic to her. She picked her way through the stolid groups, the children and squaws staring at her finery, at the queer color of her hair. The value of the enterprise pricked at her consciousness. And she was going to help it; in her own way, but that was the womanly way! She wished that she had thought of it before.

Her bright darting glance discovered MacLean under one of Ling's mesquits. He was poring over some of his own hieroglyphs in his stenographic pad. One of her bright detached smiles reached him. He followed her direction, his mouth puckering.

Before she reached the ramada, she saw that another woman was there. She caught an impassioned gesture. Her only surmise rested on Innes. The visitor, following Rickard's eyes, turned. Gerty saw that she was dark; she looked the half-breed. The brown woman drew back as the white woman entered. Gerty smiled an airy reassurance. She herself would wait. She did not want to be hurried. She told Rickard that she had plenty of time.

"There is something you want to tell me?" Rickard's patience was courteous but firm. He would hear her errand first. Gerty, remembering MacLean's banishment to the mesquits, the imploring attitude of the stranger, determined that she would not be sent away.

"Will you excuse me, señora? It will be only a minute."

She was to tell her errand, and briefly! Gerty swept past the intruder.

"Sit down, Mrs. Hardin?"

Resenting the inflection, she said she would stand. Her voice was a little hard, her eyes were veiled, as she told her mission. Her usual fluency dragged; she felt a lack of sympathy. She saw Rickard look twice toward the Mexican; she knew she was not holding his attention.

Biting her lip, she acknowledged that Ling was doing the best he could, at least the best he knew how, but of course, he had his limitations. He needed an assistant; his hands were over-full. She remembered the phrase in time to hurl it to its place; she wanted to justify her presence in camp. In short, she proposed a commissary department, herself in charge.

Rickard had a weak moment. Outside, the place was teeming with Indians to be enrolled and placed in camp. Forestier, the Indian Outing Agent, who had come in on the train with three of the tribes, was waiting in the neighboring tent. Rickard wanted some new work begun to-morrow; there were but a few hours left of this day. There were letters, despatches to be got off.

"I'd like to feel I was of some use," urged Gerty again, this time prettily, taking him back into her friendship again. "My heart is bound up in this undertaking; if I'm allowed to stay, I'd like to help along. This is the only way I can, the woman's way." It was a proud humility. Did not Rickard think that the best way, the only way? She knew he would think so, indeed!

"Aren't you taking a good deal on yourself, Mrs. Hardin?"

Then she forgave his hesitation quite, as it was of her he was thinking. "Not if it *helps*." Her voice was low and soft, as if this were a secret between them.

"It's not so easy as you think." He could see Forestier leave his tent, glance toward the ramada. Then he saw him join MacLean by the mesquits. This was no time to argue a petty question. It would do no harm to try. "Why, of course, anything you want, Mrs. Hardin." And, remembering her former position, he added: "The camp's yours as much as mine."

A glad smile rewarded him. She went out, reluctantly. She knew the ways of those half-breeds! She could understand a little Spanish, so she made her step drag. The silence behind her was disquieting. The brown woman with the wreck of beauty in her tragic eyes was staring after her; she did not see Rickard's gesture.

There was a new significance in MacLean's absence from the ramada. What could that woman have to say that MacLean must not hear? She did not see the mewling babes, half naked, who gaped at her as she passed the squaws. The stolid groups parted for her, and she moved through, oblivious to their color and charm, to the historic import of it all. For the first time, the weak tenure on her old lover came to her. Not a sign had he yet given of their understanding, of the piquant situation. Themselves, old sweethearts, thrown together in this wilderness. What had she built her hopes on? A word here, a translated phrase, or magnified glance. She would not harbor the new worry. Why, it would be all right. She used Tom's phrase, the one she hated, in solemn unconsciousness. Life had evidently planned that from the first. Fate insisted on repairing her mad mistake.

At her tent, letters were waiting to be written; letters to her grocer in Los Angeles, one to Coulter, in Calexico.

She was going to begin her régime by serving good butter—iced butter. No more oily horror melting on a warm plate. She remembered a new brand of olives put up in tins; Rickard, she remembered, loved ripe olives. She would show them all what a woman with executive ability could do.

CHAPTER XXVIII

BETRAYAL

"SIT down, señora. Don't be frightened. We won't let him hurt you." Rickard vulgarized his Castilian to the reach of her rude dialect.

Her work-sharpened fingers moved restlessly under her reboso. She pulled it together as though the day were not scorching. Her eyes questioned his sympathy. A flash of desperate courage had left her weak and tremulous. She stood by the long pine table looking hopelessly down on the señor whose eyes had twice looked kindly at her.

"Sit down," he repeated, and motioned to a chair.

For long years her misery had been silent; her tongue could not tell her story. She shook her head. "Take your time, take your time," counseled the manager. He feared a burst of hysteria.

There was a sound of feet outside the ramada. The Indians, passing and repassing, brought a gleam of anger to her eyes. She recalled her wrongs; they lashed her into fury. Familiar as was Rickard with the peons' speech in their own country, he could not keep up with her history. Lurid words ran past his ears. Out of the jumble of abuse, of shame and misery, he caught a new note.

"You say Maldonado, *himself*, sells liquor to the Indians?"

"Ssh, señor!" Some one might hear him! She looked over a terrified shoulder. Maldonado had told her he would kill her if she ever told—it came to her, as a shock, what she was doing, what she had done. It meant ruin for them all—for the muchachos. That had slipped out, the selling of the liquor. She could have told her story without that; she wanted to deny it. Relentlessly Rickard made her repeat it, acknowledge the truth.

"Ssh, señor, it has been so for many years, since I went there, oh, years ago. No one knows, who would suspect a rurale, a rurale who does his duty? He would kill me—"

"Stop shaking. No one is listening." Rickard forced a tone of brutality. The poor wretch, he suspected, had been trained by the whip; he threatened to send for Maldonado.

"No, I will tell you, will tell you everything, señor. It is an easy trick, señor. No one would take the word of an Indian against Maldonado, a rurale. And the drink makes the men crazy, or stupid. Afterward, he does not remember where he got the tequila. Maldonado whips him, the Indian does not know it is the same hand, and when he is turned loose, he would kiss his feet— Or perhaps, Maldonado sends him to Ensenada—who believes him when he swears the rurale who arrested him made him drunk, señor? Twice, three times, Maldonado's life was in danger—but the law made quick work of an Indian who tried to kill a rurale. He would kill me, señor—would Maldonado."

"Go on," drove Rickard.

Her bony fingers worked restlessly. She was shaking with terror.

"Is it known that he keeps liquors there?" Rickard saw he would have to help her.

"Oh, no, señor. Not even the Indians. They come, by accident. If they have no money, they are sent on. If they have—" Her curving, black-shrouded shoulders shrugged. "The walls are thick. They leave their money and their wits behind them. Sometimes, they wake a mile down the river, under the willows. They have come back to tell their wrongs to their friend, Maldonado, who promises to help them, to find the thief who has wrung those cotton pockets. It would make you laugh, señor, but if he finds it out, he will kill me."

"What makes you tell me, now?" Rickard hunted for the ulcer. He knew there was a personal wrong. "What has Maldonado been doing to you? Has he left you?"

The veil of fear was torn from her eyes. The trembling woman was gone, a vengeful wildcat in her place. "Left me, Maldonado? Left his home, where he traps the Indian with one coin in his pockets? No, señor. He brought her to our home, *there,* Lupe, the wife of Felipe, the Deguino. Felipe had found a wife in Nogales, had brought her down to the river, a mile below the oleander. She found the desert dull; she had the city's foolishness in her head. Felipe was gone a good deal. Maldonado sent him to Ensenada with some poor wretches. Maldonado was never at home then; I told him not to fool with Felipe; the Indian was dangerous; he had hot blood. Maldonado struck me—he kicked me—he said I was jealous—and hit me again." Rickard saw jealousy in the unveiled eyes of hate. She pressed her hand to her breast. Her movement betrayed pain;

whether a bruise, or a deeper hurt to the heart of her he could not guess.

She told the climax simply, her hand pressed over her bosom. "Maldonado told me to get a big meal—*tortillas* and *enchilades,* metates: I told him that it was for Felipe; I could see a black plot in his eyes. He laughed at me; when I said I would not cook for that treachery, he cursed me, he kicked me again." She threw off the reboso, dragging her dress loose. "Don't," frowned Rickard. He had seen a welt across her shoulder—a screaming line of pain.

She wound the reboso around the dishonored shoulder. "I cooked his tortillas, his dinner! There was a big meal. There was a lot of liquor—Felipe was drunk; the tequila made him mad, quite mad. He seemed to know something was wrong; he fought as Maldonado dragged him to the cell, the señor remembers the cell? The next day, Maldonado sent for two rurales, Felipe drank the pitchers of wine he put through the bars, but there was no liquor in sight when the rurales came! They started the next day for Ensenada, taking Felipe; that day, Maldonado brought Lupe home. I said she could not stay and he laughed in my face, señor. He put me outside the walls. He thought I would beg to be let in the next morning, come sneaking in like a dog that has been beaten, wash the faces of the muchachos, grind the corn for the metates, but I could stand it no longer. I beat that gate until my fingers bled. I remembered the kind face of the señor, and then I came here. You will help me, señor?"

"What is it you want me to do?" But he knew what she wanted him to do!

"Send that woman away. Make him send Lupe away.

Let me stay here until he is over his anger. He is not bad, Maldonado, when he is not angry. Make him set Felipe free; *he* will keep that Lupe from my house, from the children."

Rickard shook his head. "I shall have to look into this thing. If this is true, it's prison for your husband. You won't have to fear Lupe."

"Prison, señor? For Maldonado? You will never get him. He will swear it is not so. He will kill me; he will know that I have told. They will not believe my word against his."

She was verging toward a spasm of terror. To quiet her, Rickard said that they would have other proof. And her husband would have no more power to hurt her; Maldonado's crimes would protect her from him.

He could see the struggle in her soul; he knew she wanted to say she had been lying to him. It was not that sort of revenge she wanted; she wanted her husband. She wanted him to help her get her husband back. The revenge sought to trap Lupe—

"When he gets out, he will kill me, señor."

"Ah, but that will be a long time, señora! And you will have protection. You will get a divorce— He is your husband, señora? You are married to him?"

She screamed at him. MacLean looked up from his note-book. "A divorce?" She was approaching hysteria. "*Si,* señor, he is my husband. We were married in a church. Never would I get a divorce from my husband. No, not Lucrezia Maldonado."

Rickard back-stepped, to calm her. It would be all right, anyway. She would be protected. He would see that Maldonado did not harm her. He would look out for her and the children, and she might stay here, in camp, until the thing was settled. In the meantime, she must rest—

He wanted to get rid of her. Maldonado and his villainy must wait. The Indians were waiting to be registered. They were to be sent to their camp, tribe by tribe. Forestier was waiting for him. MacLean was waiting—

"You will let me work for you, señor?"

"There's always work. I won't have to send my washing to Yuma, and I haven't had a button sewed on for months—nor has MacLean, nor Jenks—you can darn their socks, and help Ling with the beds; we can keep you busy, señora. And you can go back to the children pretty soon."

The terror was seizing her again. Before she could begin her pleading, he called to MacLean.

"Ask Ling to find a tent for Señora Maldonado. Tell him to give her a good meal."

Her eyes appealed to Rickard over her shoulder. Her body wavered with fatigue. Her eyes were cavernous, with dark radiating shadows.

"How did you get here?"

"I walked, señor."

"Walked! You must be dead. Get to bed. You'll be all right in the morning." A twenty-mile walk to escape the cruelty of the brute whom she would not divorce because of a few priest-mumbled words! Not hers the sacrament of love, of vows mutually kept, yet he knew that he could not depend on her testimony to convict that scoundrel down the river. One glance from his eye, and she would be a shivering lump of fear again.

He must trap the rogue. Some Indian, that was the plan. He would ask Coronel. Coronel, himself, could not play the game; Maldonado would not sell liquor to the white man's friend. He was too wily for that. But some buck—Coronel would make the choice. An Indian who would go to the adobe, pretend intoxication; be clear-headed enough to betray him. That infernal place must be closed. The woman had come in the nick of time. Those tribes were to be guarded as restless children—

He went out to meet Forestier.

CHAPTER XXIX

RICKARD MAKES A NEW ENEMY AND A NEW FRIEND

THE coming of the Indians gave the impetus the work had lacked. Under Jenks, of the railroad company, a large force was put on the river; these, the weavers of the brush mattresses that were to line the river-bed. On the banks were the brush-cutters; tons of willows were to be cut to weave into the forty miles of woven wire cable waiting for the cross-strands. Day by day, the piles of willow branches grew higher, the brush-cutters working ahead of the mattress workers in the stream. In the dense undergrowth, the stolid Indians, Pimas and Maricopas and Papagoes, struggled with the fierce thorn of the mesquit and the over-powering smell of the arrow-weed. As tough as the hickory handles they wielded, they fought a clearing through dense thickets, in the intense tropic heat.

It was a glittering day. A copper sun rode the sky; the desert sand burned through the shoe leather. Down stream, the Brobdingnagian arm of the dredge fell into the mud of the by-pass, dropping its slimy burden on the far bank. Twenty-four hours of sun, and the mud bank would resemble a pile of rocks that wind and sun again would disintegrate into a silt. Down the long stretch of levee, the "skinners" drove their mules and scrapers; two pile-drivers were setting in the treacherous

A NEW ENEMY AND A NEW FRIEND

stream the piles which were to anchor the steel-cabled mattresses to the river-bed. It was a well-organized, active scene. Rickard, in his office, dictating letters and telegrams to MacLean, Jr., felt his first satisfaction. Things were beginning to show the result of months of planning. Cars were rushing in from north and east; every quarry between Los Angeles and Tucson requisitioned for their undertaking.

A shadow fell on the pine desk. Ling, in blue ticking shirt and white butcher apron, waited for the "boss" to look up. He stood wiping the perspiration from his head, hairless except for the long silk-tapered queue.

"Well, Ling?"

"I go tamale." His voice was soft as silk. "I no stay."

It was a thunderclap. There was no one to replace Ling, who was drawing down the salary of a private secretary.

"You sick?" demanded Rickard. Lose Ling? It would be more demoralizing to the camp than to lose an engineer.

"Ling no sick."

"Maybe you want more money?"

"Plenty get money." The yellow lean fingers spread wide apart. "Money all lite. Bossee all lite. No likee woman. Woman she stay, Ling go."

"Mrs. Hardin!" Rickard woke up.

"She all time makee trouble. She talkee butter—butter, butter. All time. She clazy. She think woman vellee fine cook. She show Ling cookee plunes. Teachee Ling cookee plunes! I no stay that woman." Unutterable finality in the leathern face. Rickard and MacLean, Jr., exchanged glances which deepened from concern into perplexity. They could not afford to lose Ling. And offend Mrs. Hardin, the camp already Hardinesque?

Rickard grew placating. "Now, see here, Ling, you no understand. Mrs. Hardin a nice lady; nice home, she like things first-class. You understand things first-class?"

Sourly, Ling vouchsafed that he, too, understood things first-class. "She say bad plunes. Too much water. She bossee me all time. Mr. Lickard likee lady, keep lady, no keep Ling."

Rickard looked at his watch. He wanted to be off. He had been promising himself an afternoon for three weeks, since the day the tribes came in. He must start things moving at Maldonado's. Coronel, who had come in from Yuma yesterday, had told him of an Indian who would do the trick for him, who could withstand liquor, and pretend to reel with it. Already, he had lost some of his Indians. They might wander back; the chances were good that they had been "sent up." He needed every Indian. But more he needed Ling. He spent another half-hour in wheedling. They met at the starting place. "Ling go tamale."

"Oh, lord," groaned the manager, capitulating. "All right, Ling. I'll speak to Mrs. Hardin to-morrow."

Even that would not do. The two men made out that Mrs. Hardin was to invade his quarters that evening and teach the outraged Chinese how to cook prunes. That insult had caused the rebellion. "She come, I go." It was a statement, not a threat. Rickard succumbed.

"All right, Ling. I'll stop it." With the dignity of an oriental prince, Ling pattered out of the tent. Rickard was puckering his lips at his secretary. "I'd rather take castor oil."

A NEW ENEMY AND A NEW FRIEND 281

"Take time!" laughed MacLean, Jr.

"I can't do that," Rickard's reply was rueful. "I can't take chances with Ling. More Hardin trouble, or my name's not Casey. We'll quit for to-day, Junior. If I'm to head her off, I'll have to be moving some."

A half-hour later, MacLean saw his chief leave his tent. He was in fresh linens; and MacLean noticed that he had a pin in his tie.

"I wouldn't swap places with him this minute! She'll be as mad as a wet hen!"

Heartily, Rickard, too, was disliking his errand. But there was no shirking it. Ling must be appeased. "And, already, they have enough reason to dislike me. And here comes this to make matters worse!

"It's not their fault, it's Hardin who's inflaming them with his wrongs. Lord, what does the man want? Here was his precious scheme going to pot for lack of funds, and bad management, and he goes whining to Marshall for help, and now he's sore because he got what he asked. He wants to be the high-muck-a-muck; he pretends it's the valley salvation. If it were that, he'd be whistling, instead of kicking."

Mrs. Hardin, from her bed by her screen window, saw him coming. She slipped into a semi-negligee of alternate rows of lace and swiss constructed for such possible emergencies. She did not make the mistake of smoothing her hair; her instinct told her that the fluffy disorder bore out the use of the negligee. She was sewing, in her ramada, when Rickard's knock sounded on the screen door.

Despite his protests, she started water boiling in her chafing-dish. He had not time for tea, he declared, but she insisted on making this call of a social nature. She opened a box of sugar wafers, her zeal that of a child with a toy kitchen; she was playing doll's house.

Rickard made several openings for his errand, but her wits sped like a gopher from his labored digging. He suggested that she was working too hard.

"Oh, I love it," she declared. "It justifies my being here. I know you must think women a nuisance here at camp, Mr. Rickard. I like to do my little best. And Ling needed help. We get along pretty well. He is crude, of course. What could you expect? I've taken the liberty of sending out for some extra things. And that reminds me, has my bundle been heard from? Isn't that the most mysterious thing? It left Chicago, why, it must be months ago."

Rickard said that the missing bundle had been last heard from in Tepic; by some stupid mistake, it had got into the hands of the Mexican officials, "who were playing ball with it!"

"The mistake came in having it sent here; this is Mexico; everything gets balled up the instant it crosses the line. If you'd had it sent to Yuma now—but you were speaking of orders, camp orders—"

"I'm not going to trouble you with that," cried Gerty, filling up his cup with an aromatic blend of tea she had sent for to Los Angeles. So far, it had been wasted on the men of the Service, boys, most of them. She felt more at home with Rickard than ever before. The quizzical, amused glance of appraisement was gone, replaced by an earnestness she misread. She met his mood with womanly dignity; she tutored her coquetries, withheld her archness. She remembered a day when her flirtations had deflected her whole life; she no longer said "ruined." One battle lost? "Time to fight another!" She placed a wafer or two on his protesting plate.

He brought up Ling's contrariness, and he found they were discussing the Indians. There were a hundred questions she wanted to ask about them. Was it true the popular impression that they caked their heads with mud to—clean their hair? It was true? How dreadful! She liked to believe that it was some religious custom, a penance of some kind.

Rickard saw another opening. He related his plan of having the camp on the Arizona side of the river to save duties on food stuffs; they ate, the Indians, in Arizona, and slept in old Mexico: "It saves the O. P. a nice little sum every month. It's not an easy thing to manage a commissary, as you know—"

The new hole was dug, but the gopher was out of sight. She spoke of a new book the critics were praising.

He found he would have to discard diplomacy, blurt out his message; use bludgeons for this scampering agility.

He put down his cup; no, he would not have any more. "Thank you just the same. It is really delicious. I feel like a truant, sipping tea here. I'm forgetting my errand." He stood. She had never seen him hampered by embarrassment before. Her smile was gently encouraging, womanly sweet. She really admired him, more than any one she had ever known. His reserve called to her always, to reach his ideals, ideals she could only guess at. Her mind grasped at the concrete; she believed him impatient of external coarseness. She was always conscious of her dress, her surroundings, her table when he was present.

"My mission is a little awkward, Mrs. Hardin. I hope you will take it all right, that you will not be offended."

"Offended?" Her face showed alarm.

"It's about Ling. He's a queer fellow, they all are, you know." He was blundering like a schoolboy under the growing shadow in Gerty's blue eyes. "They resent authority, that is, from women. He is a tyrant, Ling is."

"I think you are right, Mr. Rickard. He is an unruly servant. But you could replace him easily."

"Oh, but we couldn't. It's no easy matter to get a cook while it's hot like this; and a camp cook, who can cook quantities, and yet make them palatable—"

Then what was it he was trying to say? The blue eyes met his at last squarely, a glint of warning in them he would not see.

"I have to give in to him, we all do; have to humor him. We've spoiled him, I guess."

"Yes?" Ah, she would not help him. Let him flounder!

"He wants to be let alone; he doesn't appreciate your kind help, Mrs. Hardin."

"Oh!" Her eyes were hot with tears; angry tears. She would not for the wealth of that desert let him see her cry. This was so different from what she had expected. This was what he had come to say. She could not speak, nor would not. She sat in her spoiled doll's house, all her pleasure in her toy dishes, her pretty finery, ruined. She would no longer meet his eyes; mocking, forever, let them be! She had been so proud of her managing, and here he listens to the complaints of a Chinese cook! Complaints against her, against Gerty Holmes, the girl he had once loved! He could not care if he could humiliate her so. She stared at her hands

A NEW ENEMY AND A NEW FRIEND

lying limp over the hand-whipped negligee. The azure hue of the silk slip beneath had lost its charm to her. It was the most vivid moment of her life. Not even when Rickard had left her, with his kisses still warm on her lips, had she felt so outraged. He was treating her as though she were a servant—discharging her—because she was the wife of Hardin. Her eyes grew black with anger; she hated them both; between them, their jealousy, their rivalry, what had they made of her life? She suddenly realized that she was old. If she were young, he would not flout her like this. She remembered the woman she had seen in his ramada; she had heard that the Mexican was in camp, employed by Rickard. Her thoughts were like swarming hornets.

"He's an ungrateful beast, Mrs. Hardin, if he doesn't appreciate your labors. I'd let him struggle alone. As I say, we've spoiled him.

"He has been complaining?" It was all she could say with control.

"He's a tyrant. I told him I would not let you waste your kindness one instant longer—"

Oh, she understood! A bitter pleasure to see him so confused. Rickard, before whose superior appraisement she had so often wilted! She would not help him out, never! She rose when he paused. He thanked her for meeting him half-way, and her smile was inscrutable.

"So I'm discharged?"

He misunderstood her dignity, as before he had misconstrued her flirtations.

Gerty drooped under the sudden coming of age. She knew she must be old.

"Or he would not treat me so! he would not treat me so!"

"You can't be discharged, if you've never been employed, can you? Thank you once again, and for your tea. It was delicious. I wish Ling would give us tea like that."

Boorish, all of it, and blundering! Why wouldn't he go? When he had hurt her so! had hurt her so!

Her hand met his, but not her eyes. If he did not go quickly, something would happen; he would see her crying. The angels that guard blunderers got Rickard out of the tent without a suspicion of threatening tears. She threw off her negligee and the pale blue slip; the tears must wait for that. Then she flung herself on her bed, and shook it with the grief of wounded vanity.

MacLean looked up as Rickard reentered the office.

"It went all right," nodded his chief, cheerful now that was out of the way. "She didn't mind. Tired of it already, I guess."

MacLean looked at him thoughtfully. Funny for as keen a man as Rickard to be a dolt about women. No woman would forgive that; Gerty's kind of women. Mind! Mind being turned down? He'd find out later what she thought about it. That was his blind side. And she'd been throwing herself at him ever since she came to the Heading. Everybody had seen it—hold on, everybody did not include Rickard, himself. MacLean, Jr., softly whistled.

That evening, the chief had a visitor. The wife of Maldonado, some of the fear pressed out of her eyes, brought in his laundered khakis, socks, darned and matched; all the missing buttons replaced.

"I haven't worn a matched sock," he told her, "for months. That's great, señora."

He wanted to get to bed, but she lingered. She wanted

A NEW ENEMY AND A NEW FRIEND

to talk to him about her troubles; he had cautioned her against talking about them in camp, so she overflowed to him whenever she found a chance; about Maldonado, the children; Lupe. It was getting wearying; but he could not shove the poor thing out. She wanted him to say again that Maldonado could not harm her. He reminded her of the solution; she could leave him.

"And go to hell! Oh, no, never would I do that. It would be a mortal sin."

Rickard stretched. He had to be up early in the morning.

"The señor has been very kind," the woman's gratitude resembled a faithful dog's.

"Oh, it was nothing." His lids were drooping. At five the next morning!

"The señor, he is lonely?"

"Lonely!" He laughed in her puzzled face. Great Scott, he was dying for sleep! He did not catch her drift.

"The señor, he is so kind, and he is lonely. He has no one to sew for him, to mend his clothes, to keep his tent. I am so grateful to the señor."

Had she misunderstood his suggestions about a divorce? Rickard sat up.

"You are doing very well for me. Thank you. And now, good night, señora. I'm up early in the morning."

There was something on her mind. She walked toward the entrance of the tent-house, but turned back.

"I have a sister, señor, who would be good to you, mend your clothes, when I am gone. The señor will be lonely, then, is it not so? She is grown now, almost fifteen. She is *muy sympatica,* can sew, and can cook—"

"Oh, lord—" cried Rickard.

Her refrain was insistent. "The señor is lonely; you need a *mujer.*"

"No *es posiblé,*" his answer was rough to her savage, childish kindliness.

The señor was so kind, he would be kind to her sister—

"*Por Dios,* no!" cried Rickard.

Señora Maldonado gave a sharp intake of breath, an aborted scream. Rickard, too, saw a man's figure outside the screen door. The Mexican woman pressed a frightened hand to her heart. Of course, it was the vengeful Maldonado—he would kill her—

"If I am intruding," it was the voice of Hardin.

"Come right in," welcomed Rickard. "Get along, señora." The Maldonado slipped out into the night, her hand still against her heart.

Hardin, a roll of maps under his arm, entered with a rough sneer on his face. A dramatic scene, that, he had interrupted! And Rickard who did not like to have women in camp. White women!

Rickard, still sleepy, asked him to sit down.

"Thank you, no. I wanted to speak to you about those concrete aprons. They tell me you've given an order not to have them."

"The order's from Tucson." Rickard yawned covertly.

"A child's order!" exploded Hardin. "Why doesn't Marshall come and see for himself? Brush jetties! It will never stand!"

"He is coming." Rickard wrinkled the sleep out of his eyes. "He will be here next week."

"It's a crime!" Hardin unfolded his map, spreading it over the table. A bottle of ink was upset in his eagerness. Rickard was thoroughly awake by the time

A NEW ENEMY AND A NEW FRIEND

he had mopped the purple black flood with towels and blotting-paper. Hardin recovered his map, but slightly damaged. Two of Rickard's books were ruined.

"See here," cried Hardin, still excited. "Calculate that distance. If this is a farce, Marshall ought to say so." He pulled a chair up to the ink-stained table. "Brush aprons! He's wasting our time, and the company's money."

Rickard resigned himself to a long argument. It was three o'clock when Hardin let him turn in.

When he was getting ready for bed, he remembered the melodramatic scene Hardin had entered upon. He stared comprehendingly at the screen door—seeing, with understanding, Hardin's coarse sneer—the Maldonado, breathing fast, her hand over her heart. "Of course, he'll think—good lord, these people will make me into an old woman! I don't care what the whole caboodle of them think!"

Five minutes after blowing out his candle, he was deeply sleeping.

CHAPTER XXX

SMUDGE

FROM her tent, where she was writing a letter that lagged somehow, Innes Hardin had seen Rickard go to her sister's tent. She did not need to analyze the sickness of sight that watched the dancing step acknowledge its intention. It meant wretchedness, for *Tom*. At a time when he most needed gentleness and sympathy, rasped as he was by his humiliations and disappointments—how could any woman be so cruel? As for Rickard, he was beneath contempt—if it were true, Gerty's story, told in shrugs and dashes. She had jilted him for Tom; and this his revenge? Did it hang together, if he still loved her? Loved Gerty? How was it that those clear-sighted, quizzical eyes had not at once penetrated her flimsy evasions, her deviousness? Could he ever have cared, or was the story a web of vanity? Still caring, what would be the end of it all?

She had not known that she had such feeling as the thought roused in her. It proved what the blood tie is, this tigerish passion sweeping through her, as her eyes watched that closed tent—it was love for Tom, pity for Tom. Sex honor, why, Gerty did not know the meaning of the words! Were she not a harem woman, a cheap little vain thing, she would not be flirting in a time like this—getting on the track with her coquetries.

She pulled herself away from her wire-netting window, and took up her pen. What had she been writing about? "They are working steadily on the permanent concrete gate, and pushing the wooden gate to control the autumn floods—" How long would it be before Tom would see what every one else was seeing? What would he do when he knew? Hating Rickard already, bitter as he was—

She was not so biased as he. She could see why Marshall had had to reorganize, or Faraday, whoever it was who had done it. Estrada had shown her; and MacLean. Her sense of justice had done the rest. Rickard had proved his efficiency; the levee, the camp, the military discipline all showed the general. Whether he were anything of an engineer, time would tell that. MacLean thought so, and Eduardo, but the others did not, the older engineers, hot-headed for Tom. It was a long call he was making!

Where had she left off? "The wooden gate—" her letter as wooden! And how could she vitalize it without telling the personal history which was animating the endeavor into drama? Her brother, Mr. Marshall, the new manager— Suppose Tom were to come back? She must watch for him—make some excuse to pull him in if he should come back before that other went— Hateful, such eavesdropping! A prisoner to that man's gallivanting!

For an instant she did not recognize the figure outside Gerty's tent. Her fears saw Tom. She reached the screen door in time to see Rickard lift his hat to a disappearing flurry of ruffles.

She had seen the ruffles, but she could not see the distress behind that swiftly shut door. Angry eyes watched

Rickard's step swing him toward Ling's mesquits. She was still standing, her brown hands tightly laced, when he emerged, and swung toward his ramada.

How much later was it that he came out again into that wash of sunlight, followed by MacLean, who had his absorbed look on that was almost adoration? How long had she been standing there? After they had gone, she would take a walk. The letter could wait till the morning.

From the levee that day, she had a glimpse of the Mexican woman on her knees by the river, rubbing clothes against a smooth stone. A pile of tight-wrung socks lay on the bank. Innes stood and watched her.

"I must remember to speak of her to Gerty," she determined. "She probably does not know that there is a washerwoman in camp."

Then she speedily forgot about it; forgot even her anger of the afternoon. The skinners driving their mules over the hot sands, the mattress weavers twisting willows through the steel cables, the pile-drivers pinning down the gigantic carpet as it was woven to the treacherous bed of that river, the Indians cutting arrow-weed, that dredge-arm swinging low—the diversified panorama caught her as it always did.

It was so big, the man-work! Behind the big fight lay its purpose. Not only to save the homes of that far-reaching valley, but to make room for the homes of the future. Always a thrill in that, the work for those yet unborn!

Still sleeping that land was, land that would feed a nation. Stretching north to the strange new sea, that made this one with the age of fable, reaching over into Mexico, its lateral boundaries the distant unreal mountains, here was a magic soil that piratical rains had not filched of its wonders. Here tired out men, from their tired out farms, would find homes, here the sick would find healing in its breath, safety and succor in its spaces —that dredge-arm swinging across the channel would make all that come true!

It was a week later before she remembered to speak of the Mexican woman "who could wash." The two women were on their way to their tents from the mess-breakfast. Señora Maldonado was leaving MacLean's tent with a large bundle of used clothes held under her arm.

"She washes for the men. I'm going to ask her to do my khakis for me. It's too much to keep asking those busy men to see that my bundle of wash is sent out and brought back."

"More impossible," she added, following Gerty into her tent, "is it to do it myself. It's too hot. And khakis are stiff rubbing. Perhaps this woman would be willing to do all our laundry?"

Gerty had been wondering what she would say to Innes. The speech which needed only an introduction was stirred into the open.

"You must not," her voice trembled with anger, "you must not ask that woman."

Innes was staring out of the tent door, watching the arm of the dredge as it dipped and rose from the river. She did not see the flag of rage flung in her sister's cheeks.

"I don't care at all how she mangles them, so they are clean, and *I* do not have to make them so!" She interpreted the counsel from experience. She knew the fastidiousness of Mrs. Hardin. She had no ruffles to care about. "It's a blessed miracle to find some one who will wash for you."

"I don't mean that." Each word was curt and icy. "She is not to be spoken to."

The girl asked her bluntly what she meant.

"You must not give her your washing—must not speak to her. I've not mentioned it before. I—I hoped it would not be necessary. Tom told me not to speak of it."

"*Tom* told you not to speak of it? Not to speak of what?"

Gerty hesitated. Her husband, having relieved himself of his scorn, had made her see the necessity for not repeating that scene in Rickard's tent. That did not prevent her speaking of what she herself had seen, what she surmised. But Innes must not speak of it; their position practically depended on him, now.

Innes, bewildered, asked her what in the world she was talking about?

"You must have observed—Mr. Rickard?"

The girl's ear did not catch the short pause. "Observed Mr. Rickard?"

"The coolness between us. I scarcely speak to him. I don't wish to speak to him."

When had all this happened, Innes demanded of herself? Had she been asleep, throwing pity from outdated dreams?

"I won't countenance a common affair like that." Her eyes, sparkling with anger, suggested jealous wrath to Innes, who had her first hint of the story. She had learned never to take the face value of her sister's verbal coin; it was only a symbol of value; it stood for something else.

Gerty had been suffering with abscessed pride, inflamed vanity. This was the first relief; the angry venom spent itself.

The yellow eyes were on the dredge bucket as it swung across the channel, but they did not register. She was angry, outraged; she did not know with whom. With Gerty for telling her, with Rickard, with life that lets such things be. If Gerty would only stop talking! Why would she string it out, tell it all over again? She hated the hints which the accented voice was making. She jumped up. "Oh, stop it!" She rushed out of the tent, followed by a strange bitter smile that brought age to the face of Gerty Hardin.

In her own tent, Innes found excuse for her lack of self-control. She did not like the color of scandal; she hated smudge. Gerty had *told* her nothing, only hinted, hinted! What was it Tom did not want her to know? She would not think of it. She would be glad that something had occurred to check the foolish little woman's folly. Gerty had said the whole camp knew it; knew why the Mexican woman was in camp! She did not trust Gerty in anything else; why should she trust her in that? She would not think of it.

True or not, it was better for Tom. She assured herself that she was glad that something, anything, had happened before her brother learned the drift of things. There was nothing now to worry about. She would forget Gerty's gossip.

But she remembered it vividly that week as she washed her own khakis; as she bent over the ironing-board in Gerty's sweltering "kitchenette." She thought of it as she returned Rickard's bow in the mess-tent the next morning; each time they met she thought of it. And it was in her mind when she met Señora Maldonado by the river one day, and made a sudden wide curve to avoid having to speak to her.

CHAPTER XXXI

TIME THE UMPIRE

A BLAZING sun rode the heavens. The river was low; its yellow waters bore the look of oriental duplicity. Men and horses were being driven to take advantage of the continued low water. Each day was now showing its progress. The two ends of the trestle were creeping across the stream from their brush aprons, as though sentient, feeling their way; watching the foe; ready to spring the trap when the river was off guard.

"Things are humming," wrote MacLean, Jr., to his father, who was inspecting the survey below Culiacan for the new line on the west coast. The focus was indeed visible. A few weeks of work, at the present rate, and the gap would be closed, Hardin's big gate in it; the by-pass ready; the trap set for the Colorado. The tensity of a last spurt was in the air.

It was inspiring activity, this pitting of man's cumulative skill against an elemental force. No Caucasian mind which did not tingle, feel the privileged thrill of it. To the stolid native, as he plodded on his raft all day under a blazing sky, or lifted his machete against the thorny mesquit or more insidious arrow-weed, this day of well-paid toil was his millennium, the fulfilment of the prophecy. His gods had so spoken. Food for his stomach, liquor for his stupefaction; the white man's money laid in a brown hand each Sunday morning was what the great gods forespoke. The completion of the work, the white man's victory, would be an end of the fat time. A dull sense of this deepened the natural stolidity of their labor. Hasten? Why should they, and shorten their day of opportunity? Saturday night, feasting, dancing; then a day of rest, of stupor. To-day is theirs. The gods are speaking.

Between the two camps oscillated Coronel, silently squatting near the whites, jabbering his primitive Esperanto to the tribes. His friendship with the white chiefs, his age and natural leadership gave him a unique position in both camps. Forestier consulted him; Rickard referred to him. He was too lordly to work; long ago, he had thrown his fate with the Cocopahs whose name was a synonym for majestic idleness.

"But he's worth a dozen workers," Hamlin had once told Rickard. "Get Coronel on your side. He's got influence; they do as he says." Behind that grizzled mask, Rickard surmised a pride of authorship in the reclamation project. Coronel had known Powell; he had crossed the desert with Estrada; that his proudest boast. Assiduously, Rickard cultivated the old Indian who crouched days through by the bank of the river.

The engineers felt the whip of excitement. Silent, up at the Crossing, at work on the great concrete head-gate, which would ultimately control the water supply of the valley, was prodding his men to finish before the winter storms were on. His loyalty to the Hardin gate did not admit a contingency there, but it was the thought which lurked in every man's mind. Never a man left his camp in the morning who did not look toward that span crawling across the treacherous stream, measure that widened by-pass. Would the gate stand? Would pilings driven through brush mats into a bed of silt, a bottomless pit, hold against that river, should it turn and lash its great tail? The Hardin men halloed for the gate, but looked each morning to see if it were still there. The Reclamation Service men and the engineers of the railroad were openly skeptical; Sisyphus outdone at his own game! Estrada and Rickard looked furtively at the gate, with doubt at each other. Uneasiness electrified the air.

Hardin, himself, was repressed, an eager live wire. His days he spent on the river; his nights, long hours of them, open-eyed, on his back, watching the slow-wheeling, star-pricked dome of desert sky. His was the suspense of the man on trial; this was his trial; Gerty, Rickard, the valley, his judge and jury. Gradually, the peace of the atom lost in infinity would absorb him; toward morning he would sleep. But the first touch of dawn would bring him back to the situation; the sun not so tender as the stars! Dishonored,— he had to make good, to make good to the men who loved him, to prove to Gerty who scorned failure— By the eternal, he must prove to Gerty! She must give him respect from those scornful eyes of hers. If ever he had worked, in his life, he must work for his life now! The gate grew to be a symbol with him of restored honor, an obsession of desire. It must be all right!

Rickard was all over the place, up at the Crossing with Silent at the concrete gate, Marshall's gate; down the levee inspecting the bank with untiring vigilance; watching the mat-makers on the rafts weave their cross-threads of willow branches and steel cable; directing, reporting. "Watching every piece of rock that's dumped in the river," complained Wooster. "Believe he marks them at night!"

They were preparing for the final rush. In a week or two, the work would be continuous, night shifts to begin when the rock-pouring commenced. Large lamps were being suspended across the channel, acetylene whose candle-power was that of an arc light. Soon there would be no night at the break. When the time for the quick coup would come, the dam must be closed without break or slip. One mat was down, dropped on the floor that had already swallowed two such gigantic mouthfuls; covered with rock; pinned down to the slippery bottom with piles. Another mat was ready to drop; rock was waiting to be poured over it; the deepest place in the channel was reduced from fifteen to seven feet. Each day the overpour, anxiously measured, increased. A third steam-shovel had been added; the railroad sent in several work-trains fully equipped for service; attracted by the excitement, the hoboes were commencing to come in, from New Orleans where the sewer system was finished and throwing men out of work; from Los Angeles, released by the completion of the San Pedro breakwater; from San Francisco they were turning, the excitement over. No fat pickings there!

It was a battle of big numbers, a duel of great force where time was the umpire. Any minute hot weather might fall on those snowy peaks up yonder, and the released waters, rushing down, would tear out the defenses as a wave breaks over a child's fort made of sand. This was a race, and all knew it. A regular train despatch system was in force that the inrushing cars might drop their burden of rock and gravel and be off after more. The Dragon was being fed rude meals, its appetite whetted by the glut of pouring rock.

Tod Marshall came down from Tucson in his car. The coming of the *Palmyra* and Claudia rippled the social waters at the Front for days ahead. Gerty Hardin, to whom had been rudely flung days of leisure, though she still hated Rickard, wondered if she were not glad that her hours were to be her own when the grand Mrs. Marshall came. For Marshall was a great man, the man of the Southwest; his wife, whom she had not yet met, must be a personage. Gerty's position as a helper of Ling's might have been misunderstood. Yet too proud to tell her astonished family that she wanted to desert the mess-tent, she shook herself from her injury, and "did up" all her lingerie gowns. Mrs. Marshall was not going to patronize her, even if her husband had snubbed Tom. It was hot, ironing in her tent, the doors closed. It would have hurt her to acknowledge the importance of the impending visit.

Everything carried a sting those indoor hours. She was aflame with hot vanity. Twice, she had openly encouraged him; twice, he had flouted her. That was his kind! Men who prefer Mexicans—! She would never forgive him, never!

She followed devious channels to involve Tom's responsibility. There was a cabal against the wife of Hardin. Working like a servant! she called it necessity. Everything, every one punished her for that one act of folly. Life had caught her. She saw no way, as she ironed her mull ruffles, no way out of her cage. Her spirit beat wild wings against her bars. If she could see a way out!

She really was not free to establish an honest independent life. Horticulturists speak of the habit of a plant. Psychologists take the long road and find a Mediterranean word; temperament. Gerty was a vine; its habit to cling for support. Her tendrils had been rudely torn, thrown back at herself; world-winds were waiting their chance at her—a vine is not a pretty thing when it trails in the dust— Sometimes she would shiver over her ironing-board when she thought of the dust. She knew her habit, which she, too, called temperament. Nothing to do but to stay with Tom!

Maddening, too, that Rickard would not see that he had hurt her. His bow was just as friendly as before. Friendly! Was that all it had ever been? At the mess-table, she caught his eyes turning toward, resting on, Innes Hardin. The girl herself did not seem to notice—artful, subterranean, such stalking! That was why she had come running back to the Heading! That the reason of her anger when she had hinted of the Maldonado. She learned to hate Innes. Before the girl's return, she had had a chance; she knew she had had a chance. He had been caught by youth, ah, that the truth that seared! Youth! Youth that need not fear the morning light, the swift passing months! *She* had no time to lose. Her heart felt old.

The mess-meals grew intolerable to her. She would watch for the shock of those conscious glances that she felt every one must see. She, Gerty Hardin, cast aside for a hoyden in khakis! The girl's play at unconsciousness infuriated her. Deep! Ah, she knew now her game! Riding fifteen miles down the levee to pay a pretended visit to a laborer's wife, Mrs. Parrish! As if she were interested in Mrs. Parrish! Jolting in a boxcar to see the concrete head-gate with MacLean; walking with Estrada, meeting Rickard, of course, everywhere; her yellow khakis in every corner of the camp. A promiscuous coquette, she changed the word to "careful"; playing her cards slowly; waiting for victory to make a hero of Rickard; pretending to take issue with Tom—ha, she knew her, at last!

Her first call at the *Palmyra* discovered the mistress in a wash gown of obscure cut and color, with a white apron a serving maid might wear. Knitting her pale-colored wools, Mrs. Marshall had little to give out but monosyllables. Gerty was forced to carry the conversation. Mrs. Marshall did not appear to see her visitor's correctness, the harmony of color, the good lines. Time thrown away, that laundering!

That avenue dull, time again hung heavily. The gay evenings on the *Delta* were abandoned; the men coming back from the river too tired, too warm to dance. She began to discover it was hideously hot. Perhaps, she might go out, after all—

She decided to tell her family that it was too warm to continue the commissary activity; Rickard was enough of a gentleman to let her cover her hurt; she could safely assume that! Yet it stung her to think what Innes might be thinking, what, perhaps, he had told her! Every one must be wondering, speculating! In her life, Gerty had felt keenly but twice; each time Rickard it was who had hurt her. That mocking superior eye of his! Bitterly she hated him.

"Tom," she said one night. He turned with a swift

thrill of expectation, for her voice sounded kind; like the Gerty of old. "I have always heard that Mr. Marshall has terribly strict ideas—for every one but himself, I mean!"

"That's a good one." It was the first laugh in weeks of moodiness. Hardin was thinking of the poker games.

"I'm serious. I think he ought to hear of that Mexican woman."

"Have you heard anything else?"

There was no new thread in her fabric of suspicions. To Hardin, it brought a memory of time past to be sitting thus familiarly together, Gerty in her negligee, her hair disarranged, looking up into his face. He did not suspect he was a pawn in her scheme of retribution.

"It ought not to be allowed." The blue eyes were purpling with anger. "Mr. Marshall ought to be told. It is demoralizing in a camp like this. I thought you said the governor of Lower California had sent a commandant here."

"To suppress liquor-selling and gambling." Hardin did not say that the request had come from Rickard.

"And persons without visible means of support," quoted his wife with triumph.

"That does not apply to the Mexican," frowned Hardin. He did not want to be dragged into this.

"You ought to tell Mr. Marshall," persisted Gerty.

"I tell Marshall anything against his pet clerk?" The Hardin lip shot out. "He'd throw me out of the company."

The pretty scene was spoiled. To his dismay, she burst into a storm of tears, tears of self-pity. Her life lay in tatters at her feet, the pretty fabric rent, torn between the rude handling of those two men. She could not have reasoned out her injury, made it convincing, built out of dreams as it was, heartless, scheming dreams. Because she could not tell it, her sobbing was the more violent, her complaints incoherent. Tom gathered enough fragments to piece the old story. "Ashamed of him. He had dragged her down into his humiliation." His sweet moment had passed.

He spent a few futile moments trying to comfort her. "Don't come near me." It burst from her; a cry of revulsion. He stared at her, the woman meeting his eyes in flushed defiance. The hatred which he saw, her bitterness, corroded his pride, scorched his self-love. Nothing would kill his love for her; he knew that in that blackest of moments. His affection for her was part of his life. It went cringing to her feet, puppy-like, but he called it back, whipped it to its place. That was all over now. No woman could dread him twice like that. He shivered at what he had seen. The man breathed deep as he got up and looked about him. It was over. He would not elaborate his awakening with words. He would never forget that look of dread, of hate. He left her tent.

That night, the cot under the stars had no tenant. Hardin had it out with himself down the levee. Strange that this bitter man could have the same hopeful blood in him which had whipped his pulse at Lawrence! He was still a young man, and God! How tired he was! He was in a net of bitter circumstance. What was he to do, where to go? He was too old, too tired and sore to begin over again, and the bitter irony of it! He only wanted what he had lost, the love of the woman who hated him, the respect of the valley into which his life had been sucked. God! He was tired.

He saw the dry forsaken channel of the Colorado; grim symbol of his life! Where was the youthful hope, the conviction that everything would come his way? The potential richness of the soil upturned by yesterday's shovel on the dike found him cold. That night, there was no future to his bitterness. Hunting for the fault, he found the real Hardin, not the man he had been spending his days with, the man he had expected to be, but the man the world saw passing. Perhaps life holds no more tragic instant than when we stand over the grave of what we thought we were, throw the sod over the ashes, facing the lonely yoking with the man that is. Hardin shivered unto himself; and grew old.

That valley might fulfil Estrada's vision and his labor; might yield the harvest of happy homes; but his was not there. He had been the sacrifice.

CHAPTER XXXII

THE WALK HOME

CLAUDIA MARSHALL sat at the head of her stately table in the *Palmyra,* mute as a statue but for the burning eyes which followed her Tod. To Innes, her guest, she was renewing the impression of heroic resignation. It was a tragic presence, of brooding solicitude.

Not easy to believe that this was once the most vivacious coquette of Guadalajara! The American girl had often wondered if it had been Tod Marshall's sentence, only, which had changed the butterfly into a gentle martyr. Listening to her brilliant host, she let her mind wander to the silent woman near her. What was it she was mourning, her position in San Francisco, the honors her Tod had had to relinquish? Was worldliness, thwarted ambition, her sorrow? Then why didn't she enjoy the distinctions he poured into her seemingly indifferent hands, those busy fingers knitting, knitting, paying no attention to the labels he won? She might have made a splendid circle, herself the center, if that *was* the thing she loved. Eduardo had told her once, in relating the family history, that the instant Tod Marshall had risen in Claudia Cardenas' sky, the coquette of Guadalajara had left her old orbit; she herself, forever a satellite, to this new sun. But that could not have silenced her vivacity, thrown that burning fire into her tragic eyes!

"I saw Cor'nel to-day, mother!" Innes caught the opportunity to glance at her. She had her first intuition. Claudia had flinched! *"Mother?"*

"That's a character, Miss Innes! Have you talked with him?"

"With him!" echoed Innes. *"To* him! Will he talk?"

"Ah, we are cousins, brothers!" chuckled her host. And then her discovery intrigued her; she could hear the words of Tod Marshall; he was telling anecdotes of the old Indian; faintly, she heard him—"As a fly to molasses, is Cor'nel to the river;" but her subterranean thought was with the woman at the head of the table. Childlessness! Of course. How was it that she had never sensed it before! That her sentence, her renunciation. And he calls her "mother!"

A phase of Marshall's caught her. "A Yuma, Cor'nel? I always thought him a Cocopah."

Marshall's fine head was thrown back in laughter. "Too much work, Yuma!" He was mimicking the old Indian's laconic brevities. "Marry Cocopah. Go live Cocopah. No work, Cocopah!"

Mrs. Marshall, it struck Innes, was hastening the dinner. She overheard her sending back a course. "It's too much, Tony!" And as the coffee was being passed, she could not wait longer to open her work-bag which she had carried to the table. Her steel needles began to "put in" the sleeve of an infant sack; white soft worsted, with a scallop of blue wool. The work did not absorb her attention. Seemingly, she was engrossed in her Tod. Though her fingers never faltered, her gaze followed him. Tragically centered it was to Innes Hardin; her discovery accenting that sad stare which had the persistence of polar attraction. He was her universe, of apprehension, rather than her joy. And the girl, watching, found a pitiful thought; he was also her limitation; her fond sentence. Loving him; fearing for him; having life and love meet, and end in him!

No definite horizon, in truth, here, save as her husband made, or rose above it. The world, as related to him only, came to Claudia in her Tucson hotel, or her box rooms in the *Palmyra*. Her other interest, the orphanage of Santa Rosalia at Tucson; for whose babies she cut and sewed and sent an interminable procession of tiny garments.

Priestly counsel had turned her to vicarious motherhood. The priests, never her Tod, had heard her complaints of her abridged life. The blow that had sent Tod Marshall to the desert, had forbade her motherhood. She was overflowing with maternal passion. And the doctors and priests told her that resignation, consecration, life in a minor key, soft pedal pressed, was the price she must pay for her few happy months of wifehood. Into her eyes had come the look that Innes had found tantalizing; the gaze of fervent abridgment.

She had never grown to feel at ease with her husband's countrywomen; and they could not understand her gulf of silence. The nearest approach to a woman friendship was with Innes Hardin, and this, without a bridge of speech. There had been many terrible hours before the orphans' call had been heard. Then, those her Tod did not fill, she learned to crochet into soft baby-smelling jackets for the Santa Rosalia babies. Some day, perhaps, she might be brave enough to approach Tod with her plea; perhaps he might let her take one of those helpless darlings. To do that, she must lay bare her ache to him—not yet had she found the daring. Until then, the Santa Rosalia Orphanage! Her room at the Rosales Hotel was lined with work-boxes and knitting bags filled with tender rainbow wools. Unsewn slips lay in snowy piles waiting for Tod's days of absence. They needed her undivided attention; he liked to see her listening to him. She had learned to crochet with her eyes shut that she might work without distracting him. The balls of wool lost their baby fragrance in the fumes of his tobacco; that the one dissipation she did not protest against. Late hours, excitement, might abridge the life she so passionately policed; but she would not demand the sacrifice of his cigar. The babies must have their sacques; so lavender sticks and sachet bags made a fumigating compromise.

Claudia could not lessen her sorrow by sharing it. Only by a flash of intuition could Innes have penetrated her secret. Divined, it chained her sympathy. Her look listening to Tod Marshall, her memory gathered pitiful evidence of the renunciation. Dull, never to have felt it before!

Marshall's cigar followed the coffee. Tony, the white-capped Italian cook of the *Palmyra*, was removing the cups. Innes was carrying her double interest, listening to Tod Marshall's broad sweep, getting a new viewpoint as he minimized the local scheme—feeling that silent presence at the head of the table.

Then something drove Claudia from her mind. What Mr. Marshall had said swept a disturbing calcium on Tom. What if, truly, the river fiasco could be traced to that overzealous hand? To Tom, this undertaking blotted out the rest of related big endeavor; but that was not the way her host was looking at it. He was too courteous to give her discomfort; he had not said it directly. But always it met her, rose up to smite her, wherever she was. "If this is a failure, then it's hell to pay at Laguna." That the reason of the importance of this section; as it affected other enterprise, as it was related to irrigation in the lump. Not because it was Tom, who had started it, the general who had conceived it—Marshall, who with his railroad was carrying it through. Not for personal reasons; as a block of the great western activity to fit into its place in the mosaic. More and more disturbing, her thoughts of Tom!

Can a man change equipment, method, his entire habit of life, in a five-minute walk from home to office? She had to meet a question of her host. Yes, she had heard of Minodoka. Yes, it was a big undertaking. She saw him well started toward the Salt River country before she went back to meet her fear. Was it not egotism, personal pride, that was making her cover her eyes, like any simple ostrich? *Her* brother. Assume him anybody else's brother! Grant a man a moment of apparent distinction given him by a distinguishing enterprise. That moment of distinction his betrayal, unless the method of the man is big enough to rise equal to it!

Big issues had never found this man, her host, wanting. He had pulled opportunity from a denying fate; he had *made* big issues. It gave her a strange sinking of the heart as she put him in her brother's place; the river then would not be running into a useless sea! Because he had the trick of success; his big opportunities did not betray him! Ah, now she had touched the thought. It paled her pride in being a fervid Hardin. There was a looseness in the method. The dredge fiasco

—the wild night at the levee—no isolated accidents those. Hardin's luck!

A flush of miserable shame came to her. How they had all been trying to spare her—Eduardo, these kindly Marshalls—MacLean! She loved Tom just the same, just as fondly, perhaps more tenderly, even; for the limitations of his upbringing, his education, he was not to blame! It did not justify Gerty's resentments—that was a personal feeling, a craving for distinction; hers, a wistful shame that Tom, not being equal to his opportunity, must drag it down with him, cancel forever that vision! It must not be a failure—it must succeed! She was turning, impulsively, to ask Tod Marshall if he thought, could he think it probable that they would fail, when a step that sent the blood to her face took the car's stairs at two leaps. Now, indeed, the dinner was spoiled.

"That's Rickard," Marshall came back from Salt River. "I forgot to tell you that I asked him to dinner. He couldn't get away. He said he'd run in for coffee. Hello, Rickard. Thought you'd forgotten us!"

"More coffee, Tony," ordered Mrs. Marshall, after she had greeted her guest. "A cup for Mr. Rickard."

She hadn't thought of that contingency! She found herself shaking hands with him. Could he not hear her mind, ticking away at the Maldonado episode?

Of course, he would insist on seeing her to her tent. Punctilious, always. Well, she just wouldn't. She didn't know how to prevent it, but she just wouldn't! Perhaps, she could slip out, some way. She would watch her chance. She would ask Mrs. Marshall—that was it, ask to be shown—anything. Then she would slip away.

Mrs. Marshall's needles were clicking. Her eyes

were on her Tod's face, watching for the first sign of fatigue. Tony carried in liqueurs. Rickard allowed his glass to be filled, but Innes noted that he did not touch it. She remembered that he had not refused it at her sister's dinner. She was in a mood to carp.

"No spirits, either?" She thought she detected a mockery akin to hers in Marshall's tone.

"Can I do what I won't let my men do, sir?"

"Not smoking yet, I see!"

"I think I've learned to dislike it, for myself—" added Rickard. "Can I talk shop for a while?"

They withdrew to a cushioned window seat. Innes could hear bits of their talk. Rickard, she gathered, was urging a warm protest against a policy of his superior. She caught enough scraps to piece together their opposition. "Reclamation Service," "Interference," "A clean slate—" and then "We're handicapped enough," she heard Rickard say, and then caught a quick glance in her direction.

Marshall's answer was judicial. Again Innes got the wide view, the broad sweep. She remembered what Eduardo Estrada had told her of Rickard's complications. This was what they were talking of. Marshall advocated a hospitality to their ideas, if set; "Where it is possible. 'Be soople, Davy, in things immaterial,'" he twinkled. "Remember your Stevenson? Government men are a bit stilted, and we rough railroad men can teach them a point or two, I agree with you, but we're looking far ahead, Rickard. And it's all the same thing, Laguna, Imperial. If it's to be the same system, stands to reason they want it done their way, eh? Can't see it? Wait till you're old like me."

His Claudia looked at him with quick anxiety. He

was not old. And he looked well. Sometimes, she almost believed he *was* well. That terrible sword—

Innes had found her chance. She asked to be shown over the car. Mrs. Marshall put aside her wools and led the way through Tony's domain, who would have had them linger. A large diamond blazing on his finger pointed out ingenious cubby-holes and receptacles. He wanted to tell the young lady of his wonderful luck; how he had been picked up by Mr. Marshall—half dead in San Francisco—and brought down to the Southwest. He had not coughed for a month. He tried to tell her of his brilliant salary, "one hundred and fifty, Mex.," but his mistress abridged his confidences.

"Tony would talk all night," she explained as she led the way back through the sitting-room to her sleeping compartment.

Here Innes confided her plan. She wanted to slip out. "She would not interrupt their evening; Mr. Marshall had business to discuss—"

Mrs. Marshall would not hear of it. She felt that Tod's evening had been long enough; that he should be in bed after his long day of observation on the river. But she said that Mr. Marshall would never forgive her if she let Miss Hardin go home alone. Her opposition was softly implacable.

Innes went back to the sitting-room of the car angrily coerced. Rickard was still closeted, conversationally, with his superior.

She endured a half-hour of crippled conversation. She, herself, was not easily vocal. She felt that Mrs. Marshall liked her in her own silent remote way, but they needed Tod Marshall to bridge over the national gap. Swift fraternization, as between socially equipped women, was not possible with them. She tried many subjects. There were no points of contact, she told herself.

At last, desperately, she rose to go. Of course, he must insist upon going with her. Of course!

"I was going back early, anyway. I'm to be up at dawn to-morrow."

The good-bys were said. She found herself walking rebelliously by his side. "No, thank you!" to the offer of his arm.

The night was bright with stars. "Bright as day, isn't it?" Because her voice was curt, and she had not used his name, the rising inflection helped a little! Hateful, to stumble over a rut in the road! Of course, he'd make her take his arm! Of course!

Rickard grasped her elbow. She walked along, her head high, her cheeks flaming, anger surging through her at his touch.

Stupid to press this companionship, this awkward silence on her. If he thought she was going to entertain him, as Gerty did, with her swift chatter, he'd be surprised! Any other two people would fall into easy give-and-take, but what could she, Innes Hardin, find to chatter about with this man stalking along, grimly grasping her arm? Close as they were, his touch reminding her every minute, between them walked her brother and her brother's wife—and there was the Mexican—hateful memory! Of course, she could not be casual. And she would not force it. He had brought this about. Let him talk, then!

Oppressive that silence. Then it came to her that she would ask him the question that his coming had aborted. A glance at his face found him smiling. He found it amusing? Not for worlds, then, would she speak. And they stalked along. Unconsciously, she had pulled herself away from him. He took her hand, and put it in the crotch of his arm. "That's better," he said. She wondered if he were still smiling.

Their path led by his tent. Neither of them noticed a subdued light through the canvas walls. As they reached the place, a figure darted from the door.

"Oh, señor, I thought you would never come." It was the wife of Maldonado. Her expression was lost on Innes. The face was quivering with terror.

"Mr. Rickard," Innes' words like icicles, "I will leave you here. It is quite unnecessary to come farther." Quite unveiled her meaning!

It came so quickly that he was not ready; nor indeed had Gerty's innuendos yet reached him. But the situation was uncomfortable. He turned sharply to the Mexican. "What are you doing here at this hour?"

"Oh, señor," she gasped. "It is the worst. The señor said I was not to go home; and I tried, *Dios mio,* how I tried to obey. But the children, little Rosita, not yet four? How could I know that that woman fed them, or combed their hair? I crept in, just to see—and *Dios mio!*" She covered her face with her hands.

"Come in," he took her roughly by the arm. She would wake up the camp with her crying. He put her in a chair. "Now tell your story." The woman had got to be a nuisance. He couldn't have her coming around like this. He had seen that look in the girl's eyes—the Mexican's rocking grief was theatric. He wouldn't have her coming around. It didn't look right—"Murdered? Who did you say was murdered?"

She lifted a face, frightened into haggardness. "Maldonado and the girl."

The night was stripped to the tragedy. "You found them?"

Her face was lifted imploringly to his. "The señor knew best. I should never have gone. Will they come after me? Will they come and take me?" Her terror was physical. Her teeth were chattering. She was exhausted from running. She had stumbled, blindly, the distance between the camp and her home. "Oh, señor, it was not I. By the Mother of Christ, it was not I."

Rickard was not sure. Her fear made him suspect her. "Who was it, you think?"

"Felipe," she gasped.

"But they took him to Ensenada, you said;" Rickard was inclined to think the murderer was before him.

"No, señor. He got away from the rurales—he came back. He went home—there was no one there. Some one told him where she had gone. He came to Maldonado's. Lucrezia, the eldest, opened the gate. He was terrible, she said. He rushed past her. And when he came out, his hands were red. The children heard cries. They were afraid to go in. I got there last night. I went in. They were not quite cold—I was afraid to stay. It would look like me, señor. I made the children stay behind. They could not run so fast."

"How do you know it was Felipe?" sternly asked Rickard.

"A long scar, señor, from here to here," she motioned from lip to ear. "Lucrezia had seen him. Will they take me, señor?" She was a wreck of terror.

"Not if what you tell me is true. Now, get to bed. I'll give you something that will make you sleep."

"But the children?"

"Nothing can be done to-night. Drink this." He was not sure yet that she was telling him the truth. "I'll send MacLean down in the morning." He hustled her out of the tent.

He wondered as he got into bed as to the truth of her story. Disgusting, such animal terror! Awkward hole, that. Fate seemed possessed to queer him with those Hardins!

CHAPTER XXXIII

A DISCOVERY

THE murder of Maldonado shook the camp next morning. The wife had run from Rickard's tent to Mrs. Dowker, who had put the hysterical creature to bed. All night, she babbled of her horror. There had been no sleep at the Dowkers'; the boy woke up shrieking with fright at the strange sobbing. Dowker spoke of it at the mess-tent at breakfast; an hour later, Rickard met the story there. He wondered if it had yet reached Hardin's sister. He decided to send MacLean down to the house of the oleander to get at the facts.

He was rushing MacLean through the morning's dictation, when three rurales, in brilliant trappings, rode up to his ramada. They looked like stage soldiers, small and pompous in their spectacular uniforms and gold-laced hats. The leader, entering the office, announced that they were on the track of a criminal, the murderer of a rurale, Maldonado. The crime had occurred two nights ago, down the river. The señor knew the place. There was a famous oleander—

"Do you know who it was?" Rickard felt sure of the answer. He himself thought that the murderer lay sleeping in Mrs. Dowker's tent.

The spokesman of the party, of fierce mustaches, and glittering bullion, surprised him. "An Indian, named

Felipe." He repeated the story Rickard had heard before. Felipe had escaped his guards, the companions of the speaker. They had followed him, tracked him to his home; then, conclusively on to the adobe of the oleander where Maldonado and the woman were found —butchered. It was quite clear. He had left a stupid trail behind him of noisy threats, revenge—

"Maldonado's girl herself opened the door for him; she saw him run out. Oh, he will be shot for this. Maldonado was a good officer."

Rickard did not feel called upon to question the adjective. The evil place would be closed; the commandant would see to that. He asked about the dead man's children, if they were still at the adobe—

"An Indian woman, their only neighbor, is with them. They will be cared for. Would the señor give his respected permission for notices to be posted about the camp? A description of the Indian, a reward for his capture; the favor would be inestimable."

Rickard took the placard, written in fairly correct English and Spanish. The government of Mexico was calling its people to capture "One Felipe, Indian, belonging to the tribe of Cocopahs. His skin dark to blackness, with high cheek-bones, and an old fading scar, bluish, which runs from mouth to ear. Five feet, eight inches tall, with black hair reaching below his shoulders. One hundred dollars reward for his arrest, or apprehension. When last seen, he was wearing blue cotton trousers, a faded cotton shirt. The fugitive speaks Spanish, a little broken English and several Indian dialects."

The two solemn rurales stood at attention as the resplendent officer repeated his convictions.

"He is somewhere in the river-bed, otherwise we would have found him. The thick undergrowth shelters him, señor. He is skulking somewhere between Hamlin's and Maldonado's. He has had a start of twenty-four to thirty-six hours, maybe more, but then—our horses, señor! If we may be allowed to post these notices, we will then push up to Hamlin's Crossing. A posse is scouring the country around Maldonado's. He will not escape."

Rickard gave the card back to the pompous little officer whose sword and spurs clanked as he bowed over it. He thanked the señor eternally for his attention and courtesy. He saluted again, wheeled, marching out of the ramada, with his stage-soldiers.

Rickard saw the notice later that day. It was nailed to the back platform of the *Palmyra*. He was on Marshall's trail, his chief having failed to keep an appointment with him. They were to test the gate that afternoon; Marshall was returning soon to Tucson.

Rickard found Claudia in the darkened car reading a note from her husband. With a rising inflection that did not escape him, she told her visitor that her husband had been called to Yuma on business.

"Oh, that's so," cooperated Rickard, concealing his amusement at Marshall's truancy. "I'd forgotten about that business." Claudia Marshall had reason for her anxiety. But not for wifely worry would he mention that forgotten appointment at the river!

"He may be kept late, he says." Rickard was conscious that she was watching his face. "He says not to wait up. *That* means late hours. Oh, Tod ought not! Every time, his cough comes back—" He had caught her off guard. Her fears were a crucifixion.

In Tucson, Rickard had heard a dwarfing version of over-solicitude. Since he had been with them at the river, the thing smacked to him of tragedy. He had seen the gentle rogue slip that wistful bridle before. Her eyes, to him, looked robbed. Why should she not grudge each unnatural night, insist on life at her terms instead of the full-blooded recklessness of his?

He left the car musing on marital ironies. Daring adventure to throw together a team of unmatched natures, gambling on exteriors—as teams are chosen. Without a driver, he followed his thought whimsically, what team left so to itself would not smash its harness? Terrible plunge, that! What can two people, neighbors even, know of congeniality, that mutual delight which must survive the nagging friction of every-day life? Harder for a man to know the nature of the woman he picks out, than for the girl. She has his work as a guide; she can guess at temperament and taste. What guide has a man in the choice of the home-bred girl, the only sort he himself could imagine being willing to pin his faith to? Modern life, the home, shelters the woman; she has no profession to betray her taste or disposition. In a place like this, it's different. Camp life shows up the real man or woman. A good preliminary course, that, in matrimony, love-sick couples, made to work out a probation in a rough camp, the woman to cook, the man to hunt for grub and fire-wood! Fewer marriages, perhaps, but then not so many divorces.

A group of Indian children were playing under a clump of willows, directing a mimic stream through a canal of their own making. Even the children were playing the river game! He stopped to watch their mimicry. A pool of deserted water lay caught in a depression. The little brown hands had raised a labored levee, had scooped out the return canal.

"Hold on," cried Rickard. An engineering problem had stopped their game. The stream, returning, threatened to overwhelm their breastworks. "Do it this way." The miniature of a stolid bronze buck looked up uncomprehendingly. Rickard tried Spanish. The children shook their heads. He got down on his knees, and in a few minutes straightened out the rebellious river. Many a year since he had played with kids! The little faces looking up at him, the confidence, stirred quiescent longings. He was no longer what one would call a young man. He was living so hurriedly that he was allowing life in its great, sweet solemn meaning to pass him by. It was always *mañana* with him, or *pasada mañana*. And he was getting along!

Stretching the kinks in his legs, he continued his walk. He would take a look at the levee while he was there. The youngsters' problem recurred to him. He had had a new thought back there. He pulled a note-book from his pocket, scrawling as he went. An idea pulled him stock-still. Why not, he asked himself with some excitement? Custom says *borrow-pits on the outside*. What was the origin of that custom?

"Is not our problem different?" he demanded. "A dike is placed usually to protect immediately usable land. Not so, here. Well, then, why?" The borrow-pit must be a menace on the stream side, must expose fallible softness to floods—queer he hadn't thought of that before. He must think that well over before he made a change, but it certainly did look reasonable to him.

He hailed Parrish, down the levee a distance. Parrish was the foreman of that section of levee, in charge of a big gang of Indians and hoboes. He came up running.

"Go slowly here," advised his chief. "I may change the orders. Going to open up muck ditches this afternoon?"

Parrish thought that they might, late.

"Wait to see me. Come up to camp this evening. I'll go over it by myself first. I'll talk it over with you."

Parrish asked hesitatingly would the next night do as well? He had promised Mrs. Parrish to go to Yuma to fetch some medicines she needed. She wasn't well, but if it was pressing—

"Surely, go," agreed Rickard. "But you will be passing the camp. Lay off early to-night, and start in time to have a talk with me before going to Yuma. Here, this is what I'm figuring on." He wanted to try it on the practical mind, unbiased by conventions. He drew his idea again, elaborating the suggestion of inside borrow-pits.

"I don't see why it isn't right," frowned Parrish, whose ideas grew slowly.

"I believe it *is* right. But I'll go over it carefully at the office. Drop in early. I'll give you your orders for to-morrow."

Rickard turned back toward camp, deep in his thought; so intent that a sharp cry had lost its echo before the import came to him. He stopped, hearing running steps behind him. Innes Hardin was loping up the bank like a young deer, with terror in her eyes.

"Mr. Rickard," she cried, "Mr. Rickard!"

She was trembling. Her fright had flushed her; cheek to brow was glowing with startled blood. He saw an odd flash of startling beauty, the veil of tan torn off by her emotion. The wave of her terror caught him. He put out his hand to steady her. She stood recovering herself, regaining her spent breath. Rickard remembered that this was the first time he had seen her since the murder of Maldonado, since the meeting with the Mexican woman at his tent. "What was it frightened you?"

"The Indian, the murderer. Just as they describe him on those notices, the high cheek-bones, the scar, a terrible gaunt face. I must have fallen asleep. I'd been reading. I heard a noise in the brush, and there was his face staring at me. Foolish how frightened I was." Her breath was still uneven. "I screamed and ran. Silly to be so scared."

He started toward the willows, but she grabbed his sleeve. "Oh, don't." She flushed, thinking to meet the quizzical smile, but his eyes were grave. He, too, had had his fright. They stood staring at each other. "I'm afraid—" she completed. How he would despise her cowardice! But she could not let him know that her fear had been for him!

He was looking at her. Suppose anything had happened to her! He had a minute of nausea. If that brute had hurt her—and then he knew how it was with him!

He looked at her gravely. Of course. He had known it a long time. It was true. She was going to belong to him. If that brute had hurt her!

She shrank under his gravity; this was something she did not understand. They were silent, walking toward the encampment. Rickard did not care to talk. It was not the time; and he had been badly shaken. Innes was tremulously conscious of the palpitating silence. She fluttered toward giddy speech. Her walk that day, Mr. Rickard! She had heard that water had started to flow down the old river-bed; she had wanted to see it, and there was no one to go with her. Her sentence broke off. The look he had turned on her was so dominant, so tender. Amused at her giddiness, and yet loving her! Loving her! They were silent again.

"You won't go off alone, again." He had not asked it, at parting. His inflection demanding it of her, was of ownership. She did not meet his eyes.

Later, when she was lying on her bed, face downward, routed, she tried to analyze that possessive challenge of his gaze, but it eluded words. She summoned her pride, but the meaning called her, sense and mind and soul of her. It cried to her: "I, Casey Rickard, whom your brother hates, once the lover of Gerty Holmes, I am the mate for you. And I'm going to come and take you some day. Some day, when I have time!"

Oh, yes, she was angry with him; she had some pride. "Why didn't he tell me then?" she cried in a warm tumult to her pillow. "For I would have given him his answer. I had time, ample time, to tell him that it was not true." For she wanted a different sort of lover, not a second-hand discard; but one who belonged all to herself; one who would woo, not take her with that strange sure look of his. "You'll be waiting when I come." Ah, she would not, indeed! She would show him!

And then she lay quite still with her hand over her heart. She *would* be waiting when he came for her! Because, though life had brought them together so roughly, so tactlessly had muddled things, yet she knew. She would be waiting for him!

Before he had left her, Rickard had followed a swift impulse. Those bronze lamps averted still? Was she remembering—last night? No mistake like that should rest between them. He must set that straight. That much he allowed himself. Until his work was done. But she knew—she had seen—how it was with him!

"I wonder if you would help me, Miss Hardin? Would you do something for that poor crazed woman? I wanted to ask Mrs. Hardin, but for some reason I've got into her black books. The Mexican needs help,— she ran away from her children, she thought the suspicion would fall on her—I suppose we must not blame her for cowardice. Just the little kindness one woman can give another. A man finds it difficult. And these Mexican women don't understand a man's friendship."

Her eyes met his squarely. His tantalizing smile had gone. He was making a demand of her—to believe him, his request his defense. The glances, of yellow eyes and gray, met with a shock, and the world was changed for both. Life, with its many glad voices, was calling to senses and spirit, the girl's still rebellious, the man's sure.

It was the serene hour of the day. The work of the day was done, save Ling's and the river shifts'. The wonderful slow evening of the desert was unfolding. Beyond, the distant deep-shadowed mountains, which shut them out from the world, made a jagged rent across the sky.

Rickard pulled himself free from the solemnity of that moment. They were to be friends—first! He sought her eyes. Good! They were not to be enemies any more!

He put out his hand. "Good night!" To both, it carried the sound of "I love you!" She put her hand in his, then tore her fingers away, furious with them for clinging. Where was her pride? When he had time!

She fled into her tent, his look from which all laughter had faded, following her.

Neither of them had seen Gerty Hardin watching them from her tent door.

CHAPTER XXXIV

THE FACE IN THE WILLOWS

THAT evening, in her tent by the river-bed, Mrs. Parrish thought that she heard a noise outside. She had been lying down, a wet cloth pressed over her eyes which would twitch in spite of desperate effort. She had sent Sam to Yuma for ammonia and headache powders, and for valerian; the last for her nerves.

It was only the wind rustling the river willows, but it startled her every time. She wished that she had not let him go. The headache, the twitching, was easier to stand than loneliness. She kept her nerves on edge listening for noises. That noise again! Some one was surely prowling about the tent. She raised her head, straining her ears. There was no sound without. She was unstrung. All that excitement about the murder of Maldonado had made her scary. There, what was that?

She tore the wet rag from her eyes and jumped up. A face haggard and wild was staring at her through the screen-wire door. The twilight was lingering; the long warm dusk of the desert. She could see that it was an Indian, and her blood froze; for a purple scar twisted his face.

She had seen the rurales nail a notice on the tool house down the river that very morning. She had braved the fierce noon sun to read it. The description was burned in red letters on her memory. "High cheekbones, long streaming hair. Faded cotton shirt, a scar from mouth to ear!"

"Bread," the voice grated on her. *"Dame el pan,* señora. Love of Gord, bread, señora. *Pi-*why. *La-hum-pah."*

Her flesh chilling, she was backing cautiously toward the table. He must not guess what she was seeking.

She found it difficult to enunciate. Her tongue was thick. "You understand camp? Indian Camp?" He shook his head. She was still backing, retreating toward her revolver. "Camp," she insisted. "Indians have bread, mucho. Go there. Get bread, mucho, there."

"Bread," he pleaded. "Bread, señora. *Hambreando!"*

Starving! She knew what that meant. Then he was dangerous. To save herself, she would give him bread, but she was afraid to open the door. Every Indian tragedy she had ever read shook her then with terror. She was groping blindly, her hand behind her, over the crowded surface of the table. She struck against the cold steel butt of the gun. Her fingers curled around it.

"Go away," she repeated. "Man come pretty soon." He would know what that meant. She lifted her revolver, and the face left the door.

She dared not now have a light. Her heart was bursting. If it would not pound so! She must quiet it, so she could breathe, so she could shoot. How could she be calm? She was thinking of the things the Indians do to people, to people who have not harmed them; of scalping, of tortures. Sam said these Indians were gentle; but he had said her tent would not blow down. He would not deceive her. He did not know. This

THE FACE IN THE WILLOWS

shook,—with fear, but of course he could not have crept in! She would have heard him break the door. Foolish, to be so nervous. That was only the box she had felt, the box with a woolen cloth over it, the green and yellow portière from Coulter's, Chicago. Was it Coulter's? Where *was Coulter's?* How her head pounded!

She must not let herself go like that. She must control herself. She had a long night ahead of her.

For an instant, as she relaxed her stiffened muscles toward the pine box, her sharp gaze wavered from the dark spot on the river-bank. She pulled herself together sharply; she must not let him surprise her, steal on her. She must be on guard. Her finger found the trigger again. Why had she sent Sam? Oh, why had she ever let him leave her?

The stars were coming out in numbers now. Increasingly, their lamps fell on the cleared space between the tent and the dark river-line. A broad band of star-washed sand lay between her and the skulking figure in the brush, the Indian who had murdered Maldonado. She would see him the instant he stepped out on that belt of light. If she kept her eyes fixed—they must not stray. Before he could reach her, she would shoot. She would have no scruples. He had had none for that man and woman down yonder. She wondered if they were young, if it was for bread he had killed them.

Why was she alone? She couldn't remember. It made her head hurt to think. She was always alone in this desert. Why had she made Sam bring her to such a place, when he wanted to stay home with the folks and the doctor? Why had they come? Oh, yes, she remembered. Their tent had blown down, their Nebraska tent. Funny to see it come down, the dishes all smashing. What a noise they made. It made her laugh to think of it. How it made her laugh! Ssh. She must not laugh. He would hear her over there. He would come creeping back, to leer at her.

What was that smell? Rice, burning rice and scorched codfish. She always let rice burn. She could never remember to control that blue flame, no, it was a yellow flame, long fingers of yellow fire, like the rays of the sun in the desert. Or was it Nebraska? What a smell that was! And she could not leave the door, nor take her eyes from the clump of willows because the company's automobile would be coming upon her, and she with her purple waist on.

What was she thinking of? Nothing was burning. That had happened long ago, before the scorpion frightened her, before the tent blew down back in Nebraska. She couldn't think straight, she was getting sleepy. She must shake it off. Until Sam came back from the levee with the bottles of rice. She knew what those Indians did to people, hungry Indians. They cut off your scalp. Her hairpins might save her, wire hairpins.

The Wistaria. What made her think of that? That was where the good doctor lived who knew what was the matter with her. No—that was Nebraska. But there were no tents in Nebraska. Her head hurt. She wished he would come, or Sam.

There, a movement in the brush. She must be all ready to shoot. Suppose she could not pull the trigger? Her fingers were like bits of steel. Sam would come home and find her lying there, her scalp gone. How funny she would look. Ssh, she must not laugh. The Indian did not like it. He killed anybody who laughed. Sam had told her so. From his hiding-place, she could

THE FACE IN THE WILLOWS

see the Indian shake his finger at her. No, it was a willow branch.—She must be calm!

Sam would be sorry that he had had a headache. It must have been a bad headache, or he would not have left her. He had to get that codfish for his head. No, it was rice; burning rice.

Her eyes burned. If the willows moved, could she see them? She wondered if she should blink to rest those burning balls, would he see it and rush at her, break down that door, barred with a wire hairpin?

She had been sitting there for years. Sam was never coming back. Her gun lay on her knees; her finger touched the trigger. Oh, she could not keep awake any longer. She was slipping, slipping off to—somewhere. The Wistaria. She would bite her lip. That would pull her back. But she could not find her lip. It was running away from her.

There was a stealthy creeping sound outside the tent. She could not see anything. But her eyes pained so. Perhaps he was creeping. A shadow fell between her and the stars. A cautious hand tried the latch.

She fell to low shaking laughter. Funny, he thought he could get in! He didn't know the door was barred—an Indian fooled by a wire hairpin! He could never get in. He would hear her laughing. It would make him angry.

"Lizzie!"

The laughter stopped. He knew her name. He was trying to trick her, to make his voice sound like Sam's.

Her voice was thick with strangled laughter. "Can't come in. Can't get in. Barred, hairpin."

"Lizzie!"

"Say, 'señora.' Go away. Man come back."

"Lizzie!" There was an impact of determined muscle against wood, the door-jamb splintering. A stifled scream rose toward the desert stars. The door fell in. A different sound split the air; another cry in a deeper key, and a man's body fell across her knees. Some bottles crashed to the floor. There was a swift odor of spilled ammonia, of valerian.

Something was burning again! Rice. Burning on her knees. She couldn't shake it off. Why didn't some one come and take off this dead Indian? He hadn't got her scalp. It made her laugh—hush, she must call. She fell to screaming; low terrible cries, thick and muffled, coming through her twitching and twisted mouth.

She was sitting there the next morning when they found her, the body of Sam Parrish shot to the heart, lying at her feet. Her empty gun lay on her knees; her finger at the trigger. Her eyes stared into the willows. They thought her dead until they touched her. Then she screamed!

They carried her out of the valley the next day, still screaming.

CHAPTER XXXV

A GLIMPSE OF FREEDOM

THE siding was deserted. The *Palmyra* had run out to Tucson, carrying Marshall and Claudia with her tender-hued, baby-smelling wools. Of that little party, Tony made perhaps the larger gap, Tony with his diamond blazing on his finger, his "holdouts," left-overs from the Marshall table, and his case of smuggled triple X whisky. The young fellows encouraged his stories of old San Francisco, of Bliss and his yellow tips, of wonderful dinners, of the Bush Street Theater when McCullough and Barrett were there. Ah, those the only days! A forefinger would flank Tony's wicked eye.

Marshall had gone without apprehension. They did not expect now to have setbacks, to have to extend the time set for the ultimate diversion. The days were flowing like oil.

The encampment was filling up with visitors, newspaper men who came to report the spectacular capture of the river. Gerty was finding some opportunities for her chafing-dish and lingerie gowns, but the fish felt small to her net. The attention she received assuaged little of her pride. "At any rate, Rickard will see it." On the *Delta,* for the young engineers were relaxing again toward hospitality, she was a belle. Every afternoon, she served tea to a small court.

Brandon came down, sent by the *Sun,* his old paper. Rickard had the newcomer's tent pitched next his own. He was anticipating snatches of intimacy with this cosmopolitan, whose sweetness he felt sure was the ripe result of some deep experience. His few hours in the Imperial tent had discovered to him a rare brain. He was keen to see more of him.

The day after his arrival, Brandon sent a telegram to his wife. He told Rickard about it afterward.

"I suppose I should have asked you first," he admitted. "I may have taken a liberty!"

"I think you couldn't do that," smiled Rickard. "This camp is yours, señor!"

"Impulse does not often carry me away." The trim-cut, dog-like face of the irrigationist frowned. "I should have asked you. But seeing other women here gave me the idea, I suppose. I telegraphed for Mrs. Brandon to join me here."

Deliberately Rickard controlled the muscles of his face. Every one else knew what he thought about women in camp. He hoped that he would not be quoted to Brandon.

"It is a little different, I think, from ordinary cases," Brandon was working up a justification. "Mrs. Brandon is a writer of fiction, of some note. You have run across her books, her pen name—George Verne."

Rickard's face held back the surprise of it. A smile suffused his mind. Brandon, the classicist, the *Sun's* pet man, a specialist on irrigation, related by marriage to *The Cowboy's Bride!* He acknowledged that he knew her by name, had seen her books. He had been in remote places, where English matter is scarce, and had often found George Verne usurping the shelves.

"I should think she would find this an opportunity," he agreed. He had caught a hint of returning fires in the calm gray eyes.

The thin lips were pursed musingly. "But it is pretty hard for her to leave New York. Her publishers keep her pretty busy."

Rickard's silence was not inactive. He was thinking of the diverted lives; of Brandon living out his banishment in a western desert tent; George Verne weaving her stories hundreds of miles away in a New York apartment-house.

"The separation is hard on both of us." The man was revealing his renunciations in this instant of homesickness; his guards were down. "When my trouble came, I had hoped that her work might make it possible for her to come out with me, at least half her time, that she might gather material. But they crowd her with orders; she works right through the hot summers; I don't remember when she has taken a vacation. I run out once in a while to try to stop her, to make her play a little. But my cough comes back; she has the habit of grind by this time. I'm hoping this will appeal to her as a chance; it's a tremendous setting, this!"

He chatted about valley happenings for a few minutes before leaving.

"Anything I can do for you?" inquired Rickard.

"Thank you, no. I'm off now to the Crossing to see Marshall's gate. And I want to see Matt Hamlin. He was my host once, years ago."

Rickard's mail that morning included a letter from his chief at Tucson. Marshall delivered a peremptory mandate from Faraday. The borrow-pits and muck-ditches were to be constructed according to precedent.

The stream-side excavating was to be continued. Marshall added that this order admitted no argument.

Rickard, fuming helplessly, read the letter to MacLean, Jr. "Everybody sticking his precious fingers in the pie. Tying me up with orders. What does Faraday know about it, I'd like to know?" MacLean observed a Hardin inflection.

The mail had brought other exasperations. A classmate he had been wiring for, an engineer specialist on hydraulics, was ill. There was another letter from Marshall, with enclosures. More complaints from Chicago. Rickard declared he could "smell" Washington.

Irish brought the news of the Parrish horror. The opened vein of tragedy stained the day. The double tragedy, the three sharp deaths sobered the camp, preparing for its coup.

"War!" summed up Rickard. "Our army marches over dead bodies."

The day badly begun, piled up with vexations. By evening, Rickard's temper, slow to rouse, was on the rampage. His men got out of his way. The river flotsam was piling up against the gate and making a kink in the trestle. There was a nasty bend. Rickard spent his afternoon on the by-pass, jumping from boats to rafts, directing the pile-drivers, driving the stolid bucks. By sundown, he was wet to the skin, and mad, he told MacLean, Jr., as a sick Arizona cat.

In this jaundiced juncture, MacLean, Jr., brought down his despatches to the river.

"Anything important?" cried Casey from the raft. "Read them to me. I can hear."

MacLean read of the burning of a trainload of railroad ties in a nasty wreck on the way to the break; just out of Galveston. To purge his mood, Rickard swore.

"If that isn't the darndest." He had "luck" on his tongue. His mood had been paralleling, disagreeably to his consciousness, Tom Hardin's manner. He withheld the word.

"Anything else pleasant?"

"A letter from the governor—from dad. Nothing important." MacLean had that instant decided to leave that letter on the desk where Rickard might find it by himself.

"Fire away," cried Rickard, stretching the cramp from his shoulders.

Uncomfortably, MacLean cleared his throat before he read that his father begged a small favor of Rickard. "Godfrey, the celebrated English tenor, is on my hands. His doctors have been advising outdoor occupation. I am sending him to you, asking you to give him any job you may have. He is willing to do anything. Put him at something to keep him occupied."

MacLean saw Rickard's face turn red. "Suffering cats! A worn-out opera-singer! What sort of an opera does he think we're giving down here? Why doesn't he send me a fur coat, or a pair of girl twins? Give the tenor a rôle! Anything else? Pile it all on."

"That's all." MacLean was turning away. Then, as an afterthought, he threw over his shoulder, "Oh, and one from Godfrey himself. He's in Los Angeles. He says he'll be here to-morrow." He did not wait for his chief's reply.

At the supper-table, Rickard, dry and in restored humor, alluded to the invasion of high notes. "Pity the parts are all assigned! He might have done the "Toreador,' or 'Canio.' The only vacancy—" he could safely gibe at his own complications, for the Hardins were dining on the *Delta* that evening, "is in the kitchen. I wonder how he would like to be understudy to Ling!"

The next day when the incident had been forgotten, and while Rickard was up at the Crossing on the concrete gate, Godfrey blew into camp. He was like a boy out on a lark. His brown eyes were dancing over the adventure.

"He's certainly not sick," thought MacLean, Jr. "Must be his throat." He was a little piqued over Rickard's sarcasm. What in creation was his father thinking about, anyway?

Godfrey asked to be turned loose. "I won't be in any one's way!" He explored the Heading, covered the by-pass in a river boat, went a way down the river, down the old channel through which considerable water was now flowing, made the trip down the levee work, on horseback, and came back bubbling.

"It's the biggest thing I ever saw. But say, Junior, that's what they call you, isn't it? I'm the only idle man here. Can't you give me something to do?"

MacLean was not sure but that the suggestion of Rickard's had been a jest. He felt abashed to repeat it. "I'll do anything," twinkled the handsome tenor. "I'd like the boss to find me busy when he comes in."

MacLean softened the offer. Perhaps until Mr. Godfrey learned the ropes he could be of general use. They were short-handed the present moment—there was another hesitation—in the kitchen! Ling, the Chinese cook, was overcrowded—so many visitors—

"Great," crowed Godfrey, slapping him on the shoulder. "I don't want to feel in the way. I want to earn my board. And it's not bad to keep on the right side of the cook. No one can beat me beating eggs."

His spirits were infectious. "Not many eggs in this camp!" grinned MacLean.

"Lead me to the cook!" declaimed the newcomer. "Chin chin Chinaman!" he sang at a daring pitch. "Chin chin Chinaman, chop, chop, chop!" His voice had the world-adored quality, the vibrant stirring thrill which is never tremolo.

"He'll do," thought the youth. He foresaw concerts on the deck of the *Delta*.

That evening, the dinner was helped on its way by the best paid singer of England. In an apron, borrowed of Ling, he was "having the time of his life." Ling, pretending to scold, had been won immediately. Rickard, hearing of the jolly advent, forgot his vexation, and immediately on his return made his way to the mesquit enclosure—to greet the friend of George MacLean.

It was a comic opera already to Godfrey. He had won over Ling by doing all of the tedious jobs. Had peeled the potatoes, opened the cans of tomatoes, washed the rice and scoured the pans. As Rickard, obscured by the mesquit hedge, reached the enclosure, the newcomer was entering by the riverside.

"Hi, there, you," cried Ling. "Where you put my potato skins? Save potato skins. Me plant skins by liver, laise plenty potatoes—bimeby."

Godfrey laughed uproariously. He pounced on a red slab of bacon rind and was making for the outside, Rickard vastly entertained.

"Hi, there," yelled Ling. "Hi, stop. No thlow bacon away. Save bacon. Me make hot cakes, grease pan."

"Not on your life," Godfrey swept the irate Ling and the entering stranger in khaki a deep theatric bow. "Ling no get bacon. Me plant bacon by river. Me raise hogs!"

Thus met Rickard and the tenor, who captured the camp that night with his singing. After dinner, MacLean carried off his prize to the *Delta,* where Godfrey earned his welcome. In a dark corner, Brandon was feeling the edge of his disappointment. George Verne was blocking out a new book, so she had wired. She was too busy to come. Gerty Hardin forgot to flirt with the engineers; she had discovered a new sensation. The wonderful voice twisted her heart-strings; it told her that the heart that has truly loved never forgets, and she knew that she could never have really loved, yet, because the youth in her veins was whispering to her that she could still forget. Godfrey saw a mobile plaintive face turned up to the gibbous moon; he swept it with thrills and flushes. She was a wonderful audience; she was also his orchestra, the woman with the plaintive eyes. He played on her expressions as though she were a harp.

Later, he was presented to Mrs. Hardin. She told him that the camp would no longer be dull; that she had tea every afternoon in her ramada. She convicted him archly of British-hood. "She knew he must have his tea!"

"You American women are the wonders of the world! Nothing daunts you. In the desert, and you give afternoon teas. I'll be there every day!"

He gave her open admiration; she looked young and wistful in her soft flowing mulls, the moonlight helping her. She fell into a delicious flurry of nerves and excitement. Later, she wandered with him from a rude gaping world into a heaven of silvered decks and gleaming waters. He told her of himself, of his loneliness; his music had dropped him to self-pity.

Gerty Hardin heard her bars drop behind her. She snatched her first glimpse of freedom.

CHAPTER XXXVI

THE DRAGON SCORES

THE *Palmyra* was once again on its siding. Marshall was at the Front again; having made another of his swift dashes from Tucson. This time he expected officially to close the gate. Claudia was with him. She never left the car, unless it were to step out to the platform to see what she could from there of the river work, immediately returning to her wool work in the shaded compartment.

Hardin and Rickard had been devoting anxious weeks. A heavy rainfall and cloudburst in the mountains of northern Arizona had swollen the feeders of the Gila River which roared down to the Colorado above Yuma. The eroding streams carried mountains in solution which settled against the gate, a scour starting above and below it. Relief had to be given on the jump. A spur-track was rushed across the by-pass above the gate, as the closing of the ill-fated gate with the flash-boards was no longer possible. A rock-fill was the only means of closure. In the distant quarries men were digging out rock to fill the call from the river.

Marshall came down to see the completed spur. Before he reached the intake, the first rock train had moved on to the spur-track. The trestle had settled, the train thrown from the rails and wrecked.

"That's not the way I planned to dump that rock!" was Rickard's comment. "Now, we'll have to stop and straighten out that trestle."

"If we'd had those rock-aprons, this'd never have happened," stormed Hardin, who was standing on the bank when the trestle gave way.

They were already repairing that disaster when the *Palmyra* was cradled on its siding. Marshall from one platform, Tony, white-capped from the rear, started out for the river. Claudia settled herself for a quiet morning.

When Innes Hardin came in later, she felt that she was interrupting a fierce orgy. But Mrs. Marshall would not let her go. "I can knit just as fast when I talk."

The shades were all pulled down. To Innes' protest, her hostess declared that "she could see with her fingers." Innes had never asked the destiny of the little knitted jackets; earlier in the acquaintance she had surmised a pressing haste for some sister, or niece; a tender date. She had seen several downy sacques completed; but still those black needles clicked.

Later, Marshall came in from the damaged trestle, bringing Rickard and Crothers. The chief was in buoyant spirits, as though the accident had played to his hand, instead of against it.

"I've brought company to lunch, mother," his mellow voice called through the car.

Only one caught the look of pain that twisted the severe features of Claudia Marshall. Instantly, Innes saw it disciplined into a welcoming smile. And then she herself fell to flushing, and chilling, as a lithe-muscled figure came directly to her. His eyes—where was the look she had feared, of possessive tenderness? The quizzical gleam was gone. On guard! A solemn business, loving, when you know that it means—Life! On guard, though, to *her!* She pulled her fingers from his strong lingering clasp, and joined Mrs. Marshall, who was again busily knitting, until Tony's crisp whiteness crackled into the apartment.

Rickard had his soldier look on. She was watching him covertly as he talked with his host and Crothers, as though she were not there; as though something were not waiting for him to claim! She told herself that she would have no character if she did not deny him, when he came for her. How could he be talking, oblivious of everything else in the world except that river? Was that—loving? Could she think of anything else when he was in the same room with her? Was that the difference between men and women? Woman's whole existence! He was a soldier of the modern army. It came to her, a sort of tender divination, that he would not divide his thoughts, even with her, with Love, until his battle was won. He owed his mind clear and on duty to the work on hand. Well, couldn't she understand that? What her accusation against Gerty? Sex honor —keep off the track! Wasn't that her own notion? Oughtn't she to be proud of him?

She had brought a nest of waspish thoughts tumbling about her ears. Gerty! He had loved Gerty. Her resentment was alive again. Perhaps, it was not true. Perhaps, some day he would tell her that it was not true, had never been true. He couldn't love her, if his thoughts had ever lingered, with that same seriously solemn look on the false little face of her sister-in-law.

A slur to a chef could one talk of else but food while banqueting! Tony's white cap danced around the table after he had seated them, urging their appetites. Mrs. Marshall tried to suppress him; Marshall and Rickard wickedly abetting his capering. He forced a commendation of his bouillon from dreamy Innes; the recipe, he boasted, was his own. Tod Marshall's query as to the Spanish peppers evoked a long history. The lunch was served to a running accompaniment of his reminiscences, when he had been a restaurateur, and the great Samuel Bliss one of his patrons. He was working up a crescendo of courses. With the importance of a premier, he bore in a majestic, seasoned plank carrying a thick steak. Another trip to the kitchen returned a primrose sauce.

"Tony will be insulted if you do not all mention the Bernaise," Marshall had suggested during the chef's absence.

Rickard declared without straining his veracity that it was the best Bernaise he had ever tasted. Tony's face worked with emotion.

"It is because no one knows how to mix a Bernaise—bah, the bad stuff I've eaten! When I go to a big city, I go to the finest hotel. Good clothes, a diamond ring," his finger shot up to his nose. "And who would refuse to give me a table to myself? Who would believe that it is a cook? I say, 'Your best wine, and the steak thick, and a sauce Bernaise!' Never have I tasted it but once fit to serve to a gentleman like Mr. Marshall—or Mr. Bliss. They make it with poor vinegar. You can not make the sauce Bernaise without the best Tarra-r-rragon vinegar." His r's hurtled out like a burst of artillery. "Everywhere you can not get the real Tar-r-ragon vinegar. Ah!" His face grew wolfish and eager. "Tony knows. Tony always carries it with him for the great gentlemen like Mr. Bliss, Mr. Marshall—"

"Some bread, Tony," clipped in Mrs. Marshall. "You can not teach him his place," she complained in the interval, "if you let him talk like this!"

"Oh, but you don't want to, mother!"

Innes saw again the look of pain. Did he think her life complete, in its guarding of his own reckless one! Innes thought pitifully of the little knitted jackets. Hadn't he ever sensed—those?

Tony trotted back with the bread. He was eager with speech, but Rickard was beginning a river anecdote, of his introduction to Godfrey, the story of the bacon rind. Marshall was at once interested in the tenor.

"We must have him down some night to sing for us, eh, mother?"

"Oh, I wish he wouldn't call her that!" yearned Innes.

A rich salad of mayonnaise and canned shrimps was rejected, to the chef's despair.

"Why, you'll incapacitate us, Tony." Marshall waved it away. "I want to get back to Tucson alive. Now, a cup of coffee, not another thing on your life—or I'll cut your salary. I want Mr. Rickard to do some work this afternoon! Now be quick with the coffee."

Deep gloom covered the retreat of the salad.

The coffee was brought in with ascetic simplicity. But Tony was not to be crushed. While Marshall was talking to Rickard, he insinuated a platter of cream puffs toward the ladies.

Marshall caught the sly action. He stopped. "You can have one—but only one, Rickard," he commanded. "If Tony does not mind me, you must."

"If you will excuse me," Rickard was rising. "Tony, will you *owe* it to me? There really is other work to be done to-day. You are setting a bad example in camp,

Mr. Marshall, you and Tony. We are not sybarites here." His good-by to Innes was guarded. Why should she drop her eyes, she asked herself angrily? Nothing there that the whole world might not see! Marshall went out to the platform with his engineer. Immediately he came back, smiling, "Look here, girls!"

Claudia and Innes Hardin followed him to the platform. Under the kitchen window, a group of young engineers were eating indiscriminate "hand-outs." MacLean, unabashed, waved a lukewarm stuffed pepper at his chief. Bodefeldt, caught red-handed, crimsoned under his desert tan when Innes' glance isolated him, his mouth full of cream puffs, his hand greasy from fried bananas.

"He's a prince," cried Bangs, of the Reclamation Service.

"He can afford to be on that salary," cried MacLean, with roguish intention. "I'd be generous on a hundred and fifty a month."

"Mex.," cried Bangs. "That's only seventy-five."

"It's a hundred and fifty," spluttered the white cap from the window. "I spend it in Mexico; I get twice as much for a dollar down there."

"Don't let them tease you, Tony," laughed Marshall. "You'll spend that hundred and fifty in Mexico next week."

They were standing in the shade of the *Palmyra,* Claudia on the platform shading her eyes, Innes on the step below. It was a soft still afternoon. There was no wind; not a cloud blurred the sky. The burning heat of summer had passed, giving place to a warmth that was like a caress. The fierceness of the savage desert had melted to her days of lure. Beyond, the turbid waters of the Colorado bore a smiling surface. There was nothing to hint of treachery.

It was a minute of pleasant lassitude, snatched from the turmoil. Rickard had succumbed to the softness of the day and his mood. He was enjoying the thought of Innes' nearness, though she kept her face turned from him. He knew by the persistence of those averted eyes that she was as acutely conscious of his presence as he was, restfully, of hers. Deliberately, he was prolonging the instant.

"Well?" said Marshall. The group moved. Rickard turned toward his hostess. Just then a strange thing happened. A stir on the river had caught the alert eye of Tod Marshall. He swore a string of picturesque Marshallian oaths. Rickard's eyes jumped toward the by-pass. The placid waters had suddenly buckled. Majestically, the gate rose and went out. They watched it variously, the groups by the *Palmyra;* the catastrophe too big for speech. Months of work swept away! The gate drifted a hundred feet or more, then stopped as though sentience, or a planned terminal, were governing its motion. Some unseen obstruction caught it there, to mock at the labors of man.

Innes, aghast, had turned toward Rickard. His face was expressionless. There was a babel of excited voices behind them, Bodefeldt, MacLean, Tony, Crothers, Bangs, all talking at once. Her eyes demanded something of Rickard. A fierce resentment rose against his calmness. "He knew it," she rebelled. "He's been expecting this to happen. It's no tragedy to *him!*" There was a stab as of physical pain; she was visualizing the blow to Tom.

She heard Marshall's voice, speaking to Rickard.

THE DRAGON SCORES

"Well, you're ready for this." She did not hear the answer, for already Rickard was heading for the by-pass. Marshall and the young engineers followed him. The women were left staring. An odd sound came from the rear of the car.

"What is that?" demanded Claudia.

They found Coronel sitting on the ground, his knees drawn up to his chin. His mud-crusted head was turned riverward. His age-curdled eyes, fixed on the spot where the gate had been, did not see them. A moaning issued from his shut lips. His paint-striped shoulders were shaking with dry sobs. He had been watching, waiting for fifteen years. It was all over, now, to him. The Great Dragon had conquered.

Innes moved toward him. Coronel cared, Coronel and Tom! The Indian sat, wrapped in his grief. To the girl the worst, too, had happened. She had refused to believe in the possibility of failure. Her brother's optimism had swept her along. That wreck down yonder was worse than failure; it was ruin. It involved Tom's life. It was his life. This would be the final crushing of his superb courage—her thoughts released from their paralysis were whipped by sudden fear. She must find him, be with him. She did not see the look of sympathy on Claudia Marshall's face. She felt alone, with Coronel. The next instant, she was speeding like a young colt toward the encampment.

Estrada met her on the run. "Have you heard?" she cried. Estrada said he had just been talking to Rickard. He looked sorry, she reflected after she left him, sorry for her; but not surprised. "No one is surprised but Coronel, Coronel and I."

Had Gerty heard? The pity that she must know! She

would not be tender to Tom; her pride would be wounded. She must ask her to be tender, generous. Her footsteps slackened as she came in sight of the tents.

She heard voices in the ramada, a man's clear notes mingling with Gerty's childish treble. "Godfrey!" Her mind jumped to other tête-à-têtes. Of course! Abundant opportunity, with herself and Tom at the break all day! So that was what was going on. And she not seeing! Just a cheap little woman! If not one man, then another! Conquests, attention! Horrid little clandestine affairs!

The meeting was awkward. Speedily, Innes got rid of the news. She caught an odd look glittering in Mrs. Hardin's eyes. The same expression Rickard had worn when the gate went out! As though his slate had been cleared, as though her sister-in-law saw an obstacle drop from her path.

Mrs. Hardin shrugged. Her shrugs were dainty, not the hunching variety. She merely moved her shoulders, the action as elusive as a twinkle.

"I believe I'll go out." Plaintively, she made the announcement as though it were just evolved. "Now, the camp will be horrid. Everybody will be cross, and everybody will be working. Perspiring men are not inspiring men!"

As she left the tent beyond, Innes could hear the vibrant voice of Godfrey persuading Mrs. Hardin to stay there a few weeks longer. She could hear him say, "This will delay the turning of the river at the most but a few weeks. Rickard told me so a week ago. And think what it would be here without you!"

"They were all expecting it!" resisted Innes Hardin. She turned back toward the river. She must find Tom.

CHAPTER XXXVII

A SUNDAY SPECTACLE

TROUBLE with the tribes, innocent and childish in its first aspect, was well grown before it was recognized. Disaffection was ripe, the bucks were heady, the white man's silver acting like wine. Few of the braves had dreamed of ever possessing sums of money such as they drew down each Sunday morning. They were paid a white man's wage, and to each group of ten went another man's pay, *"lagniappe,"* to be paid to a squaw cook for the squad. The extra sum had excited from the first a gentle insurrection. Had they dared, they would have divided it among themselves, but the obloquy of "squaw man" confronted them. The discussion was weekly; over their pipes and their fires that sum was passed, itching their palms.

It was a solemn processional, smacking of ceremonial, which filed into Rickard's ramada every Sunday. Pay time was the climax of their week, the symbol of the revel which followed. All day, the bucks danced and glutted.

Rickard began to suspect liquor again. The commandant and Forestier protested. There was no way of their getting liquor. Still Rickard shrugged, incredulous. In the Indian camp, Sunday was a day of feasting, followed by a gorged sleep; the next day, one of languor, of growing incohesion.

Rickard spoke of it to Coronel who was his "go-between," as MacLean, Jr., dubbed him, a valuable interpreter, because he transcribed the spirit of an interview. Coronel's patois, mongrel and pantomimic, was current coin among all the tribes.

"Like small baby," hunched the old shoulders. "Happy baby. Pretty soon stop."

With the next wages went a reprimand, then a warning. Still followed bad Mondays. It was easy to see that no work was to be expected from them on that day, their all-night feasting insufficiently slept off. Rickard then issued a formal warning to all the tribes.

The white men were being held antithetically by their habits of carousal; Rickard, doling out the weekly wage, had been observing the pitiable look of determination on the faces of the volatile hobo. "The look of 'I can bear no more; I shall move on.'"

"Poor devils!" he exclaimed to MacLean as Number Ten, the hobo without a name, shuffled out, bearing his money in his hand and a farewell leer on his face. His number, bound by a circle, his mark and title, decorated each bridge and pier, so his boast ran, between New Orleans and San Francisco, and then again, New York. He was on his second round, and he had never bought a ticket in his life.

"Poor devils," he repeated as the desert's perspective claimed the tramp. "They always think that they are not coming back. It's a mean trick we play on them."

"What's the trick?" queried MacLean absently, who was thinking of Innes Hardin. He had seen her on the river with his chief the evening before; and the flash of betrayal from the eyes of Rickard, the girl's shy quenched gleam of surrender, had been a shock to him. Until that instant, he had thought she lined up with the rest of the Hardins in hating Rickard. So that was what had been going on under his nose! It looked settled to him; he would not have believed that no word had been spoken.

He had wondered since what variety of fool he had been making of himself. Trying to oust a man like Rickard—a *man*. That was the particular sting. He was reproaching himself for bloodlessness as he counted out moneys for his chief that afternoon. Surely, had he any spirit, his disappointment would have flared into bitter enmity against the man who had stolen what he was coveting. For Innes Hardin was a queen! He had never seen any one like her. Queer, he could not make himself hate Rickard. Something must be wrong with himself, to be able to sit there in the old familiar way, without bitterness in his heart.

"They think they are free men; free to go and come. And we own them, body and soul. They might as well be slaves for all they can do."

MacLean frowned. "I don't think I understand." He put aside his problem for a while. He would settle that later.

"Lord! MacLean, didn't you see 'Ten's' face?"

Dimly, MacLean summoned a gaunt heat-seared visage; an unshaven, stubbled face of leering defiance. "He won't come back again."

"But he will. He's got to come back. He can't get through Yuma. That's the trick. We have the screw on them. Yuma's practised. She won't let a man with a week's wages in his pockets slip through her talons.

They all mean to go. Lord! I see it in each of their faces as they come in here. As I pay them off, their eyes say: 'I've got enough to be quit of you with your hell-hole. You can go to the devil for all the work you'll get out of me.' They don't say it because they're afraid, not of me, but of Yuma. They're afraid of Yuma. And when she's sucked them dry, they slink back here for one more week of it."

MacLean drew in his lip, frowning at the memory of the stubbled face as it had glared at Rickard.

"You remember Jack, the hobo?"

"Arnica Jack?" In spite of his resolution to be miserable, MacLean laughed. The hobo's weak ever-turning ankles made him the butt of the hobo camp. A bottle of arnica in his coat pocket, the insidious smell of the stuff which clung to his clothes, had drawn the inevitable sobriquet.

"He didn't come in to-day. Poor devil! He's trying to stick it out, and not draw his wages. You run a chance of being put off in the heart of the desert when you ride out on a brake-beam from Yuma. You've got to have a little 'dough' in your pocket to wheedle a man with a team, or a soft-hearted brakeman. Else it's death. We've got it on them, a dead sure cinch."

"Why haven't I seen any of this?" demanded MacLean, sitting up, very red.

"It's not on the surface. They go out swaggering Sunday; they come back cringing Monday. That's all there is to it. But the situation with the Indians is more serious. They're getting liquor in here, some way, the Lord only knows how. Maybe Coronel is right; he declares they are simply gorged with food, dead from their stuffed orgies. Anyway, they're not fit for burning Monday morning. I've just sent them word by Coronel that it's got to quit, or they do."

"Suppose they do?" MacLean was startled. Not an Indian could be spared at that stage of the game.

"Bluff!" Rickard got up. "It's caught white men before this. They won't take the chance of losing that money. I'm off now to the Crossing. There's a hitch at the concrete gate. I'll be back this afternoon. I'll leave you in charge here."

"I'll hold down your seat." He did not remember his lagging enmity until Rickard's dancing step had carried him out of sight. MacLean spent an hour unraveling the puzzle of it. If a man really loves a woman,—his question hurled a doubt at the integrity of his affection. Stoutly, he defended that. Yet, he should hate Rickard. His veins must run ice-water. An Ogilvie sort of man he was!

The next morning, Wooster broke into the ramada where MacLean sat clicking his typewriter.

"Where's Casey?"

"Gone to the Crossing. Anything up?"

"Everything's up." Wooster flung his hat on the table. He stood, legs wide apart, his hands thrust into his pockets, looking down on Rickard's secretary. "He's done it now. Sent some all-fired, independent kindergarten orders to the Indians. Says they have to be in bed by ten o'clock, or some such hour on Saturday and Sunday nights. Indians won't stand that! Any tenderfoot ought to know that. At this stage of the game, when we can't afford to lose a man. It's a strike, their answer. That's what his monkeying has brought down on us."

"They're not going to quit?"

"They've sent word they won't work on Mondays, and they will go to bed when they choose Saturday night. Losing one day a week! We can't stand for that."

"That's not so bad." MacLean was relieved. "I thought they were all going. He'll find a way out." He remembered then that he was speaking of his rival. This was an opportunity to put him in the wrong. Instead he was flaming to partizanship. No backbone! He found himself taking the side of the man he should be hating. "He's no man's goat." Only sense of justice, this!

"Luck's been playing into his hands," spat Wooster. "But this will show him up. This'll show Marshall his pet clerk. Tell Casey there'll be no Indians to-morrow." He sputtered angrily out of the office.

Rickard seemed pleased when MacLean made the announcement a few hours later. "Good! Now, we have something to work on."

"You are losing the work of five hundred men for one day a week," urged MacLean, observing him as curiously as though he were a stranger.

"We had already lost them. They have not given us a day's work on Mondays for weeks past, and we've had to give them a full week's pay. You can't deduct for lazy work, not unless you've an overseer for each man."

His secretary was weighing him. "What do you intend to do about it?"

"Call their bluff," grinned Casey, showing teeth tobacco had not had a chance to spoil. "Boycott them." He was at his table, already, writing. He had forgotten to remove his duster or his hat. He was unconscious of his secretary's new appraisement.

A SUNDAY SPECTACLE

"But you can't afford to take the chance—" began MacLean, forcing a tepid hostility.

"Oh, can't I?" His tone suggested, "You're playing on the track, kid."

Reddening, the boy persisted. "But the others—the engineers, *can* you afford to? Suppose you lose?"

Rickard threw down his pen. "I've got to have workers, not dabbers! If I'm to lose the Indians, the sooner I know it the better. I don't want to know what the others think. I've got to go straight ahead. Don't think I've not seen their faces. Take this note to Wooster. Tell him to take Coronel and see Forestier."

On his way, MacLean felt like the match that is to set off a charge of dynamite. Wooster would go straight up in the air. Those Hardin men would make an uproar that would be heard at Yuma!

He found Wooster at the river-bank, with Tom Hardin. The two men were watching a pile-driver set a rebellious pile for the new trestles. Two new trestles were to supplement the one which had been bent out of line by the weight of settling drift. The pile-driver had no Sabbath, now. The piles must be placed before rock could be poured between. Marshall's plan was being followed, though jeered at by Reclamation men and the engineers of the D. R. Company.

"Stop the mattress weaving and dump like hell!" had been his orders.

No one believed that the soft silt bottom of the river which cut out like salt would hold a pour of rock. Marshall, aided by Rickard, schemed to fight power with haste. Faster than the current could wash it downstream, the crews would rain gravel and rock on to the treacherous river-bed.

"And there's always the concrete gate when everything else fails," Marshall was fond of repeating when he saw polite incredulity in opposing faces.

"Boycott the Indians, well, I'm blowed," the beady eyes sparked at Hardin. "Now, he's cut his own throat."

"By the eternal!" swore Hardin. MacLean left the two engineers matching oaths. "If he wins out on this!" he was speculating as he made his way back to his copying, "I'll back him against anything. Wonder how he feels, inside, about it? I know just how I'd feel. Scared stiff."

There was an ominous quiet the next day. Not an Indian offered to work at the river. A few stolid bucks came to their tasks on Tuesday morning; they were told by Rickard himself that there was no work for them. Rickard appeared ignorant of the antagonism of the engineers.

Wooster watched the Yumas carry their stormy faces back to their camp.

"Garl darn it," he cried. "There's his chance, and he lost it."

An unfathered rumor started that Rickard was in with the Reclamation Service men; that he wanted the work to fail; to be adopted by the Service. MacLean broke a lance or two against the absurd slander. He was making the discovery that a man's friendship for a man may be deeper than a man's love for a woman. It was upsetting all his preconceived notions. He was backing his hot young will for Rickard to win out. He got to blowpoint that evening with Bodefeldt. He avoided Wooster and Silent and Hardin. It inflamed his boyish loyalty to find that he was losing his old friendships. He was a Rickard man. He was made to feel the reproach of it.

Wednesday dawned dully. Not an Indian reported. Squatting in their camp, they listened to "Fig Tree Jim" and Joe Apache, the insurgent bucks. Coronel passed from camp to camp, his advice unpopular. "They would get their pay, and stay out Monday beside. Joe Apache said so."

Scouts sent out to watch the work on the river reported it was crippled. The white man would be sending for the Indian soon. The waiting braves sat on their haunches, grinning and smoking their pipes.

On Thursday, Forestier, who must feed his reservation Indians while away from the reservation, grew anxious. He tried arguments with the Indians; then with Rickard. That engineer had just been closeted with Marshall who was taking a swift run out to Tucson that day. Rickard would not budge from his position. The Indians must work Monday, or not at all. He refused to discuss the situation with Forestier, or any one. He was apparently engrossed with the setting of the piles. That the brush-cutting was held up, the work on the levee halted, he waived as unimportant. The look of the Hardin faction was getting on his nerves; he was learning to swear and smile at the same time.

Marshall carried a worried face from the Heading. He must back his man in this! And he never forgot the levee. Still, if he should fail— He determined to arrange to pull some track crews from Salton and the West Coast to send to Rickard for emergency.

Saturday night, the camp went gloomily to bed. On the Indian side, there was no revel, no feasting or dancing. Forestier was closeted with Rickard.

"I'll have to take them back to their reservations," he said. "I can't keep them here, we can't afford to.

They've got to be fed. You know, Rickard, the howl that'd be raised if the thing gets out twisted. Sentimental, the Indian feeling is, you and I know that, but it'd be uncomfortable. The man who'd kick an Indian out of his back yard would go to Washington to start up a scandal if any blamed buck says he was starving."

"Hold them here a few days, you can," Rickard was worried, himself. Forestier could not keep them out of their reservations if they were not earning money. He knew that. Already, he was needing them badly at the river. Something, will or reason, he was not sure, would not let him give in.

"Just two or three days," he urged Forestier.

"I'll try." The face of the Indian agent was not reassuring. Rickard did not turn in until after midnight, planning alternatives. He was sleeping hard when MacLean, at dawn, dashed into his tent.

"Quick, what does this mean?"

Rickard was scrambling into his clothes. It was the river, of course. The trestles had been carried out? He was into his khaki trousers and slippers. He made a dive into his shirt as he followed MacLean to the tent door, his head working through the bag of cloth to the light-well at the top.

"Look over there," cried MacLean. "What do you think of that?"

It was a splendid spectacle, and staged superbly. For background, the sharp-edged mountains flushing to pinks and purples against a one-hued sky; the river-growth of the old channel uniting them, blotting out miles of desert, into a flat scene. On the opposite bank of the New River, five hundred strong, lined up formidably, their faces grotesque and ferocious with paint, were the

A SUNDAY SPECTACLE 365

seven tribes. The sun's rays glinted up from their firearms, shot-guns, revolvers, into a motley of defiance! Cocopahs, with streaming hair, blanketed Navajos, short-haired Pimas, those in front reining in their silent pinto ponies, and all motionless, silent in that early morning light.

"What does it mean?" whispered MacLean. Rickard did not answer. He had one nauseous instant, as he looked toward Innes' tent. Then he noticed a movement in the throng; he saw it was the pressing of newcomers toward the front of the brilliant mass. Brown naked chests gleamed with wet paint. Black shirts, striped with white and yellow and red, made a strange serpent effect. Ropes of beads weighted down their shoulders; ribbons streamed from their arms.

The barbaric spectacle stood immovable. The stir came from the near bank. The camp was rising. From each tent, a face thrust out casually, stayed to watch, startled. The unsettled condition of the days past had prepared the stage for some climax; the surprise loomed savage and threatening.

MacLean was watching Rickard's face. The manager had drawn back into the shadow of his tent. He expected to see them wheel and ride out of camp; this then their ultimatum. He did not fear worse trouble, now that nauseous half-second was over; they had too much to lose; there was no one to organize, to mobilize. Still, they were Indians—he was trying to make out their faces; the whites, surprised—the squads divided, at the levee, up at the Crossing!

MacLean had turned to watch the Indians; he heard a chuckle. Rickard broke into laughter.

"See, the white horse, no, in front—"

"By jove," MacLean slapped his thigh. "Coronel! They had me buffaloed. What do you think it is?"

Rickard stepped out into the wash of morning air, and waved a solemn salute across the river. Gravely, it was returned by Coronel.

"What does it mean?" demanded MacLean.

"It means we've won," chuckled his chief, coming back into his tent.

"If you haven't the best—luck," substituted MacLean, self-consciously.

"If you say 'luck' to me," grinned Rickard, "I'll cane you! Get out, I want my shower. They'll be coming over here now."

An hour later, after every one in camp had looked and speculated and smiled, the first thrill passed, at the massed Indians, Coronel led in a picked group of the tribes. If the white chief would recall the boycott, the Monday strike was over. The white man's silver had won.

Rickard shook hands all around, and commended Coronel privately. "You'll get a present for this." The wrinkled face was majestically inscrutable.

"They could never do it like white men," commented Rickard after they had left the ramada. "They must get up that bit of bravado; they are like children—" He never finished his sentence. He was thinking of a little white tent, and an instant of nausea when he had first seen those waiting Indians.

CHAPTER XXXVIII

THE WHITE NIGHT

"LORD, I'm tired," groaned Rickard, stumbling into camp, wet to the skin. "Don't you say letters to me, Mac. I'm going to bed. Tell Ling I don't want any dinner. He'll want to fuss up something. I don't want to see food."

As he moved on to his tent, MacLean noted a dragging step and a feverish face. But his anxiety was dwarfed by Ling's. The Chinese immediately invaded Rickard's tent, leaving the dishing of the dinner to Godfrey. Ling found Rickard, burning with fever, stripping for a cold shower.

"Velly bad, velly bad," he exclaimed. "Hi, there, you stop," as Rickard went on stripping. "Hi, there, no cold watel. Me ketchem hot watel."

"'*Hot* watel'! I'm burning up now!"

"Here you, get into bed, hop. I ketchem warm watel. Cold watel no good, make velly sick. Hop."

Rickard hopped. He was worn to the point of yielding to any authoritative voice. The day had been exhausting. His eyes closed with weariness. He did not watch Ling's new captaincy. The Chinese, soft-slippered, pattered around the tent, and out. The sheets felt cool and comfortable. Rickard had a sensation of dropping, falling into oblivion.

The day, confused and jumbled, burned across his eyeballs; a turmoil of bustle and hurry of insurrection. He had made a swift stand against that. He was to be minded to the last man-jack of them, or any one would go, his threat including the engineers, Silent, Irish, Wooster, Hardin himself. This was no time for factions, for leader feeling. They knew he meant business; perhaps the tussle with the Indians had had good effect. But he had lost his temper with Hardin and Wooster; he didn't feel pleased with himself. It left a sting of self-discontent which pulled him back from the rest into which he was sinking. A man can enjoy the mastery over other men if he gets out of it with self-control. It seemed worse now than when he had been in the clamor and the contention of the day. Tossing feverishly on his bed, the day's perspective gave no order, no progress. His body was hot, his head on fire.

His grouch focused on Wooster. "The gall of him!" He recalled the snapping black beads of eyes as they resented Rickard's criticism of his handling of the rock.

"Who's superintendent here?" had growled Wooster.

"It is a pity that I must superintend your superintending," had been his answer. "You will obey my orders, or quit."

"He's had an ax for me ever since I came; he's been sore ever since I won over the Indians. He thought he was going to see me crushed. The whole camp would have crowed had those Indians marched out. Lord, what a head I have!"

Ling came in, towing a portable tub of galvanized tin, a bucket of steaming water in his other hand.

"If you think you're going to get me into that, you're mistaken," Rickard raised his head to scowl at the bucket. Ling had the tact not to answer. Quiet as a cat, he placed the tub by the bedside, and emptied the bucket. Pattering to the door, he took from an unseen waiting hand, another pail of rising steam, and a large yellow-papered tin of mustard.

"You needn't think you're going to boss me," Rickard flared with impotent resistance. "Mustard! I've not taken that since I was a small boy. I'm not going to put my foot in it, do you hear?"

Ling would not hear. He was moving noiselessly around the tent, blind and deaf to scowls and grumbling. Rickard watched him collect blankets and towels. His rebellion was deflected. What an amusing race it was, at cooking, nursing or diplomacy equally facile!

"Who was that outside the door?" The hand suddenly reassured to him.

"Mlister Godfley." Ling, the laconic, went on with his preparations. When he had finished, he stopped suddenly in front of the bed. Rickard was off guard.

"Here you, ketchem bath. Hop."

"A bath, get in that? Not on your life," defied Rickard. But he knew he was as putty in Ling's hands.

"Hop, velly quick," commanded Ling.

As Rickard did not hop, he was pulled out of bed by soft Chinese, work-wrinkled fingers. After a sputtering resistance to the sting of the hot mustard, he lay back, an unexpected relaxation meeting his supineness. The first sting over, the pain began to melt from his bones, from his strained aching muscles. His irritability began to dissolve. He decided to forgive Ling, who had left the tent.

His eyes closed. He caught an instant's doze. Ling's entrance wakened him.

"This salad water's all right! I'm going to stay here all night."

The Chinese had a hot, pungent smelling drink in his hand.

"Oh, say," groaned the engineer. "I don't have to drink that!"

"All lite tamale," replied the calm doctor. "Hi, there, get up. Hop. Pletty quick. Take heap cold. Velly bad."

In bed, Ling's hot drink inside him, the day with its irritations fell away. He could see now the step ahead that had been taken; the last trestle was done; the rock-pouring well on; he called that going some! He felt pleasantly languid, but not yet sleepy. His thought wandered over the resting camp. The *Delta* was no longer entertaining; the days were too strenuous for that. Frank Godfrey must be finding them dull. And then Innes Hardin came to him.

Not herself, but as a soft little thought which came creeping around the corner of his dreams. She had been there, of course, all day, tucked away in his mind, as though in his home waiting for him to come back to her, weary from the pricks of the day. The way he would come home to her, please God, some day. Not bearing his burdens to her, he did not believe in that, but asking her diversions. Perhaps she would sing to him, or play to him, little tender tunes he could understand. He had never had time to keep up with the new-fangled music which sounded to his ear like a distinct endeavor to be unmusical and bizarre. All the melodies have been used up; Mozart and those old boys had hogged them. The moderns have had to invent a school of odd discords and queer rhythms. Innes would tell him about that! Some day! Contentment spread her soft wings over him. When Ling came stealing back, his patient was asleep.

The tent was a wash of white light when he woke; the moon was filtering through the white canvas; a band of pale radiance was streaming through the screen door. Rickard wakened as to a call. What had startled him? He had been sleeping heavily, the deep sleep that knows no dreaming. He listened, raising himself by his elbow. From a distance, a sweet high voice, unreal in its pitch and thrilling quality, came to him. It pieced on to his last waking thought. For an instant, he thought it was Innes.

Awake, the rhythmic beat coming clear and sweet to him, he knew it was Godfrey; Godfrey, somewhere on the levee, singing by the river.

"What a voice that fellow has!" He wondered what it was he was singing. "The quality of the angels, and the lure of the sirens besides!"

There was a haunting thrill to the air; something he should remember. He used to be able to carry tunes; was it too late, he wondered, to sharpen his musical memory? The soft side of life he had left alone, music, ease, poetry; they went with women, and his swift marching life had had no time for them. Women and little children. Was it too late to begin? Had he worked too long to learn to play? What was that tune Godfrey was singing now? He knew that; it was about the age of seventeen. It brought him again to Innes Hardin. He pulled aside his curtain which hung over the screening of his tent and looked out into a moon-flooded world.

The stars were dimmed, thrust into their real distances by the world's white courier. Rickard's eyes fell on a little tent over yonder, a white shrine. "White as that fine sweet soul of hers!"

Wandering into the night, Godfrey passed down the river, singing alone. His voice, the footlights, the listening great audiences were calling to him. To him, the moon-flooded levee, the glistening water, made a star-set scene. He was treading the boards, the rushing waters by the bank gave the orchestration for his melody—*La Donna è Mobile*. He began it to Gerty Hardin; she would hear it in her tent; she would take it as the tender reproach he had teased her with that afternoon in the ramada.

He forgot her as he sang, the footlights, the great audiences claiming him. They called him back! *"Bis! bis!"* He gave it again. Still, they called for him. He must come back! He gave them for encore a ballad long forgotten; he had pulled it back from the cobwebs of two decades; he had made it his own; reviving it to a larger popularity; they were selling records of it now on Broadway. In South America, in Mexico, in lonely ranches, distant barrancas, the far-spread audiences listened to his imprisoned voice, by modern magic released to them.

Detached, as an observer he worshiped his wonderful gift; impersonally, it was guarded; he could speak of it without vanity. Pity, the fellow who wrote the simple air was dead; it was enriching publishers; those "canned music people!"

The audience, South American, English, Mexican, was calling. Australia, now, was clapping her hands. That last verse again.

"But, my darling, you will be,
Ever young and fair to me."

The hush, that wonderful hush which always greets that ballad, falls on the house again.

It came, the soaring voice, to Tom Hardin, outside Gerty's tent on his lonely cot. He knew that song. He had shouted it with the fellows at college, passing through the Lawrence streets at night. The words came running back to meet him. "Woman is changeable." Had he sensed the words then? "Woman is changeable." All of them then, not alone Gerty. For she had loved him once, he had seen her face flushing answer into his. Changed altogether, the changeable. Disdained by his wife, a pretty figure a man cuts! If his wife can't stand him, who can? He wasn't good enough for her. He was rough. His life had kept him from fitting himself to her taste. She needed people who could talk like Rickard, sing like Godfrey. People, other people, might misconstrue her preferences. He knew they were not flirtations; she needed her kind. She would always keep straight; she was straight as a whip. Life was as hard for her as it was for him; he could feel sorry for her; his pity was divided between the two of them, the husband, the wife, both lonely in their own way.

Then his bitterness softened to the new air Godfrey was singing. He could hear his mother's voice humming it over her task in her rough pioneer kitchen. He lay quite still listening, life crowding before his open eyes. No use coaxing sleep, with the moon making day of the night. His memory was a harp, and Godfrey was plucking at the strings.

On the other side of the canvas walls, Gerty Hardin

lay listening to the message meant for her. The fickle sex, he had called hers; no constancy in woman, he had declared, fondling her hair. He had tried to coax her into pledges, pledges which were also disavowals to the man outside.

Silver threads! Age shuddered at her threshold. She would not get old, oh, why would he not sing something else? She hated that song. Cruel, life had been to her, none of its promises had been kept. To be happy, why, that was a human's birthright; grab it, that was her creed! Before you get old, before the pretty face wrinkles, and men forget to look at you with the worship beauty brings. She wanted to die before that happened—she would push age away from her—she could. But before that awful time which offered no alleviation, she must be happy, she must taste of success, hear the plaudits of the crowd left behind. When God made the world, He did not make enough happiness to go around; one must snatch it as it passed. There was a chance yet; youth had not gone. He was singing it to her, her escape—

"Darling, you will be,
Ever young and fair to me."

It was not true. The song was a lie. He would not love her when she was old. Men don't. They want roses and bright eyes, youth. Cruel, men are. But she had a few years yet. She would live those years, not spend them with regrets.

She had a wild thought of running out to him, to cry her joy, her bitterness in his arms! He was waiting for her, hoping for her down by the levee; his love was like a schoolboy's in its eagerness. But the sulky figure of Tom guarded her door. Tom was like Innes, always watching her with distrust, suspicion in his eyes. Whatever she would do, they would have driven her to it. She was going to be happy—to be happy before she was old!

Godfrey, singing to Gerty Hardin, had awakened the camp. Once roused, the brilliant night made sleep impossible. Innes, in her tent, too, was listening. Once, in her childhood, she had wakened to the sound of near music, sweet, unearthly, in its soaring lightness, now antiphonal, now in unison. To-night, so Godfrey's song pierced her dreams, and brought back that unreal childish night, another white night such as this. She opened her curtain to the wide spread of silvered desert; the moonlight streamed in on her bed.

"Darling, you will be,
Ever young and fair to me!"

So that is the miracle, that wild rush of certain feeling! Yesterday, doubting, to-morrow, more doubts—but to-night, the song, the night isolated them, herself and Rickard, into a world of their own. To-night, it did not even pain her that he had been the lover of Gerty Hardin, faithful through years, as Gerty had hinted, to a love that was not ever to be rewarded; nor that it had passed to her so lightly. Accidental, propinquitous, seemed his love for her. Not based on congeniality, or knowledge of sympathies. She was not vocal with him —what did he love in her? A trick of smile or speech?

Better that, even, than that he had yielded, simply, to the human need of loving! Even that did not have a sting for her this night. Life with him on any terms she wanted. To-morrow, the proud rebellions might return; now, she could see the risk of losing him! She had not the trick of persuasion; only one way she knew! When he was her own, they might face their differences, then kiss them away! Daring, then witchery! For she wanted to charm her husband; that, the proudest conquest of all. The wonder it was that all women could not see it that way. To win over again, to conquer against commonplaceness, against satiety—to bewitch one's own!

Godfrey was returning to Australia's clapping hands. The desert, Gerty Hardin, were forgotten in the ardor of his singing. To pour out song like that, to make a world listen, be the voice that summons memory! Such a night as this —*"Tanto amor—!"*

On his army cot, Wooster stirred restlessly between his coarse cotton sheets. Something was disturbing him. He was heavy with sleep. But something was the matter with the night. He covered his ears, but the irritation crept through. He raised his head from the pillow, the small snapping eyes accusing the unknown disturber of his peace.

"Those Indians!" he muttered, dragging the sheet over his ears. "Drunk again!"

"Tanto amor!" Godfrey was looking down on the river.

Such a night! It poured wine into the veins of one! Such a voice! To pour it out, thrilling himself over the call of it! Touching something, what was it he touched?

That gleam of moonlight on the river, footlights of fairies. Ah, holy night! *"Tanto amor!"*

Caught in his own spell, Godfrey passed down the levee. And the camp slept again. But even the dreams of Wooster were of love.

CHAPTER XXXIX

THE BATTLE IN THE NIGHT

GATHERING on the bank were the camp groups to watch the last stand of the river against the rock bombardment. The reporters from the outside, pads and pencils in hand, were there, and Brandon; Molly Silent, with little Jim in her arms, who had crept down from the Crossing, full of fears. Out there, somewhere on the trestles, on one of those rock cars was her Jim. She sat on the bank by Innes and Mrs. Marshall, who at last had laid aside her knitting. Tony, his white cap askew, danced from group to group, finding poor audiences. Later, he forced a heartier reception when he returned, bearing sandwiches and hard-boiled eggs, his Indian "help" carrying a pot of steaming coffee.

"That's a capital idea, Tony," commended Rickard, stopping for a snatch of lunch. "Tell Ling to do the same; here, MacLean, you tell him. We'll keep coffee and bread and beans going all day. A lunch-counter on the bank." He was off, his hands full of sandwiches.

A great wave broke into an obliterating eruption of spray. A cry burst from Molly Silent. "Oh, I thought it was gone. There's Jim. He's on the car that's pulling in!"

"Give me the boy," Mrs. Marshall reached out her unpractised arms. "Run down and speak to your husband." She shook her head ominously at Innes as the mother stumbled heavily down the bank. "This excitement is bad for her. Before Christmas, she tells me." She held the little body close to hers. Innes, watching her rapt look, felt her eyes warm up with tears.

Molly toddled back, radiant.

"I saw him!" she glowed.

"I got him asleep!" whispered Mrs. Marshall. "Don't take him; you'll awaken him. Isn't he looking a little pale?"

There was a fear in the face which leaned over the sleeping child. "He's not right. I don't know what's the matter with him. I'd take him out, but I can't leave Jim—so soon. It isn't until Christmas. I'll have to go then. Do you think he looks sickly?" Her anxious eyes questioned the two women.

Heartily, Innes said she thought he was looking stronger.

"Let me take him out," suggested Mrs. Marshall. "We'll be going this week. I'll take the best of care of him; there's a splendid children's doctor in Tucson."

"Oh, do!" cried Innes. And what a charity for Mrs. Marshall, her empty arms aching for what they that moment held!

"Oh!" cried Molly, pain and relief in her tone.

"Think about it," whispered Mrs. Marshall. "You don't have to tell me now."

Molly lifted her head from a scrutiny of the pallid baby face to see Mrs. Hardin, floating by in her crisp muslins. A few feet behind stalked Godfrey, his eyes on the pretty figure by his side. Innes, watching too, turned from his look, abashed as though she had been peering through a locked door.

Gaily, with a fluttering of ruffles, Gerty established herself on the bank, a trifle out of hearing distance. Innes saw her raise an inviting smile to the Englishman who stood looking uncertainly from her to the river. He dropped beside her on the sand. As Innes pulled her eyes away from them, she met those of Molly Silent, who had also been staring at Tom Hardin's wife.

A hard little smile played on the lips accented with Parisian rouge. The blue eyes were following the two men who were directing the bombardment; the childish expression was gone; her look accused life of having trifled with her. But they would see—

"Don't look so unhappy, dearest," whispered the man at her side. "I'm going to make you happy, dear!"

She flushed a brilliant, finished smile at him. Yes, she was proud of him. His success buoyed her faith in her destiny. Everybody knew Godfrey; his voice had subdued whole continents. He satisfied her sense of romance, or would, later, when she was away from here, a dull pain pricking at her deliberate planning. She was tired, tired of scheming, planning; unfair it seemed to her that some women have all that she had had to struggle for tossed into their careless laps. She was proud. She could not be a nobody, crushed by humiliations and adversity. She had not brought any of his trouble on Tom Hardin. It was he, he and Rickard who had ruined her life. Not quite ruined! She was stepping out before it was too late. Godfrey found her young, young and distracting. His life had been hungry, too; the wife, up there in Canada somewhere, had never understood him. Godfrey was ambitious, ambitious as she was. She would be his wife; she would see the cities of the world with him, the welcomed wife of Godfrey; she would share the plaudits his wonderful voice won.

His eyes were on her now, she knew, questioning, not quite sure of her. She had worried him yesterday because she would not pledge herself to marry him if he sued for his divorce. Her intuition told her that something was uncertain, his affection for her, or that other woman's tie, if he hinged his divorce on her promise. "I'm not sure of you! Will you give me your word? When I am free, you, too, will be free, waiting for me?"

She had shivered away from his question. Terrible that life put that obstacle, that dreadful process in her way. Always life blocked her. His doubt gave her doubts of him. Would he be faithful, a silver-voiced Godfrey; absent, other, younger women hanging on his voice? It did not hurt to keep a man guessing. She had told him to ask her that after the courts had set him free. She could not have him sure of her. Men tire when they are sure; Rickard had been too sure of her.

An exclamation from him recalled her. She found that he was no longer staring at her; his eyes were fixed on the trembling structure over which a "battle-ship," laden with rock, was creeping.

"Jove!" he cried. "Those men are heroes."

Everything irritated her to-day. She felt out of sorts, though she was going to be happy! She was going to grasp, and keep what was within reach of her hand. But this river, this dirty sordid work, was getting on her nerves. Even Godfrey now was staring at the trestles as though they were circus rings! Rickard crossed her vision, on the run, his face grotesque with soot and perspiration. She saw him stoop to speak to the group of women; he stood for a minute by Innes. The grime shielded his expression, but she had seen the girl's face! Her own eyes darkened with anger. But she was going to be happy. Her teeth clicked over that slogan. No one should stand in the way, Hardin, or that other. Rickard would see that she had never cared for him—hateful that it must be long before she could show him. She wanted him to know it right away, before those two flung their secret in her face, before Innes secretly triumphed over her.

Rickard, she could see, was turning in her direction. She sent another brilliant, dazzling smile at Godfrey, who remembered to smile back at her. She wanted to have Rickard see them together, absorbed in each other. It would pique his vanity, perhaps, to see how little she cared. He would see that he had been only one of many to her. She sent a tender little whisper after the smile.

But Godfrey had been growing restless. It began to irk him, to tease his superb muscle to be the only man without work—"sitting on the bank like Cor'nel down yonder!" He answered Gerty, turning away to her annoyance to hail Rickard.

"Going all right?"

"Bully," cried Rickard, not stopping.

"Haven't you something for me to do? Can't I help?"

"We can use everybody," Rickard called back over his shoulder.

Uncomfortable to find that that voice still had power to make her tremble. Even when she loved Godfrey. For she did love him. She intended to love him. Else what did life mean? Those broken beginnings, those false starts? It was hate, she told herself, hate that shook her, when Rickard came near. With all her soul she hated him.

Godfrey was itching to be off, but he would not offend Mrs. Hardin. After a deliberate interval, she got up, shaking out her ruffles. "One gets stiff sitting so long. Don't let me keep you."

He saw he had hurt her. "I want to stay with you, you know that, dearest. But it doesn't feel right to see them all working like niggers and me loafing here. You don't mind?"

Oh, no, Gerty did not mind! She was tired, anyway! She was going back to her tent!

"Won't you wait for the closure?"

Her laugh was airy and detached. "Oh, they are always closing that river. They will always be closing it. It's no novelty. You can tell me all about it."

He thrust a yellow paper into her hands. "I sent that off to-day. Perhaps you will be glad?"

She flung another of her inscrutable smiles at him, and went up the bank, the paper unread in her hands. Godfrey's uncertain glance followed her. He had vexed her, some way. He should follow her, see her to her tent. She expected those little attentions. He loved to please her, but his eyes went back, yearning, to the river. Those men working like tigers—! He was down the bank in a trice.

"Give me something to do!"

The long afternoon wore away. On a giant rock on a flat car, Silent stretched his muscles, and looked at his watch. Mortally tired he was. He thought of his bed, and a cup of steaming coffee. An hour more! They were now dynamiting the largest rocks on the cars before unloading them. The heavy loads could not be emptied quickly enough. Not dribbled, the rock, but dumped simultaneously, else the gravel and rock might be washed down-stream faster than they could be put on. The job called for an alert eye and hand working together. Many cars must be unloaded at once; the din on Silent's train was terrific. His crew looked like devils, drenched from the spray which rose from the river each time the rock-pour began; blackened by the smoke from the belching engine. The river was ugly in its wrath. It was humping itself for its final stand against the absurdity of human intention; its yellow tail swished through the bents of the trestle.

"It isn't what I'd call pretty," yelled Wooster to Bodefeldt, as they passed in a flat car. The noise of the rock-pouring began again.

"Not a picnic," cried Bodefeldt.

But there was a thrill in it. They were working against the most formidable force in nature, against time, and moreover without precedent. Not one of them would risk a hazard as to the next move of the wily Dragon. A swift rise, and swift rises of the Gila were always to be feared, and their barrier would be flung down the channel as a useless toy. Haste was their only chance. The breath of the workers came quick and short. The order came for more speed. Rickard moved from bank to raft; knee deep in water, screaming orders through the din; directing the gangs; speeding the rock trains; helping Wooster, who was driving large gangs of Mexicans and Indians. The river must not be allowed to creep around the bulwark, to catch them unawares; the work must not halt for an instant; the force of the thwarted river growing fiercer with each pour of rock.

THE BATTLE IN THE NIGHT 385

Haste against strength, or the victory the river's! Hardin oscillated between the levee and dams, taking orders, giving orders. His energy was superb. His heavy run was like a bulldog's, full of ferocious purpose. Marshall halted him as he thumped past, straight from the levees.

"It's going all right," he assured the man who had humiliated him. His sense of wrong was sleeping; the battle developed the real soldier. "The levee will stand if we can work quick enough."

"Good!" cried Marshall. "We'll win yet, old man!"

It had grown dark, but no one yet had thought of the lights, the great Wells' burners stretched across the channel. To Marshall's war-trained ear, the glut of raining rock sounded like cannonading. It was a queer scene, the dark pocket of battle-ground, the clouds of smoke, the dashing mountains of spray; men rushing to and fro like masked dwarfs, trains thundering on to the trestles. Suddenly, the lights flared out.

Marshall found himself standing by Captain Brandon, who had his note-book in his hand. The dark had stolen on him; but he kept on scribbling his report to the *Sun*. He did not hear Marshall's inquiry.

Behind them, coming closer, broke a rhythmic beat. Molly Silent's waiting ear heard it, too—it was the night shift coming on! She hastened clumsily to the rock-filled end of the trestle, and waited for Silent to leave his train.

As he let himself down from the cab, she could hear him say that it was about time. "I'm all in." Just then, the Dragon lashed its mighty foaming tail; the trestle shook as though it were a mouse in the sharp teeth of a terrier.

The engineer who was taking Silent's place, drew back.

"That's your train," said Silent, who did not yet see his wife.

There was another lash of the angry tail. The engineer shook his head. "It don't look good to me." A whistle blew. The trestle was still shuddering as though in the grip of an earthquake.

"I've been an engineer for twenty years, but God Almighty Himself'd not take me out on that bridge tonight. I'd give up my job first."

"It's up to me, then," said Silent. And then two arms were thrown around his neck.

"Why, lassie," he cried. "Why, little mother."

She clung to him. The whistle blew again.

"Why, lassie!" He put her away from him, and she saw him, though mistily, climb back into the cab, the man-work swallowing him again.

Not one of those who labored or watched would ever forget that night. The spirit of recklessness entered even into the stolid native. The men of the Reclamation forgot this was not their enterprise; the Hardin faction jumped to Rickard's orders; there was a whip of haste in the air. Brandon's old style came back to him as he wrote, standing now under the great swinging light, his report for the *Sun*. "Bertha will be reading it to-morrow!" He despatched one bulletin, and began another. His periods rolled off, sonorously syllabled. Down by the trestle, humped up like a camel, the mud washed from his hair which fell like stiff wires from his head, watched Cor'nel. He had not eaten, had not stirred from his place that day.

The rain of rocks, by midnight, had settled into a

steady storm. The momentum was gigantic. The watchers on the bank sat tense, thrilled out of recognition of aching muscles, or the midnight creeping chill. No one would go home. Mrs. Marshall and Molly Silent carried the sleeping boy into the *Palmyra,* where he was laid in Mrs. Marshall's bed.

"He'll lie till morning, once he's asleep," whispered his mother, and they crept down to the bank again. The swinging lights had turned the darkness into a pale twilight. Each searched through the uncertain light for a familiar figure, for the soldier she had lent. Wistfully, Claudia was wondering if Tod's flannels were wet. Once, he came within reach of her hand, but she dared not ask him. He was on the run. "Hell! what's the matter with that train?"

To Innes, the struggle was vested in two men, Rickard running down yonder with that light foot of his as swift as though Ling's mustard had not been needed a few days before; and Hardin with the fighting mouth tense. And somewhere, she remembered, working with the rest, was Estrada. Those three were fighting for the justification of a vision—an idea was at stake, a hope for the future. There was no fear, only a wild exultation, when she once saw Rickard jump on to an outgoing train of "battle-ships," heavily laden with rock. It was a battle of giants, to her; drastic and dramatic.

Rickard passed and repassed her, running, or again walking slowly, talking eagerly to Marshall. And had not seen her! Not during those hours would he think of her, not until the idea failed, or was triumphant, would he turn to look for her. Knowing, the thought unfolded slowly, knowing he would find her there!

The real work of the world is man-work; no matter

how she or other women might yearn, theirs not the endurance. All they can do is negative; not to get on the track! Neither with pretty ruffles, nor tender fears!

Knowing he would find her *there*. Suppose she were not there, she were off building a house when he came home to find her, craving her comfort or her laurels? Suppose she had promised to deliver a plan, and that pledge involved her absence, or her attention when the world work, the man-work released him—his story on his eager lips, her ears deaf to hear? She saw Brandon under the swinging light, and his loneliness came knocking at her door. Was it still necessary for that wife to help with the bread-getting? On some women, that problem is thrust, but her college study, her later reading, had taught her that all women should seek it. An economic waste, half of the world spending more than the other half can earn! To the woman who has been spared the problem, comes the problem of choice. Has any one, born a woman, the daring to say—"I will not choose. I will take both! I will be man and woman, too!" Suppose she were not at home when he stumbled back to her! As soon leave that corner of the bank!

Her muscles grew stiff. Once in a while, the watching women stirred, or shifted their positions, but they did not get up. They would stay where their man, Marshall, or Silent, Rickard, Hardin, could find them. Only one woman symbolized that thought, and she followed it until it curved, bringing her back to that twilight of clamor, the fight between disorder and plan, waste and conservation, herself sitting on the bank waiting.

Visibly, the drama moved toward its climax. Before many hours passed, something would happen, the river would be captured, or the idea forever mocked. Each time a belching engine pulled across that hazardous track, it flung a credit to the man-side. Each time the waters, slowly rising, hurled their weight against the creaking trestles where the rock was thin, a point was gained by the militant river. Its roar sounded like the last cry of a wounded animal to Innes' ear; the Dragon was a reality that night as it spent its rage against the shackles of puny men.

Down in the shadow of a lamp-pole, the light flaring riverward, crouched Coronel. His eyes were fixed on those approaching walls of rock. Motionless, he watched the final tussle, a grunt following each glut of rock. Somewhere, his muscles ached, but his brain did not receive their message. It was off duty. His mind was sending that car across the trestle; it was hastening the charge, that quick clattering downfall of shattered rock.

Molly Silent had seen her husband's train pull in. She watched for it to go out again. The whistle blew twice. Something was wrong. She left her place in time to see Silent, his face shining ghastly pale under the soot, pull himself up from the "battle-ship" where he had been leaning. Estrada, sent by Rickard to find out why the train did not pull out, saw him the same instant as did Molly. Silent swayed, waving them back unseeingly, like a man who is drunk.

"God, man, you can't go like that!" cried Estrada.

"Who's going?" demanded Silent, his tongue thick with thirst and exhaustion. The whistle blew again.

"*I* will!" The train moved out on the trestle, as the

whistle blew angrily twice. Only Molly and Silent saw Estrada go. Silent staggered unseeingly up the bank, toward the camp, Molly heavily following.

Workers and watchers felt a queer light playing on their faces, but no one stopped to look at the lamps swinging across the channel, or they would have seen that they were growing dim. The test of strength was coming; no time to brush the damp hair from their eyes. The river was humping out yonder; the rolling mass came roaring, flank-on, against the dam.

"Quick, for God's sake, quick," yelled Rickard. His signals sounded short and sharp. "Dump it on, throw the cars in!" Marshall was dancing, his mouth full of oaths, on the bank edge. Breathlessly, all watched the rushing water fling itself over the dam. For several hushed seconds, the structure could not be seen. When the foam fell, a cheer went up. The dam was standing. Silent, it was supposed, was bringing in his train.

Above the distant jagged line of mountains, rose a red ball. A new day began. The light fell on the faces of the fighting men; Indians and Caucasians alike black with river mud and soot. The work went on. And again the Dragon rose; a mountain of water came rolling damward.

"Hump yourselves," screamed Marshall. The signals sounded like hoarse cries.

Three trains ran steaming on the rails.

"We'll get those rocks over before the river kicks," cried Rickard. "Be ready, Irish, to run in when they come back. Don't stop now to blast the big ones. Pour 'em on!"

There was a long wait before any rock fell. Marshall

THE BATTLE IN THE NIGHT 391

and Rickard waited for the pour. The whistles blew again.

"Why in Hades," began Marshall, and then they saw what was wrong. The morning light showed a rock weighing several tons which was resisting the efforts of the pressing crew. Out of the gloom sprang other figures with crowbars.

"Why don't they try to use mountains?" swore Marshall, and the rock tottered, fell. The river tossed it as though it were a tennis ball, sent it hurtling down the lower face of the dam. The river's strength was never more terrible.

"Damn those almighty fools!" screamed Tod Marshall.

"A fluke," yelled Rickard.

Things began to go wild. The men were growing reckless. They were sagging toward exhaustion; mistakes were made. Another rock, as heavy as the last, was worked toward the edge. No one listened to the frantic signals to dynamite that rock, break it on the car. Men were thick about it with crowbars. There was another wait, the whistles confusing the men on the train. They hurried. One concerted effort, drawing back as the rock toppled over the edge. One man was too slow, or too tired. He slipped. The watchers on the bank saw a flash of waving arms, heard a cry; they had a glimpse of a blackened face as the foam caught it. The waters closed over him.

There was a hush of horror; a halt.

"God Himself couldn't save that poor devil," cried Marshall. "Have the work go on!"

Pour rocks on that wretch down there? Pin him down? Never had it seemed more like war! "A man down? Ride over him! to victory!" Soberly, Rickard signaled for the work to go on.

The rock-pour stuttered as if in horror. The women turned sick with fear. No one knew who it was. Some poor Mexican, probably.

Some one standing near Rickard said that it was Arnica Jack; he said he had seen his face. He had gone out on that train. Rickard thought of the saved salary.

"Why doesn't that train come in? What is the matter with Silent?" His signals brought in the battle-ships, moving as though they were funeral carriages.

"Where is Silent?" demanded Rickard, running down to the track. A blackened figure was letting himself down from the car. The smell of something pungent struck sharply against Rickard's nostrils. Arnica! "Where's Silent?" he demanded.

"'E didn't take hout this 'ere train." The hobo's eyes looked owlish.

"Then who?" the engineer was beginning, when it came to him. He himself had sent Estrada to question Silent! He knew what the tramp was going to tell him!

"The young Mexican, Hestrada. 'E tried to 'elp. 'E wasn't fit."

"Who was it?" Marshall had run down to see why the work paused.

Rickard turned shocked eyes on his chief. "Estrada!" The beautiful mournful eyes of Eduardo were on him, not Marshall's, horrified.

"But it came again; it kept coming. I had it while you were all talking, just now!"

If that terrible smell didn't take itself off! He hated the stupid wretch standing, open-jawed before him, because it was Estrada's and not those owlish eyes that were lying in those waters yonder.

"Rickard!" The engineer did not recognize the quenched voice. "The work has got to go on."

It came to Rickard as he gave the orders for the trains to run "and be quick about it," that Eduardo was closer to Marshall than to him. "As near a son as he'll ever have."

He turned a minute later to see his chief standing bareheaded. His own cap came off.

"We're burying the lad," said Marshall. A rain of rock struck the nerves of all of them, though less than six people knew who it was who had paid the tribute of life to the river. Rickard kept the smell of arnica in his nostrils. It nauseated him. Never would its sharp breath blow on him but that scene would shake him in all its horror,—the sad beautiful face under those malignant waters, the rocks nailing it down. "It kept coming. I had it while you were all talking—just now!"

The minute of funeral had to be pushed aside. The river would not wait. Train after train was rushed on to the trestles; wave after wave hit them. But perceptibly, the dam was steadying. The rapid fire of rock was telling.

Another ridge of yellow waters rose. Every eye was on that watery mountain; it appeared to wait, as if summoning its strength for a final onslaught. The river's stillness was ominous to the sweating men who watched as they labored that bulge of yellow water. Car after car ran on to the track; load after load of clattering rock was dumped. The roll of water came slowly, dwindling as it came; it broke against the trestle weakly. For the first time, the trestle never shuddered. Workers and watchers breathed as a unit the first deep breath that night. There was a change.

Hardin came rushing down to the track where the rock cars ran on to the trestles.

"It's stopped rising!" he bellowed.

"Then work like hell!" bawled Rickard.

There followed some minutes of intensity when the rock-pour was almost continuous. Was not that another bulge of yellow waters, swelling there to the east? Every eye was on the river where it touched the rim of the dam. Suddenly, a chorused cry rose. The river had stopped rising!

"Don't stop! She may hump yet!" Rickard was splitting his voice against the cheers. The whistles screamed themselves hoarse.

"We've got her!" screamed Hardin. "She's going down!"

And then a girl, sitting on the bank, saw two men grab each other by the hand. She was too far away to hear their voices, but the sun, rising red through the banks of smoke, fell on the blackened faces of her brother and Rickard. She did not care who saw her crying.

A small sound started down the river. It grew into a swelling cheer, the pæan of victory. It demoralized into wild yells. Suddenly, the noise stopped. Simultaneously, Marshall and Rickard had held up their hands. The whistles had blown.

"What was that for?" demanded Mrs. Marshall.

"I suppose they can't afford to waste any time." Innes' reply was uncertain. She, too, was wondering.

Rickard, they could hear, again, screaming directions. The battle was won; but it must be kept won. But no cheering! The men didn't know who it was who was buried out yonder.

When things were well under way, Rickard discovered that his head was hot, his skin chilly. He would lay off for an hour. He would put Hardin in his place, Hardin or Irish.

He found Hardin, who was having his minute of reaction. This was not his triumph. Sullenly, he accepted Rickard's place. Rickard turned back. "Had you heard? That was Estrada out there."

Hardin's expression followed him, the gloom of sullen egotism passing slowly from the face of unwilling horror. He had not spoken, but his look said: "Not Estrada! Any one but Estrada!"

"Any one but Estrada! He's about the only man in this camp without enmities," thought Rickard, and then he wondered if any one had told Innes Hardin. He went in search of her, passing Coronel, whose head rested on his chest. His snores could be heard above the noise of the rock bombardment.

Mrs. Marshall, weeping, was being led back to the car by her husband. Innes, he could see, had heard! Her eyes, fixed on the conquered waters, were seeing Estrada, buried out there.

Rickard turned away without being seen. The minute he had been waiting for was not his. It belonged to Estrada.

CHAPTER XL

A DESERTION

WHEN the afternoon waned, and Godfrey did not follow her, Gerty was roused to uneasiness. Had she angered him by refusing to make the definite promise? Could it be love, the sort of love she wanted, if he could stay away like this when they could have the camp to themselves, every one down at the break, no Hardins running in every minute? Their first chance, and Godfrey slighting it! Something was wrong. The Godfrey who had rushed on work like a glad hungry tiger, was incomprehensible to her. Something must have happened.

She ruffled down to a disordered mess-tent. Wooster and one of the Reclamation Service men were leaving as she went in. She had the table to herself. MacLean, Jr., untidy, his clothes wet and dirty, came in to snatch a bite, as she passed out, gay, indifferent. No Godfrey in sight! Nor waiting for her in her tent. He would surely come that evening, knowing that she would be alone! She arranged without conscious thought the setting for a scene of pretty domesticity in the ramada. After an hour or more, she tossed down the fluffy sewing and picked up a novel, her work within reach of her hand. The approach of her own climax dulled the printed sensations.

The little watch Tom had given her for an almost forgotten birthday set the pace for her resentment. Nine, ten, eleven! How dared he treat her so? She blew out the lamps when she found that she was shaking with anger, and undressed in the dark. She could not see him, if he came now, her self-control all gone! But she could not go to bed. She stood in her darkened tent, shaken by her angry passions. Cruel, these men to her. That black moment stripped her thoughts to nakedness. If she had any other refuge, she would never forgive him, never. But what else could she do? Where could she go? Those lonely, straitened widowhoods! Not for her. She had been poor long enough. Even her little importance, as the wife of Thomas Hardin, was gone. She dared not lose her hold on Godfrey. It came to her then, how slight her hold on him was. A rover with a conquering voice like that! Keep him tied to her wrist like a tamed falcon?

Suppose that he were only trifling with her? What was that paper he had thrust in her hand? Where had she laid it? Had she dropped it on the way from the river? She groped for a match, and lighted a candle. Not in the dress she had on, for none of her gowns had pockets. Not on the floor, nor on the piano! There! She had dropped candle grease all over the green mandarin skirt, but she didn't care. A fond message, perhaps, and she had lost it—out there somewhere, food for horrid talk! Her bureau drawers were ransacked in a frenzy of fear and haste. Suddenly, she remembered putting it in her handkerchief box.

Candle grease dripped over the yellow paper. It was a copy of a telegram to Godfrey's lawyer. "Start divorce proceedings at once. Any grounds possible. Back soon. Godfrey."

The frightened blood resumed its normal flow. If he had done this, for her, then she had not lost him. But she had seen what a desert her life would be, if she let him slip through her fingers. She couldn't endure Tom Hardin. And Rickard—they would expect her to play the glad grandmother to their young romance! She couldn't get away quick enough.

It was then the courage came to her. She would not be there to be told of it. An apparent elopement, why had she never thought of that before? That would cement their bond. Her scruples could grow on the road. Oh, she could manage Godfrey! They would startle the world, a continent! Godfrey was well known. It would seem splendid; they would believe her happy. She would be happy! When she could get away from them all, she would forget the look that sobered Rickard's eyes when they fell on Innes. That still had power to sting her. Away, she would find that it was only anger. She did not care for him—she hated them all. If Godfrey gave her happiness, she would keep him transported. She knew she could. If only she did not feel so tired! So strangely old!

She blew out the candle, and went to the door of the tent-house. A low line of smoke clouds shut out the river. Lines of hatred took possession of her face. No one could have called it childish or pretty then. There they all were, the people who had wrecked her life, the Hardins, Rickard, Godfrey even, whom they would take from her if they got the chance. She would not give them that chance! She would go with him. She whipped herself into a pale imitation of excitement, telling herself that Godfrey's importance would make their affair internationally conspicuous.

She was going to be happy. Perhaps that would cloud the mockery of Rickard's quizzical eyes. She was quite sure that she hated him. And Tom? She would not let herself think of him! Had he not sacrificed her youth, taken her into a country which ravages a woman's beauty, keeping her there until her chance to escape, her youth, is almost gone? Her years smote her. She remembered that she must go to bed if she were to have any looks in the morning.

When Godfrey came to her the next afternoon, penitent, refreshed after a long morning's sleep, he found a charming hostess. Self-controlled, she listened to the story of the capture, and deflected his apology. Serpentwise, she smiled at him and called him a great foolish boy! She was shy about his telegram. She fled through a forest of phrases and he found he was running after her.

"You must go!" Enchantingly distant when he tried to reach her hand! "We can't keep this up." How tired she felt!

"I can't go without you," he cried. He had discovered her interpretation of his telegram, and it delighted him; he began to believe it his own intention. "I can't leave you. You will elude me. I shall carry you off with me. I can't leave you to your scruples, Gerty, dear. I respect you for them, darling, you know that. But I've got to keep near you to strengthen your will."

She shut her eyes because she could not force fervor into them; his were demanding it. How easy it had been! He was as plastic clay in her hands. He thought that she was suffering. Life had been hard on her. Poor little girl!

"I know. You shrink from it all. Don't you think

I know, dear? You dread the steps that will free you—for he has been your husband—you remember that; you will forget how he has treated you. You need me beside you to help you. Let's cut the knot. That makes it all easy. To-night!"

"Not to-night. Maybe, to-morrow," whispered Gerty, and then she managed a few tears, and he was allowed to kiss her. It was all arranged before he left the ramada. They were to leave together the next day.

She had let him sketch their trip to New York. She did not tell him that she was going to stay in Los Angeles until the divorces were obtained, unless she had to go to Reno. Plenty of time for scruples to send forth long branches of regret between Yuma and Los Angeles; her object would be accomplished by their leaving together. He would feel that he owed her his name.

Of course, Gerty must do it the conventional way! She would have used rope ladders had they been needed. The conventional note was pinned to her bureau scarf.

Innes was with Tom when he found it. They came in together from the river. Neither had noticed the odd looks from the men as they passed through the encampment. A dozen men had seen Hardin's wife leave for the North with Godfrey.

Gerty's letter told Tom that it was all over. She had tried to stand it, to be true even through his cruelty, but a feeling stronger than she was made her true to herself, and so true at last to him! Falsely dramatic, every word of it, romantically cruel.

Innes' revulsion lacked speech. The fulfilment of her intuitions left a smudge; indelible, she knew when she looked at Tom's face. She stretched out her hand mutely for the letter. The common blatter sickened her. She could offer no comfort. His eyes told her it was worse than death.

He struck off her hand when it touched his shoulder. Gerty's hand had coerced him that way. He was done with softness.

His silence oppressed her. This was a man she did not know; inarticulate, smitten. She told herself that even a sister was an intruder—but she was afraid to leave him alone. She went out, pitifully, questioning those tense face-muscles. She took a station by her own tent door. She would not go down to dinner. Tom, in that mood, frightened her. For hours, she watched his tent. When it grew dark, she could no longer endure it. He did not answer her knock. She found him where she had left him. But it was a different Hardin. The backward look now for him. He had buried, in those hours, his optimism. His life was lived. Gerty's blow had made of him an old man.

She forced herself toward the volcano's edge; and the swift eruption scorched her. It was the pitiable wreck of dignity, of pride. His words were incoherent; his wrath involved his sister, crouching in tears. When he was done, he began hurling clothes and brushes indiscriminately into his Gladstone.

"You are not going after them?" She had not gathered his plan.

"Yes, I'm going after them," he shouted. "I'm not wanted, you mean. An uninvited guest. I'll give them a chance for reciprocity."

She caught his arm. "Tom," she pleaded, "you can't go like this. Wait until you are calm. Until you can see this clearly." She thought then that he meant to kill Godfrey.

His plan, when at last she pieced together his distorted idea, was so sullen, so determined, that her slight weapons could not cope with it. He had promised to protect Gerty, he kept repeating. Well, he would keep his vows, if she didn't. He drew, she could see, a grim satisfaction from that antithesis. He would keep *his* vows. He would make that scoundrel promise on oath to divorce the other woman and marry the woman whom he had dishonored. Unless he got that promise, Hardin swore to kill him. Pacing up and down the canvased cage of a tent, he delivered himself of his fury.

Innes shrank from him, the man she did not know. The coarse streak was uncovered in all its repulsiveness. Old Jasper Gingg's face leered through the features of his descendant. Dementia and atavism glared through his eyes. His hate was disfiguring. "I'll protect my wife. I'll keep my vows."

He turned on Innes suddenly. She was crying, a huddled heap on the couch. "I've had enough crying—between you and Gerty. Will you get out? I've got to have some sleep."

Through her sobs, he could make out that she was afraid to leave him. He stood staring at her, frowning at her fright, her intrusion.

"Well, then, I'll go. I'm used to having to leave my own tent. A dog's life." He flung out into the night.

She cried to him to come back, that she would go. "Don't, Tom! Tom!" Her voice rang through the encampment. The echo warned her. She saw questioning slits of light from tents across the trapezium. She shut the door.

A DESERTION

She stood in the room he had left; the desecrated home of Tom Hardin. It was the wreck she had foreseen. She would sit up for him. She could not sit there watching that hateful, leering mandarin skirt, daubed with candle-drippings; those sketches; everything recalled Gerty Hardin's wistful baby smile. She could not bring herself to lie on that couch. She thrust her arms into Tom's overcoat, buttoning it around her, and went out to wait for him. His own cot was there.

A light shone from Rickard's window. The peace of the stars, the light from the window, smoothed out her terrors. She could picture Tom walking out his trouble, crying out his hurt to those same distant stars.

How fierce the resentment against pain! The atom beating his head in revolt against the universe! That particular sting, Tom's; another kind of sorrow the next man's heritage! But the stars know it, those worlds of burned-out griefs; to them how tenderly humorous, she thought, must be each individual resistance. A short span, a little joy, perhaps; a little sorrow; rebellion;— and then the stars again.

To-night, it was all sorrow. Down there, under the rocks, lay Estrada. Tripped to his end by the prophecy of the general, the son the corner-stone of his undertaking! In the river of his plan the best of them lay sleeping!

Who can measure the influence upon youth the legends of its country, the effect of its brave early history? Would any of those coming later fail to find the thrill in the story of the man who had visioned the idea, the son whose eager service to a comrade had consecrated it?

A short span:—and a little joy, perhaps! Her eyes

sought the light from Rickard's window. A little joy,—
and then the stars—again!

Slowly, the universe cradled her. She was in her
first deep sleep when a step passed her. A hand fumbled uncertainly over the surface of the door; knocked
gently. A heavy bundle dropped to the threshold.
Again the figure passed the occupied cot, and paused,
going on again, more softly.

No quickened pulse told MacLean, Jr., that it was
Innes Hardin sleeping in her brother's cot.

CHAPTER XLI

INCOMPLETENESS

STUMBLING and blind, Hardin pushed without volition toward the river which was sending its peaceful waters once again to the gulf. When he awoke to himself and the night, he was on the levee.

His bitterness was coloring both strands of his life. Strange, that a man's attainment can bring him neither pride nor joy, his own achievement winning him dishonor in a double sense! The triumph of that mound of earth, of those turned waters, was not his. Gerty had felt it; else she had not flouted him. In everything he had failed. Life held only jeers for him.

Nothing in Hardin's experience, or in his specialized reading had helped him to a philosophy of life; the books men live by were not his; and his crude egotism, as raw to-day as when he was twenty-five, in the moment of his trial tripped him to his fall. In all his jaundiced world, there was no rosy finger of light. His wounded shadow obscured the universe. His suffering, he felt, was unparalleled, because it was undeserved. What had betrayed him? His bitterness was crying to the stars. Where was the fault?

He kept telling himself that it was not true. He would wake up and find himself in his tent, under those same mocking stars; he would discover it to be a hideous dream. Why for him this bite of hate, cried his bleeding ego? It was as though life, which he had been pursuing, had turned suddenly on him, savage and virulent, had bitten him to the bone. It wasn't true, cried his resistance, because it wouldn't be right! This crash violated all his plans, warped his world, accused his judgments. This the Hardin who had followed a deliberate trail ever since that morning of resolution in this yet unawakened desert? In what had that man failed, where had he missed? Misfortune, trouble, he had thought of vaguely as a punishment for sin, or negligence, as do most eager spirits, before it comes! Himself! Tom Hardin,—why, life had scarcely begun! Why, since that moment, his path had known no turning; one woman, one ambition; selflessness. Something was wrong; the umpire caught napping!

His training betrayed him into a thicket of amaze, of protest. His mental processes kept him in a circle of tangled underbrush. What was physical pain, he cried, to the torture of his mind? What the agony of death?

Stumbling along the levee of his buried hopes, by the peaceful chained river of his dedication, it came to him, the Ultimate, the end of it all. Until then death had been kept in its decent background. The one incontrovertible fact of the universe stared him now in the face. Heretofore, his struggle had been set to the tune of life; now, the rest of the way, he was facing death. For what is death but the failure to live? That was where he, Hardin, had failed. He touched at a thought of brotherhood, the realization dim. Death had come to Eduardo swiftly; but others it follows, cloaking its face, slowly stalking its victim down! Now he knew what would be *his* companion the rest of the way!

Brandon, walking out a philosophic, bloodless vigil, came upon the distorted, reeling fugitive. The starlight showed the face tortured. No safety for that staggering derelict without a pilot! He grabbed Hardin by the arm, and with gentle force, directed his steps. He talked of himself, his voice tuned to the stillness of the night.

"I like to walk before I turn in. I go to sleep quicker. I have no dreams then. 'No dreams, dear God, no dreams.' That is the mile-post of age, I think. We cling to our dreams in our youth. When we begin to grow old, we pray for sleep, which is the beginning of the prayer for death. It is our preparation for the long sleep." He would not see the scowl that disfigured Hardin's features.

"I often think of that blessing of ours. Wondering if men could endure what they like to call their supreme blessing, life, if we were not able to sleep away half of it. We die half of our life, eagerly, that we may live the other half. Strange, that!"

Hardin thought that he was too full of pain, of intolerance to listen, but the calm voice reached his fleeing thoughts. The final sleep, release? Sharply, he looked at Brandon's straight clean profile, ascetic in its intellectual purity, sweet as a woman's. What had *his* life been? Brandon kept on with his quiet reflection, but Hardin was wandering afield. His thoughts were growing centrifugal, sympathetic. Brandon, too, had failed!

He found that his companion had been talking about the river's capture. He caught a phrase now and again, but his thoughts hovered over his own hurt as vultures over a dying body.

"That was a great battle," Brandon was saying. "And this the sort of field on which our future battles will be fought. It's modern warfare. In a few years the names of those generals will be forgotten. We call ourselves civilized, yet we put up statues to a man who bombards and burns a town of savages. We'll learn to do things differently. We'll learn our real values. When the world begins to crowd up, we'll find the value of these waste places. And we'll give titles to men like the older Estrada." Hardin was thrown against another wrong. He forgot that Brandon was droning. Suddenly, a personal note was sounded. He woke to hear Brandon's conclusion:

"You think you will, but you won't. You won't do anything to him. You won't want to."

Hardin stood still. He stared at Brandon. What was he talking about? It sounded like necromancy. He had said nothing of Godfrey.

"You won't harm him." Brandon linked his arm through the withdrawn one of Hardin and pressed him into step.

"You saw them?" Of course, everybody knew by this time that Gerty had left him! They had taken no pains to spare him, throwing publicly their scorn of him in his face!

"I was at the station. I think I know how you feel. How any man would feel. Plan it, kill him with your hands. Hate him; get it out of you. Kill him before you go to sleep." Hardin was staring like a sleep-walker. "Get it out of your system; it's poison. When you leave me"—but Brandon did not intend that to be soon—"go home and write to them both. Then you can sleep. Tomorrow, it will be done. Then burn the letter. Satisfy the animal, or it will be at your bedside waiting in the morning. I always write out my anger, before I sleep. Do you remember the Lincoln story? I've adopted that."

Hardin shut his ears to the anecdote with rude intention. Stories! What had he to do with after-dinner stories a night like this? Brandon was walking a little faster. He intended to tire out Hardin. He finished his whimsical reminiscence. "Yes, I always burn those letters. But I write them first. It's a good way, the Lincoln way."

Hardin turned on him, his twisted features unpleasant to see. "You think I mean to hurt him, kill him. We are not living in dueling times. I wouldn't touch the— skunk."

An ulcer had been pricked. His voice was calmer. The plan came out, the ugly revenge of distorted chivalry and hate and duty. Brandon's low murmurs of attention passed for assent. Hardin did not notice that they were within sight of the encampment, nor that Brandon wheeled to retrace their steps. He took Brandon back into the beginnings of things, his cramped youth, his ambition, his awakening in that very desert, his final dedication to one woman, one idea. It was a passionate self-eulogy, the relief of the wounded self-esteem. Everything had mocked him. What use were such sacrifices, if this be the end? He demanded an answer of the eternal. As well be a beast—the punishment no worse!

His fury had shouted itself hoarse, stridulous. She was still his wife—he still had a duty to perform, he maintained, the duty of protection. It was grotesque, a Frankenstein of rage, but there was no smile in Brandon's heart. He waited for the storm to exhaust itself.

Even when Hardin had finished, he hesitated; his words must be water, not fuel to those scorching fires.

"It's good as far as you see it," he was beginning.

"Of course, it's right," thundered Hardin. "She's not to be thrown aside, my wife—"

"No, but Godfrey's wife is." Brandon added no comment.

"Well, what of that? That's his lookout, isn't it? He should have thought about that before. I'll stand by Gerty, God Almighty, until the end."

He walked on sulking.

"*Your* wife. Because she is *your* wife. It's the pronoun, not the sex, or the relation. She's yours, that is, she was. Oh, we recognize the marriage ceremony, we men to-day, but we go farther, we acknowledge the unwritten sacrament, inclination. If she no longer wants to be your wife, she's not your wife, Hardin. You don't want her. Let her alone. You have no more right to her, or to her life, after yesterday, than though she were a dollar on another man's desk. You're not a savage. And she's not a child. She knows the world. She can protect herself, oh, better than you can."

Hardin flung out a protest to this startling twist of facts. Brandon let him get tangled in his angry rush.

"The river," began Brandon, as though they had been discussing it. "You have done this thing, but yours is not the credit, the published honor. It's Marshall's and Rickard's. Yet the thing is done as you wanted it, approximately. I heard that it was you who went after Faraday. Now the success stings you. *Yours* is neither the power nor the glory. The pronoun again, Mr. Hardin!"

Beside them ran the river, guileless, now, in its captivity. The flat world stretched away from them until it ran into a blur of rising shadow, of dim mountain ranges. The world was sleeping; only the stars watched. In spite of his resistance, the quiet came creeping into Hardin's soul. His muscles were relaxing; he was slipping toward sleep.

"I've wondered, too," Brandon took a slower tempo, "if we could not see men better by searching for their apex. Perhaps you've never looked at life that way?"

The ugly lip flared. Hardin couldn't see what Brandon was driving at. He'd never had time to sit still and look at life! He'd just lived! Just worked along!

"What are we doing? Climbing up a mountain. Whatever we call this journey of ours, ambition, labor; life. We climb up; we creep down. We are taught to climb up, plenty of teachers for that, all the way along. No one shows us when to begin to crawl down. When we reach the apex, that's the trial. Why? We don't know it's the apex. We've achieved all we can. Achieved or failed. We fail, anyway, there, because we find we can't climb any more. We're in the habit of climbing; we've a lust for it. No slippers and easy chair yet for us. We tell ourselves it's slothful not to climb. We keep on, and we fall. We must learn to creep; we are leaving our apex. That's when we need help, a voice out of a book, or a friend's to help us and say, 'You've not failed! You went as far as you could. You've done your part. The young men will do the rest, the ones who come after. They'll take the place you leave. Why, man, you yourself, took another's. Creep down cheerfully. You've lived. It's the eternal plan.'"

Hardin did not speak, but his eyes had left the ground.

"Look at this desert. I reckon that there's no man who knows better than I do just what you've done. You've gone ahead when others laughed at you. You've worked when others slept."

Hardin's head lost its shamed droop. Some one knew what he had done. Gerty had known, too, but she was ashamed of him. To her, he had failed.

"Don't covet all the parts, Hardin. You started it, you and Estrada. He's had less fun out of it, even, than you. I know that you sacrificed your position to get the thing pulled through. It was a grand thing to do, better than putting the harness on the river. I'm proud to know you."

The stormy blood began its normal flow. He could look at the river, now, not ashamed. A few minutes later, he remembered to ask, "What do you mean by my part?"

"Your ego, Hardin. Our ego. It tells us in our youth to do everything, that all the parts are calling for us. But one man can't fill more than one part. Then it's time to get off the stage. Make room for the young men; they're waiting for their chance. Why, Hardin, *you* don't have to write your name all over this desert! It's here! The world may mention Marshall, or Rickard when they speak of the Colorado, but there's not a man in this valley, nor one who comes after, who'll fail to take off his hat to Tom Hardin!"

Hardin stopped with a jerk. "Do you think that's true?"

A steady smile, paternal in its sweetness, answered him. "I know it's true. But what difference does that make? *You* know. You are on good terms with yourself. That's all we ought to want. It's a fact. Creep down cheerfully."

The two men struck homeward. The chill that precedes the desert dawn was in the air.

"I yearned for completeness, too," mused Brandon. "We're made that way. I thought that that was what life was. A complete thing. We begin to believe in that when we are tugging at our mother's skirts. When we grow older, we fight for it. Not until we reach our apex, not until we begin to think about death, do we discover that there is no such thing as individual completion. Did you ever hear of a rounded life, or a complete one? We live too long, Hardin, or die too soon. It's creeping paralysis, or an accident in the street. We never finish anything, even ourselves! We were never intended to, that's my philosophy. Our ego blinds us to that. We can only help the scheme along."

"Go on talking," said Hardin. Brandon had thrown him back to his own centrifugal and nebulous thought.

He was trudging now, his step grown weary, in the direction of the encampment. He could see in the distance his deserted tent. But his mood had softened. The stream of his shackling connoted his success, as this man had said. The valley beyond, yielding its harvest of happy homes, that had he done. Perhaps, after all, he had not altogether failed. And, at last, he looked up at the stars.

Before they reached the camp Brandon spoke again. "I can remember when I discovered that that was not the plan. I'd just had my knockout. I could not see any reason in it. For my wife to have to stay behind me, to support me until I was strong enough to get started, or could find a berth out here—it wasn't the thing I wanted! I wasn't pleasant to have around. I moaned a good deal to Bertha about failure. I was a failure, as a hero! I had to go to Boston to sell a piece of property. If I sold it, I thought I could take Bertha west with me. I did not sell it. I went in to a symphony concert after the deal fell through. I was full of rebellion; the apex had come too soon. I guess it always seems that way, whether we're fifty, or twenty-nine. The music itself, the sounds did not soothe me. I was thinking of my paper, my ambition. Ambition in a desert? It had a mocking sound. I wanted to support my wife!

"I wasn't listening to the music. I found I was watching the antics of the man with the violoncello. He'd sit for a while and never make a sound. It struck me as queer that a man could be willing to spend a lifetime learning to play a thing like that, spend an afternoon to come in, just once in a while! Just a few notes a day! I suppose you'll laugh at me, for we get our lessons different ways. I got mine from that 'cello player. It came to me then, the apex philosophy. I got a view at the scheme of things. Men's incompleteness, the brotherhood of man, our broken segments making up the whole; I remember when I left, I was trying to whistle a theme from that great *Pathetique!* I never shall forget that afternoon. I think of that 'cello player, think of my life that way. We are all playing in the symphony, some of us carry the tune a little further, some of us, like the 'cello player, content to fill out the harmonies."

They had reached the encampment. "I believe I'll turn in," gruffed Hardin.

"Good night." Brandon struck off to his tent.

Hardin found Innes asleep, huddled in his overcoat. He did not waken her. On his threshold he stumbled over a clumsy bundle. Paper, torn, paper wrappings, crackled under his fingers. He carried it into his tent and shut the door before striking a match, so as not to waken her. In the dark, he fumbled through the room for a match. Before lighting a candle, the flickering match in his hand, he pulled down the tent shades lest the light arouse Innes. He didn't want any more woman talk! He was stumbling off to bed when his eyes fell on the fat parcel. The shape intrigued his curiosity.

It was soiled and racked from traveling. The labels read "Jalisco; Nogales; Guadalajara; Tepic." He searched for the original address. At last he made out a blurred and muddied "Hardin." Scrawled in by recent fingers was "The Crossing, Mexico."

On the table he unwound its dirty wrappings. A covering of cheese-cloth lined the paper shells. Hardin's weary eyes questioned the odd-looking cushion. His fingers ran over the rigid curves. It came to him then, what it was. Gerty's form! And he sat it up on its waist-line.

Through Mexico, jostled from town to town; written about, speculated on, sorely needed every time one of those dainty gowns was made, "those pretty flimsy gowns of Gert's!" At last it had come to the Heading!

He stared at it vacantly.

Something was happening within him; a childishness he could not control. The shuddering storm swept over him as a dry autumn wind that strips the trees gaunt.

He staggered to the candle and blew out its wavering flame. Picking up the shape, he stole with it into the next room. He knelt by the bed that had been Gerty's. And the grandson of old Jasper Gingg cried out his hurt, with his arms around that unyielding waist, his head against that stuffed bosom.

CHAPTER XLII

A CORNER OF HIS HEART

THE second evening after the closure Rickard was dining with the Marshalls in their car. The *Palmyra* was preparing to leave the siding. She was to pull out the next day. Already Marshall was restless. Tucson was calling him; Oaxaca was calling him! And he was due in Chicago for a conference with Faraday.

Rickard had been protesting against his new orders. It hurt him to curtail his force. "Not until the concrete gate is finished, and the whole length of levee done, will I feel safe."

"Faraday says to go slow," repeated Marshall. "He's got something up his sleeve. It may be taken off his hands. If that's the case, we've done our part."

"I like to leave my work finished, not hanging in midair," grumbled the engineer. "He'd hate to do this over again. I would! You will advise him when you see him next week, Mr. Marshall? Don't let him cut down on the force we have now. Let us keep," and then he smiled, "as many as we can!"

For the hobo ranks were thinning as late snows beneath the sun. Up North, a city was rebuilding. In Mexico, new mines were being opened up. The west coast of Mexico was calling to those restless soldiers who march without a captain.

"They are going out by way of Calexico," Rickard was still smiling over some memories of desertion. "They've learned that they can hoof it to Cocopah, and from there sneak in on the work trains. Work crews are more vulnerable than regular brakemen; they have more imagination. To them, these returning hoboes are heroes. It was they who saved the valley, not you, Mr. Marshall! That's their opinion."

"I preferred my 'snap' myself!" returned Marshall. "Have you cut down on the Indians?"

Rickard nodded, remembering how Hardin had opposed himself yesterday to the number of men retained; as being twice too many! The same Hardin! An awkward relationship swung toward the two men. Hardin, it was easy to see, was striving to remember his gratitude to the man who had stopped the river. He himself had different reasons for wishing to be fair to Tom Hardin! His name was brought up by Tod Marshall. "She was light potatoes," he dismissed the woman. "But she's broken the man's spirit."

Rickard, it was discovered, had nothing to say on the subject of the elopement.

"I'm sorry his sister is not here to-night," began Marshall mischievously.

"I did ask her, Tod," Claudia hastened to interrupt her lord. "But she would not leave her brother her last evening."

"Her *last* evening?" exclaimed Rickard. "Is she going away?"

Marshall subdued his twinkle. "We are carrying her off. She is to visit Mrs. Marshall while I am on the road."

"Just a few days," put in his wife. "She feels that

her brother wants to be by himself. I think she is right."

And the *Palmyra* made early runs! He must see her that night. He would leave as soon as he decently could. Tony's dinner was endless to him.

Mrs. Marshall found opportunity in her guest's abstraction to explain to her husband that at last Mrs. Silent had consented to let her take the boy, Jimmie, "out" with her.

"She's not well herself. Another!" She arched her eyebrows meaningly.

Rickard gulped down his coffee, boiling. Tony was looking with tragic concern at the untasted dessert on the engineer's plate. "Mrs. Marshall, will you let me run away early?" Why should he give any excuse? They knew what he was running away for!

He made his way to the little white tent on the far side of the trapezium. The door was open, the lamp-light flaring through. He could see Coronel struggling with the straps of a brass-bound trunk. Innes, by the door, was bidding good-by to Señora Maldonado.

He could hear her voice as he drew near. "You'll let me hear from you? How you are getting on? And the children?"

He forgot to greet the Mexican. She stood waiting; her eyes full of him. Surely, the kind señor had something to say to her? He had taken the white girl's hand. He was staring into the white girl's eyes. Something came to her, a memory like forgotten music. Silently, she slipped away into the night.

Rickard would not release Innes' hand; her eyes could not meet the look in his.

"Wasn't she good to come? She rode, horseback, all the way up here just to say good-by to me. She is going to Nogales to live, taking the children. She thinks she has a good chance there. She asked me to tell you." Her chatter, too, dropped before his silence. He kept her hand in his.

"Come out and have a walk with me! It's not too late?"

Her foolish, chattering speech all mute!

"The levee?" asked Rickard. Still holding her hand, he drew it through the loop of his arm.

"You were not going to tell me you were going?"

No answer to that either! How could she tell him she was going when she knew what she knew!

"You were running away from me?" He leaned down to her face.

If she dared, she would be pert with him; she would not have to *run* away from him!

"You know that I love you! I have been waiting for this minute, this woman, all these lonely years."

Her head she kept turned from him. He could not see the little maternal smile that ran around the curves of her mouth. Those years, filled to the brim with stern work, had not been lonely. Lonely moments he had had, that was all. She could understand how a man like Rickard would find those moments lonely. There, he and Tom stood together. He was asking her to fill those minutes; those only. But he did not know that. He would not know what she meant if she told him that he was asking her to fill a corner of his heart!

"Nothing for me?" He stopped, and made her face him, by taking both of her hands in his.

She would not look at him yet, would not meet the look which always compelled her will, stultified her speech. She had something to say first.

"We don't know each other; that is, you don't know me!" She was not going to let them make that mistake, let him make that mistake!

"Is that all?" There was relief in his voice. For a bad moment he had wondered if it was possible, if Estrada—"I don't know you? Haven't I seen you day by day? Haven't I seen your self-control tried, proved—haven't I seen your justice, when you could not understand— Look at me!"

She shook her head, her eyes on the sand under her feet. He could scarcely catch her words. They did not know each other. He did not know her!

"Dear! I don't know whether you love red or blue, that's a fact; Ibsen or Rostand; heat or cold. Does that matter? I know you!"

An upward glance had caught him smiling. Her speech was routed. "I'm—the—only girl here!"

"Do you think that's why I love you?"

"Ah, but you loved Gerty!" That slipped from her. She had not meant to say that!

"Does that hurt?" Abashed by her own daring, yet she was glad she had dared. She wanted him to deny it. For he would deny it? She wondered if he were angry, but she could not look at him.

The minutes, dragging like weighted hours, told her that he was not going to answer her. It came to her then that she would never know whether Gerty's story were wholly false, or partly true. She knew, then, that no wheedling, wife's or sweetheart's, would tease that story from him. It did not belong to him.

His silence frightened her into articulateness. He must not think that she was foolish! It was not that, in itself, she meant. The words jostled one another in their soft swift rush. He—he had made a mistake once before. He had liked the sort of woman he had thought Gerty was. She herself was not like the real Gerty any more than she was like the other, the woman that did not exist. He would find that they did not think alike, believe alike, that there were differences—

"Aren't you making something out of nothing, Innes?"

That voice could always chide her into silence! Her speech lay cluttered in ruins, her words like useless broken bricks falling from the wall she was building.

He took her hand and led her to a pile of rock the river had not eaten. He pulled her down beside him.

"Isn't it true, with us?"

"It is, with me," breathed Innes. Their voices were low as though they were in church.

"And you think it isn't, with me!" Rickard stood before her. "Is it because I trust you, I wonder? That I, loving you, love to have the others love you, too? Don't you suppose I know how it is with the rest, MacLean; how it was with Estrada? Should I be jealous? Why, I'm not. I'm proud! Isn't that because I *know* you, know the fine steady heart of you? You hated me at first—and I am proud of that. I don't love you enough?" He knelt at her feet, not listening to her pleading. He bent down and kissed one foot; then the other. "I love them!" The face he raised to her Innes had never seen before. He pressed a kiss against her knee. "That, too! It's mine. I've not said my prayers since I was a boy. I shall say them again, here, you teaching me." His kisses ran up her arm, from the tips of her limp fingers. His mouth, close to hers, stopped there. He whispered:

"You—kiss me, my girl!"

Slowly, unseeingly, as though drawn by an external

will, her face raised to his; slowly, their lips met. His arms were around her; the world was blotted out.

Innes, minutes later, put her mouth against his ear. It was the Innes he did not know, that he had seen with others, mischievous, whimsical, romping as a young boy with MacLean on the *Delta*.

"I love—red," she whispered. "And heat and sunshine. But I love blue, on you; and cold, if it were with you,—and the rest of the differences—"

He caught her to him. "There are not going to be any differences!"

THE END

ZANE GREY'S NOVELS

May be had wherever books are sold. Ask for Grosset & Dunlap's list

THE LIGHT OF WESTERN STARS

Colored frontispiece by W. Herbert Dunton.

Most of the action of this story takes place near the turbulent Mexican border of the present day. A New York society girl buys a ranch which becomes the center of frontier warfare. Her loyal cowboys defend her property from bandits, and her superintendent rescues her when she is captured by them. A surprising climax brings the story to a delightful close.

DESERT GOLD

Illustrated by Douglas Duer.

Another fascinating story of the Mexican border. Two men, lost in the desert, discover gold when, overcome by weakness, they can go no farther. The rest of the story describes the recent uprising along the border, and ends with the finding of the gold which the two prospectors had willed to the girl who is the story's heroine.

RIDERS OF THE PURPLE SAGE

Illustrated by Douglas Duer.

A picturesque romance of Utah of some forty years ago when Mormon authority ruled. In the persecution of Jane Withersteen, a rich ranch owner, we are permitted to see the methods employed by the invisible hand of the Mormon Church to break her will.

THE LAST OF THE PLAINSMEN

Illustrated with photograph reproductions.

This is the record of a trip which the author took with Buffalo Jones, known as the preserver of the American bison, across the Arizona desert and of a hunt in "that wonderful country of yellow crags, deep canons and giant pines." It is a fascinating story.

THE HERITAGE OF THE DESERT

Jacket in color. Frontispiece.

This big human drama is played in the Painted Desert. A lovely girl, who has been reared among Mormons, learns to love a young New Englander. The Mormon religion, however, demands that the girl shall become the second wife of one of the Mormons—

Well, that's the problem of this sensational, big selling story.

BETTY ZANE

Illustrated by Louis F. Grant.

This story tells of the bravery and heroism of Betty, the beautiful young sister of old Colonel Zane, one of the bravest pioneers. Life along the frontier, attacks by Indians, Betty's heroic defense of the beleaguered garrison at Wheeling, the burning of the Fort, and Betty's final race for life, make up this never-to-be-forgotten story.

GROSSET & DUNLAP, PUBLISHERS, NEW YORK

STORIES OF WESTERN LIFE

May be had wherever books are sold. Ask for Grosset & Dunlap's list

RIDERS OF THE PURPLE SAGE, By Zane Grey.

Illustrated by Douglas Duer.

In this picturesque romance of Utah of some forty years ago, we are permitted to see the unscrupulous methods employed by the invisible hand of the Mormon Church to break the will of those refusing to conform to its rule.

FRIAR TUCK, By Robert Alexander Wason.

Illustrated by Stanley L. Wood.

Happy Hawkins tells us, in his humorous way, how Friar Tuck lived among the Cowboys, how he adjusted their quarrels and love affairs and how he fought with them and for them when occasion required.

THE SKY PILOT, By Ralph Connor.

Illustrated by Louis Rhead.

There is no novel, dealing with the rough existence of cowboys, so charming in the telling, abounding as it does with the freshest and the truest pathos.

THE EMIGRANT TRAIL, By Geraldine Bonner.

Colored frontispiece by John Rae.

The book relates the adventures of a party on its overland pilgrimage, and the birth and growth of the absorbing love of two strong men for a charming heroine.

THE BOSS OF WIND RIVER, By A. M. Chisholm.

Illustrated by Frank Tenney Johnson.

This is a strong, virile novel with the lumber industry for its central theme and a love story full of interest as a sort of subplot.

A PRAIRIE COURTSHIP, By Harold Bindloss.

A story of Canadian prairies in which the hero is stirred, through the influence of his love for a woman, to settle down to the heroic business of pioneer farming.

JOYCE OF THE NORTH WOODS, By Harriet T. Comstock.

Illustrated by John Cassel.

A story of the deep woods that shows the power of love at work among its primitive dwellers. It is a tensely moving study of the human heart and its aspirations that unfolds itself through thrilling situations and dramatic developments.

Ask for a complete free list of G. & D. Popular Copyrighted Fiction

GROSSET & DUNLAP, 526 WEST 26th ST., NEW YORK

STORIES OF RARE CHARM BY
GENE STRATTON-PORTER

May be had wherever books are sold.   Ask for Grosset and Dunlap's list

LADDIE.
Illustrated by Herman Pfeifer.

This is a bright, cheery tale with the scenes laid in Indiana. The story is told by Little Sister, the youngest member of a large family, but it is concerned not so much with childish doings as with the love affairs of older members of the family. Chief among them is that of Laddie, the older brother whom Little Sister adores, and the Princess, an English girl who has come to live in the neighborhood and about whose family there hangs a mystery. There is a wedding midway in the book and a double wedding at the close.

THE HARVESTER.   Illustrated by W. L. Jacobs.

"The Harvester," David Langston, is a man of the woods and fields, who draws his living from the prodigal hand of Mother Nature herself. If the book had nothing in it but the splendid figure of this man it would be notable. But when the Girl comes to his "Medicine Woods," and the Harvester's whole being realizes that this is the highest point of life which has come to him—there begins a romance of the rarest idyllic quality.

FRECKLES,   Decorations by E. Stetson Crawford.

Freckles is a nameless waif when the tale opens, but the way in which he takes hold of life; the nature friendships he forms in the great Limberlost Swamp; the manner in which everyone who meets him succumbs to the charm of his engaging personality; and his love-story with "The Angel" are full of real sentiment.

A GIRL OF THE LIMBERLOST.
Illustrated by Wladyslaw T. Brenda.

The story of a girl of the Michigan woods; a buoyant, lovable type of the self-reliant American. Her philosophy is one of love and kindness towards all things; her hope is never dimmed. And by the sheer beauty of her soul, and the purity of her vision, she wins from barren and unpromising surroundings those rewards of high courage.

AT THE FOOT OF THE RAINBOW.
Illustrations in colors by Oliver Kemp.

The scene of this charming love story is laid in Central Indiana. The story is one of devoted friendship, and tender self-sacrificing love. The novel is brimful of the most beautiful word painting of nature, and its pathos and tender sentiment will endear it to all.

GROSSET & DUNLAP,   PUBLISHERS,   NEW YORK

GROSSET & DUNLAP'S
DRAMATIZED NOVELS
THE KIND THAT ARE MAKING THEATRICAL HISTORY

May be had wherever books are sold.   Ask for Grosset & Dunlap's list

WITHIN THE LAW. By Bayard Veiller & Marvin Dana. Illustrated by Wm. Charles Cooke.

This is a novelization of the immensely successful play which ran for two years in New York and Chicago.

The plot of this powerful novel is of a young woman's revenge directed against her employer who allowed her to be sent to prison for three years on a charge of theft, of which she was innocent.

WHAT HAPPENED TO MARY. By Robert Carlton Brown. Illustrated with scenes from the play.

This is a narrative of a young and innocent country girl who is suddenly thrown into the very heart of New York, "the land of her dreams," where she is exposed to all sorts of temptations and dangers.

The story of Mary is being told in moving pictures and played in theatres all over the world.

THE RETURN OF PETER GRIMM. By David Belasco. Illustrated by John Rae,

This is a novelization of the popular play in which David Warfield, as Old Peter Grimm, scored such a remarkable success.

The story is spectacular and extremely pathetic but withal, powerful, both as a book and as a play.

THE GARDEN OF ALLAH. By Robert Hichens.

This novel is an intense, glowing epic of the great desert, sunlit barbaric, with its marvelous atmosphere of vastness and loneliness.

It is a book of rapturous beauty, vivid in word painting. The play has been staged with magnificent cast and gorgeous properties.

BEN HUR. A Tale of the Christ. By General Lew Wallace.

The whole world has placed this famous Religious-Historical Romance on a height of pre-eminence which no other novel of its time has reached. The clashing of rivalry and the deepest human passions, the perfect reproduction of brilliant Roman life, and the tense, fierce atmosphere of the arena have kept their deep fascination. A tremendous dramatic success.

BOUGHT AND PAID FOR. By George Broadhurst and Arthur Hornblow.   Illustrated with scenes from the play.

A stupendous arraignment of modern marriage which has created an interest on the stage that is almost unparalleled. The scenes are laid in New York, and deal with conditions among both the rich and poor.

The interest of the story turns on the day-by-day developments which show the young wife the price she has paid.

Ask for complete free list of G. & D. Popular Copyrighed Fiction

GROSSET & DUNLAP, 526 WEST 26th ST., NEW YORK

JOHN FOX, JR'S.
STORIES OF THE KENTUCKY MOUNTAINS

May be had wherever books are sold.   Ask for Grosset and Dunlap's list.

THE TRAIL OF THE LONESOME PINE.
Illustrated by F. C. Yohn.

The "lonesome pine" from which the story takes its name was a tall tree that stood in solitary splendor on a mountain top. The fame of the pine lured a young engineer through Kentucky to catch the trail, and when he finally climbed to its shelter he found not only the pine but the *foot-prints of a girl*. And the girl proved to be lovely, piquant, and the trail of these girlish foot-prints led the young engineer a madder chase than "the trail of the lonesome pine."

THE LITTLE SHEPHERD OF KINGDOM COME
Illustrated by F. C. Yohn.

This is a story of Kentucky, in a settlement known as "Kingdom Come." It is a life rude, semi-barbarous; but natural and honest, from which often springs the flower of civilization.

"Chad." the "little shepherd" did not know who he was nor whence he came—he had just wandered from door to door since early childhood, seeking shelter with kindly mountaineers who gladly fathered and mothered this waif about whom there was such a mystery—a charming waif, by the way, who could play the banjo better that anyone else in the mountains.

A KNIGHT OF THE CUMBERLAND.
Illustrated by F. C. Yohn.

The scenes are laid along the waters of the Cumberland, the lair of moonshiner and feudsman. The knight is a moonshiner's son, and the heroine a beautiful girl perversely christened "The Blight." Two impetuous young Southerners' fall under the spell of "The Blight's" charms and she learns what a large part jealousy and pistols have in the love making of the mountaineers.

Included in this volume is "Hell fer-Sartain" and other stories, some of Mr. Fox's most entertaining Cumberland valley narratives.

Ask for complete free list of G. & D. Popular Copyrighted Fiction

GROSSET & DUNLAP, 526 WEST 26th ST., NEW YORK

B. M. Bower's Novels
Thrilling Western Romances

Large 12 mos. Handsomely bound in cloth.   Illustrated

CHIP, OF THE FLYING U
A breezy wholesome tale, wherein the love affairs of Chip and Della Whitman are charmingly and humorously told. Chip's jealousy of Dr. Cecil Grantham, who turns out to be a big, blue eyed young woman is very amusing. A clever, realistic story of the American Cow-puncher.

THE HAPPY FAMILY
A lively and amusing story, dealing with the adventures of eighteen jovial, big hearted Montana cowboys. Foremost amongst them, we find Ananias Green, known as Andy, whose imaginative powers cause many lively and exciting adventures.

HER PRAIRIE KNIGHT
A realistic story of the plains, describing a gay party of Easterners who exchange a cottage at Newport for the rough homeliness of a Montana ranch-house. The merry-hearted cowboys, the fascinating Beatrice, and the effusive Sir Redmond, become living, breathing personalities.

THE RANGE DWELLERS
Here are everyday, genuine cowboys, just as they really exist. Spirited action, a range feud between two families, and a Romeo and Juliet courtship make this a bright, jolly, entertaining story, without a dull page.

THE LURE OF DIM TRAILS
A vivid portrayal of the experience of an Eastern author, among the cowboys of the West, in search of "local color" for a new novel. "Bud" Thurston learns many a lesson while following "the lure of the dim trails" but the hardest, and probably the most welcome, is that of love.

THE LONESOME TRAIL
"Weary" Davidson leaves the ranch for Portland, where conventional city life palls on him. A little branch of sage brush, pungent with the atmosphere of the prairie, and the recollection of a pair of large brown eyes soon compel his return. A wholesome love story.

THE LONG SHADOW
A vigorous Western story, sparkling with the free, outdoor life of a mountain ranch. Its scenes shift rapidly and its actors play the game of life fearlessly and like men. It is a fine love story from start to finish.

Ask for a complete free list of G. & D. Popular Copyrighted Fiction.

GROSSET & DUNLAP, 526 WEST 26TH ST., NEW YORK

MYRTLE REED'S NOVELS

May be had wherever books are sold. Ask for Grosset & Dunlap's list

LAVENDER AND OLD LACE.

A charming story of a quaint corner of New England where bygone romance finds a modern parallel. The story centers round the coming of love to the young people on the staff of a newspaper—and it is one of the prettiest, sweetest and quaintest of old fashioned love stories, * * * a rare book, exquisite in spirit and conception, full of delicate fancy, of tenderness, of delightful humor and spontaniety.

SPINNER IN THE SUN.

Miss Myrtle Reed may always be depended upon to write a story in which poetry, charm, tenderness and humor are combined into a clever and entertaining book. Her characters are delightful and she always displays a quaint humor of expression and a quiet feeling of pathos which give a touch of active realism to all her writings. In "A Spinner in the Sun" she tells an old-fashioned love story, of a veiled lady who lives in solitude and whose features her neighbors have never seen. There is a mystery at the heart of the book that throws over it the glamour of romance.

THE MASTER'S VIOLIN,

A love story in a musical atmosphere. A picturesque, old German virtuoso is the reverent possessor of a genuine "Cremona." He consents to take for his pupil a handsome youth who proves to have an aptitude for technique, but not the soul of an artist. The youth has led the happy, careless life of a modern, well-to-do young American and he cannot, with his meagre past, express the love, the passion, and the tragedies of life and all its happy phases as can the master who has lived life in all its fulness. But a girl comes into his life—a beautiful bit of human driftwood that his aunt had taken into her heart and home, and through his passionate love for her, he learns the lessons that life has to give—and his soul awakes.

Founded on a fact that all artists realize.

Ask for a complete free list of G. & D. Popular Copyrighted Fiction

GROSSET & DUNLAP, 526 WEST 26th ST., NEW YORK

TITLES SELECTED FROM
GROSSET & DUNLAP'S LIST
RE-ISSUES OF THE GREAT LITERARY SUCCESSES OF THE TIME

May be had wherever books are sold.　　Ask for Grosset & Dunlap's list

BEN HUR. A Tale of the Christ. By General Lew Wallace

This famous Religious-Historical Romance with its mighty story, brilliant pageantry, thrilling action and deep religious reverence, hardly requires an outline. The whole world has placed "Ben-Hur" on a height of pre-eminence which no other novel of its time has reached. The clashing of rivalry and the deepest human passions, the perfect reproduction of brilliant Roman life, and the tense, fierce atmosphere of the arena have kept their deep fascination.

THE PRINCE OE INDIA. By General Lew Wallace

A glowing romance of the Byzantine Empire, showing, with vivid imagination, the possible forces behind the internal decay of the Empire that hastened the fall of Constantinople.

The foreground figure is the person known to all as the Wandering Jew, at this time appearing as the Prince of India, with vast stores of wealth, and is supposed to have instigated many wars and fomented the Crusades.

Mohammed's love for the Princess Irene is beautifully wrought into the story, and the book as a whole is a marvelous work both historically and romantically.

THE FAIR GOD. By General Lew Wallace. A Tale of the Conquest of Mexico. With Eight Illustrations by Eric Pape.

All the annals of conquest have nothing more brilliantly daring and dramatic than the drama played in Mexico by Cortes. As a dazzling picture of Mexico and the Montezumas it leaves nothing to be desired.

The artist has caught with rare enthusiasm the spirit of the Spanish conquerors of Mexico, its beauty and glory and romance.

TARRY THOU TILL I COME or, Salathiel, the Wandering Jew. By George Croly. With twenty illustrations by T. de Thulstrup.

A historical novel, dealing with the momentous events that occurred, chiefly in Palestine, from the time of the Crucifixion to the destruction of Jerusalem.

The book, as a story, is replete with Oriental charm and richness, and the character drawing is marvelous. No other novel ever written has portrayed with such vividness the events that convulsed Rome and destroyed Jerusalem in the early days of Christanity.

Ask for complete free list of G. & D. Popular Copyrighed Fiction

GROSSET & DUNLAP, 526 WEST 26th ST., NEW YORK

CHARMING BOOKS FOR GIRLS

May be had wherever books are sold.　　Ask for Grosset & Dunlap's list

WHEN PATTY WENT TO COLLEGE, By Jean Webster.

Illustrated by C. D. Williams.

One of the best stories of life in a girl's college that has ever been written. It is bright, whimsical and entertaining, lifelike, laughable and thoroughly human.

JUST PATTY, By Jean Webster.

Illustrated by C. M. Relyea.

Patty is full of the joy of living, fun-loving, given to ingenious mischief for its own sake, with a disregard for pretty convention which is an unfailing source of joy to her fellows.

THE POOR LITTLE RICH GIRL, By Eleanor Gates.

With four full page illustrations.

This story relates the experience of one of those unfortunate children whose early days are passed in the companionship of a governess, seldom seeing either parent, and famishing for natural love and tenderness. A charming play as dramatized by the author.

REBECCA OF SUNNYBROOK FARM, By Kate Douglas Wiggin.

One of the most beautiful studies of childhood—Rebecca's artistic, unusual and quaintly charming qualities stand out midst a circle of austere New Englanders. The stage version is making a phenomenal dramatic record.

NEW CHRONICLES OF REBECCA, By Kate Douglas Wiggin.

Illustrated by F. C. Yohn.

Additional episodes in the girlhood of this delightful heroine that carry Rebecca through various stages to her eighteenth birthday.

REBECCA MARY, By Annie Hamilton Donnell.

Illustrated by Elizabeth Shippen Green.

This author possesses the rare gift of portraying all the grotesque little joys and sorrows and scruples of this very small girl with a pathos that is peculiarly genuine and appealing.

EMMY LOU: Her Book and Heart, By George Madden Martin.

Illustrated by Charles Louis Hinton.

Emmy Lou is irresistibly lovable, because she is so absolutely real. She is just a bewitchingly innocent, hugable little maid. The book is wonderfully human.

Ask for complete free list of G. & D. Popular Copyrighed Fiction

GROSSET & DUNLAP, 526 WEST 26th ST., NEW YORK

AMELIA E. BARR'S STORIES
DELIGHTFUL TALES OF OLD NEW YORK

May be had wherever books are sold.   Ask for Grosset and Dunlap's list.

THE BOW OF ORANGE RIBBON. With Frontispiece.

This exquisite little romance opens in New York City in "the tender grace" of a May day long past, when the old Dutch families clustered around Bowling Green. It is the beginning of the romance of Katherine, a young Dutch girl who has sent, as a love token, to a young English officer, the bow of orange ribbon which she has worn for years as a sacred emblem on the day of St. Nicholas. After the bow of ribbon Katherine's heart soon flies. Unlike her sister, whose heart has found a safe resting place among her own people, Katherine's heart must rove from home—must know to the utmost all that life holds of both joy and sorrow. And so she goes beyond the seas, leaving her parents as desolate as were Isaac and Rebecca of old.

THE MAID OF MAIDEN LANE; A Love Story. With Illustrations by S. M. Arthur.

A sequel to "The Bow of Orange Ribbon." The time is the gracious days of Seventeen-hundred and ninety-one, when "The Marseillaise" was sung with the American national airs, and the spirit affected commerce, politics and conversation. In the midst of this period the romance of "The Sweetest Maid in Maiden Lane" unfolds. Its chief charm lies in its historic and local color.

SHEILA VEDDER. Frontispiece in colors by Harrison Fisher.

A love story set in the Shetland Islands.

Among the simple, homely folk who dwelt there Jan Vedder was raised; and to this island came lovely Sheila Jarrow. Jan knew, when first he beheld her, that she was the one woman in all the world for him, and to the winning of her love he set himself. The long days of summer by the sea, the nights under the marvelously soft radiance of Shetland moonlight passed in love-making, while with wonderment the man and woman, alien in traditions, adjusted themselves to each other. And the day came when Jan and Sheila wed, and then a sweeter love story is told.

TRINITY BELLS. With eight Illustrations by C. M. Relyea.

The story centers around the life of little Katryntje Van Clyffe, who, on her return home from a fashionable boarding school, faces poverty and heartache. Stout of heart, she does not permit herself to become discouraged even at the news of the loss of her father and his ship "The Golden Victory." The story of Katryntje's life was interwoven with the music of the Trinity Bells which eventually heralded her wedding day.

Ask for complete free list of G. & D. Popular Copyrighted Fiction

GROSSET & DUNLAP, 526 WEST 26th ST., NEW YORK